CAMBRIDGE SURVEYS OF ECONOMIC LITERATURE

D1125617

THE ECONOMICS OF INDIVIDUAL AND POPULATION AGING

CAMBRIDGE SURVEYS OF ECONOMIC LITERATURE

The literature of economics is expanding rapidly, and many subjects have changed out of recognition within the space of a few years. Perceiving the state of knowledge in fast developing subjects is difficult for students and time-consuming for professional economists. This series of books is intended to help with this problem. Each book will be quite brief, giving a clear structure to and balanced overview of the topic and written at a level intelligible to the senior undergraduate. The books will therefore be useful for teaching, but will also provide a mature yet compact presentation of the subject for the economist wishing to update his knowledge outside his own specialism.

First books in the series
E. Roy Weintraub: Microfoundations: The compatibility of microeconomics and macroeconomics
Dennis C. Mueller: Public choice
Robert L. Clark and Joseph J. Spengler: The economics of individual and population aging

The economics of
individual and population aging

ROBERT L. CLARK
Associate Professor of Economics, North Carolina State University

JOSEPH J. SPENGLER
Professor of Economics, Duke University

CAMBRIDGE UNIVERSITY PRESS
CAMBRIDGE
LONDON   NEW YORK   NEW ROCHELLE
MELBOURNE   SYDNEY

Published by the Press Syndicate of the University of Cambridge
The Pitt Building, Trumpington Street, Cambridge CB2 1RP
32 East 57th Street, New York, NY 10022, USA
296 Beaconsfield Parade, Middle Park, Melbourne 3206, Australia

First published 1980

Printed in the United States of America
Typeset by David E. Seham Assoc., Inc., Metuchen, NJ
Printed and bound by Vail-Ballou Press, Inc., Binghamton, NY

Library of Congress Cataloging in Publication Data
Clark, Robert Louis, 1949–

The economics of individual and population aging.

(Cambridge surveys of economic literature)

Bibliography: p.

Includes index.

1. Old age – Economic aspects. 2. Aging – Economic aspects. 3. Retire-
ment– Economic aspects. 4. Aged– Economic conditions. 5. Old age assistance. I.
Spengler, Joseph John, 1902– , joint author. II. Title.
HQ1061.C52 301.43′5 79–19495
ISBN 0 521 22883 2 hard covers
ISBN 0 521 29702 8 paperback

CONTENTS

PREFACE

This study summarizes and assimilates research by international scholars in economics, demography, and the other social sciences in order to provide a conceptual framework for the economics of aging. The objective of this analysis is to identify and describe the principal economic issues associated with individual and population aging and to assess the existing knowledge respecting the economic and social problems emerging with aging. The integration of interdisciplinary research is of special importance in any examination of gerontological issues, and we have been sensitive to this mandate. However, our primary focus has been on economic complexities of individual life-cycle allocation decisions and the macroeconomic problems that arise from age-structure changes.

The review is international in scope, as we trace the development of concern for population aging in Europe, the United States, and other industrialized countries. Theoretical concepts and changing demographic conditions are illustrated with data from various countries. Cross-national econometric studies are reported along with time-series and cross-sectional research on individual countries. National differences in the response to aging, the institutions that provide income maintenance to the elderly, and the economic conditions of the elderly are noted. In some cases, a single country is examined in detail to indicate a particular aspect of the economics of aging. Most frequently, the United States is chosen because of the availability of data, the greater number of empirical studies employing U.S. data, the familiarity of the authors with U.S. institutions, and the essential universality of aging phenomena.

Throughout the manuscript, we have attempted to assess the current state of the literature bearing on economic concepts relating to aging phenomena and to indicate fruitful avenues for further research. It is our hope that scholars interested in economics or gerontology can productively utilize this text to identify important problems, become acquainted with previous research on these questions, and generate ideas for future study.

Many colleagues at Duke University and North Carolina State University have contributed to the improvement of this manuscript. We owe a special debt of gratitude to Juanita Kreps, who has worked with us on related projects and whose thinking is reflected in many sections of the book. George Maddox and George Brosseau have been instrumental in formative stages of our research on the economics of aging and have been helpful in the integration of interdisciplinary findings into the volume. Some of the material included in the volume was previously published in a condensed version in the *Journal of Economic Literature*.

Robert L. Clark
Raleigh, North Carolina

Joseph J. Spengler
Durham, North Carolina

November, 1979

1

Recognition of the economics of aging

The economics of population aging is essentially a new concern for economists as well as other social scientists. Individual aging, of course, has always been a concern of man, both as an observer and as an individual undergoing the process of aging. Belletristic and other literature relating to man is replete with references to aging concerning its incidence among individuals and within the family. Of this we find representative evidence, for example, in Simone de Beauvoir's *The Coming of Age,* in relevant articles in the July–September 1977 *Educational Gerontology,* and in many interpretations of individual aging and its treatment by poets, novelists, and philosophers.

Even so, important research on aging is of relatively recent vintage. Don C. Charles writes (pp. 237–8) that "research (other than medical) on old persons is almost exclusively a phenomenon of the post–World War II period, although some work began prior to that – as early as the 1920s. Philosophers did, of course, give some thought to what we today call man's life cycle (e.g., see Cyril P. Svoboda's account of "Senescence in Western Philosophy," pp. 219–35). Svoboda reports, for example, that Aristotle, one of the classical world's most careful observers, "posited that it is natural for the body to reach its prime around age 35 and to 'advance' until about age 50," and then begin to decline (p. 223). The "soul," he said, reached its perfection at age

1

50. Some authors mentioned the functional usefulness of older persons and their experience, but without always correlating this aspect closely with specific age. At the other extreme, we find descriptions such as that of mythological Tithonus or Jonathan Swift's "Struldbrugs."

Indicative of the growing concern with aging and relating problems is the fact that in the first (1933–4) edition of *The Encyclopaedia of the Social Sciences* there was no article on "aging."[1] In what amounts to a second edition, *The International Encyclopedia of the Social Sciences* (1968), there was a 26-page article dealing with the psychological, social, and economic aspects of "aging."

Given the low life expectancy found prior to the seventeenth and eighteenth centuries, the fraction of a population over, say, 60, would be small. For example (see United Nations, 1968, pp. 148, 182; United Nations, 1973b), with life expectancy at birth between 30 and 40 years, the fraction of a stationary population aged 75 and over would be between 1 and 2 percent, whereas the fraction 60 and over would lie roughly between 7.5 and slightly over 11 percent. With the population growing, this fraction would be lower. In populations with low life expectancies, therefore, older persons would not be conspicuous as in a modern society in which, with numbers stationary and life expectancy at 70.2 years, 6 percent would be 75 or more years old, and nearly 21 percent would be 60 and over. Such changes are reflected in the historical development of the age structure in America, as only 2.6 percent were 65 and over in 1850, compared with 6.8 percent in 1940 and about 19 percent were the population to become stationary.

Population aging – increase in the relative number of older persons (e.g., those over 60 or 64) – would not become pronounced until a population virtually ceased to grow and life expectancy at birth had moved to a sufficiently high level (e.g., over 40). Moreover, the problem of collectively providing adequate support for aged persons who had retired from the labor force would not, as a rule, become pronounced as long as the ratio of persons of productive age to those aged 60 and over was considered sufficiently high.

Sensitivity of an economy to the ratio of persons of productive age to those beyond productive age is conditioned by the nature of the family support system. This sensitivity is greater when a major source of the support of welfare recipients and retired persons is a collective or national social security system whose resources are supplied mainly or entirely by employed persons of working age instead of by members of the traditional family sometimes supplemented by occasional work on the part of retired persons (Hareven, pp. 19–21; Hareven and Vinovskis; also Achenbaum; Treas; cf. Parnes and King). When support is supplied collectively, the number of beneficiaries and the amount of support supplied are much greater (e.g., see Browning). In part because contributions are involuntary, they assume several forms, and their incidence is widely distributed among members of the labor force.

The economic significance of the age structure commanded little attention in the nineteenth century. In his comprehensive *The Population Debate,* E. P. Hutchinson refers only to Hans von Mangoldt's discussion of age structure in his *Volkswirthschaftslehre* (1868), in which J. E. Wappäus's age data for 14 countries are commented on. Mangoldt pointed out that a population's average productivity depended upon the ratio of persons of working age to the total population (pp. 37–40), a ratio that varied inversely with the relative number of young people. He contrasted the fraction of France's population aged 14–60, 64.3 percent, with Prussia's, 59 percent (p. 38). He noted also the economic advantage of reduced child mortality (pp. 38–9). In summarizing economic thinking prior to the twentieth century, Hutchinson concludes that "not much attention was given the ratio of workers to total population. For population was generally taken loosely as equivalent to labor supply" (p. 396).

The importance of the age structure as the fundamental governor of the ratio of beneficiaries to contributors was not stressed until the 1930s after the implications of subreplacement fertility for the future age structure were illustrated through population projections. As early as 1895, Edwin Cannan (pp. 108–24) forecast that the population of England and Wales would be virtually stationary by the 1940s and at a stationary maximum by 1995, but he did not draw attention to the decline in the ratio of persons of working age to those of retirement age. With the reexamination of the population prospect in the late 1920s and 1930s, theretofore stressed mainly in France, and the growing likelihood that population growth might cease, the implications of this trend for the dependency problem, especially the security of the aged, began to command attention. Economic implications of changes in age structure were pointed out in 1930 by L. I. Dublin and A. J. Lotka in *The Money Value of a Man*.

The first careful study of the then U.S. population prospect was set in motion by President Herbert Hoover when in December 1929 he named a committee to survey social changes under way and to identify emerging problems confronting the American people. One of these inquiries, by W. S. Thompson and P. K. Whelpton, projected the future U.S. population on the basis of then prospective trends. In this report, issued in enlarged form in 1933, the authors emphasized the unfavorable impact of the relatively rapid increase in the population over 65 years of age upon the pension system, the degree of aged dependency, entrepreneurial creativity, and economic progress (pp. 165–71) – conditions associated with the supposed approach of a stationary population (see also Whelpton). In the 1930s Enid Charles prepared several projections of prospective changes in the size of the future British population and its age composition – projections indicating a decrease after the 1950s in the ratio of the population 15–59 years old to that 60 and over (E. Charles, pp. 84–93). After World War II the League of Nations sponsored a study of the population of Europe and the Soviet Union, 1940–70, by F. W. Notestein and his associates at the Office of Population Research, Princeton. They called attention (Notestein et al., Chapters 4–8) to implications of declining fertility and changing age structure for manpower and dependency problems in some European countries, implications of which Sir William Beveridge took some note in his famous report (pp. 397–400). After World War II inquiries into population prospects were undertaken in a number of countries. In its report issued in 1949 the British Royal Commission on Population drew attention to the social effect of population aging, the "burden of dependency," and so on (Chapters 9, 11, 13). In 1956 and 1973 the United Nations issued a study on the implications of the aging of populations.

Our concern in the present review of literature relating to aging is with studies relating to the *age of population,* a process governed only in part by individual aging. In recent years numerous articles and books on medical, sociological, political, economic, and other aspects of aging have appeared. Illustrative of their variety are Dr. Nathan Shock's bibliographies of current publications in gerontology and geriatrics appearing regularly in the *Journal of Gerontology,* and collections based on them. Illustrative also are the items reported quarterly in *Population Index* and the emerging literature pertaining to dependency, pensions, and related problems affected by population age structures.

Treatment of population aging and its literature is complicated by the fact that population aging is a concomitant of the approach of a population to stationarity, and that some effects of each phenomenon are reenforced by those of the other (Spengler). In this report, however, attention is focused upon literature relating wholly or essentially to economic aspects of population aging.

Upon the discovery of a new area of inquiry in a social science, publications dealing with newly noted aspects of this area continue to increase, perhaps logistically, until the subject is exhausted or is found in need only of adjustment for new information. Such appears to have been the history of geriatric and gerontological literature in general as well as that of literature relating directly or indirectly to the nature and consequences of population aging. Studies, of course, may become more refined as data or theories are reexamined.[2] The voluminousness of the literature makes some review of it useful, in that scholars may thereby be freed of the need for completely canvassing what has been written and be able to isolate issues seemingly in need of further examination. In the reviews of the literature presented in the eight chapters following, such screening is attempted, together with some indication of the findings. Although virtually all of the relevant literature is of post-1920s vintage, our attention has been directed mainly to that appearing since the 1950s. This examination is international in its scope, for the emergence of population aging is not limited to a few countries. The analysis notes the determinants of aging and the economic response to this process as presented in the international economic, demographic, and social science literature. Data from individual countries are used to illustrate theoretical and methodological issues and to assess empirical relationships. The following paragraphs indicate the content focus of each of the next eight chapters.

In Chapter 2 we indicate that population aging (i.e., increase in the relative number of persons over 60 and 65) is traceable mainly and essentially to decline in fertility or gross reproduction under modern conditions. The impact of prospective improvement in life expectancy at older ages appears to be quite limited, given current conditions, modes of living, and the state of medical and related sciences. Accordingly, labor force and related phenomena, especially those relating to income, are likely to continue to be dominated by the behavior of fertility. Indeed, however long the life span, its impact upon population aging can be offset by increases in fertility.

In Chapter 3 we review the literature bearing upon the way in which various changes in the age structure directly or indirectly affect the capacity of a population to support those of dependent age, especially older dependents. Also reviewed are references to age structure and retirement policies and how the latter need to be adjusted to the given age structure. Some attention is directed also to papers relating to optimum population growth from the standpoint of age structure as distinguished from pressure of numbers upon resources in the Ricardo-Mill tradition.

Chapter 4 is devoted to a review of works relating to the current and recent status of the elderly, mainly in the United States. These works do not relate significantly, however, to the pre-1930 evolution of family and aged support systems (e.g., see Treas, Rubinow, 1934a,b and his bibliographies). This chapter is intended to illustrate the relative and absolute income position of the elderly in a developed country. The availability of recent data to the authors determined, in part, the choice of the United States for this example.

Two sets of changes affected these support systems and helped to give rise to interest in the development of pension systems in and after the mid–nineteenth century, initially in Europe and especially in Germany with its governmental provision against old age dependency in 1889. First, with the development of the industrial system and the breakdown in agriculture of patriarchal and similar systems which afforded the aged some support, there was less support for the aged outside the confines of the immediate or larger family. Moreover, prolongation of work life became more difficult with imposition of limits on the hiring of older workers and reduction of opportunities for their continuation with their current employers in less demanding employment – a practice that still prevailed in the United States around 1900 when 90 percent of the males aged 55–65 and about 68 percent of those over 65 were employed, often at jobs less onerous (e.g., "Sweeper") than those they had formerly held (see Hareven, pp. 19–21).

Second, although life expectancy at age 60 increased slowly – in Sweden from about 15 years in the 1880s to slightly over 16 years in 1910–20 – the number of survivors to age 60 gradually did increase. For example, in the United States where in 1900–2 only 46,452 of 100,000 newly born white males attained age 60, by 1974 the corresponding number of survivors had risen to 77,734. Accordingly, there were more aged in need of support.

Prolongation of later life thus reenforced the need for collective and governmental provision for support of the aged already made desirable by the earlier and gradual breakdown of existing family and aged support systems. Many believed it would be too difficult to build such a system solely on private initiative and individually oriented insurance and annuity systems. Today, in many European countries as well as in Canada and the United States, under social security and similar systems a worker upon retirement receives the equivalent of one-half or more of average earnings in manufacturing (Haanes-Olsen, pp. 3–14).

In Chapter 5 we review literature relating to relations between age and stage in the life cycle on the one hand, and individual economic activities and conditions, on the other. The division of life into stages is not new; it has entered into man's view of life and social policies over the centuries. Such division is of great importance in respect to socioeconomic policy and the ordering of life. Also of importance and stressed in modern life-cycle theory is the degree to which activities and planning in one stage of the life cycle affect those in later stages. Of corresponding importance is the degree to which planning of man's life in life-cycle terms actually influences his activities, together with the degree to which socioeconomic policies increase or reduce individual planning in life-cycle terms (e.g., the degree to which a social security system tends to discourage individual capital formation). Of individual and collective significance, therefore, is extension in the prospective length of the later stages in man's life cycle (Arrow).

In Chapter 6 we review literature relating to labor-force participation on the part of older persons, as well as changes in the incentives and disincentives that affect labor-force participation on the part of older as compared to younger persons. Data relating to labor-force participation as reported in Table 6.1 indicate that participation among males 55–64 remained about as high in 1948 as around 1900 and that participation among those over 64 was only about 40 percent lower than it was around 1900. Since 1948, however, participation has continued to decline among males both 55–64 and over 64; it has increased among females 55–64. A number of statistical studies of labor-force participation along with age of retirement reveal the relative importance of incentives and disincentives to retirement. These are further clarified by the literature reviewed in Chapter 7 – literature bearing upon personal and market determinants of retirement such as health, persistence of unemployment, and decline in occupations accommodating older workers (e.g., agriculture). Financial and individual determinants are also examined.

Chapter 8 is devoted to the growth and impact of the social security system throughout the world. The analysis concentrates on the individual effects. The development of private pension systems and their effects are also examined. Finally, a macroeconomic review of the aging problem is undertaken in Chapter 8. The potential impacts of population aging on consumption, investment, and savings are assessed. In addition, evidence pertaining to the productivity and mobility of an older work force is examined.

2

Population aging: sources

Population aging is represented by an increase in the relative number of older persons (e.g., those over 60 or 65 years of age) in a population; it is reflected also in the associated increase in the median age of the population. Population aging thus is a counterpart to population "youthening" and the associated decline in the median age of the population (United Nations, 1951, 1956, 1973; U.S. Bureau of the Census, May 1975). Population aging tends to emerge in a mature low fertility population, whereas "youthening" may characterize a high-fertility population experiencing declining mortality among the young (Spengler, 1968).

Inasmuch as awareness of the demographic sources of population aging is conditioned by the sensitivity of available demographic measures, we shall point first to the development of these measures. Later we shall review population changes that led to the emergence of population aging and conditions associated with it. Socioeconomic characteristics of older populations (U.S. Bureau of the Census, Nov. 1975), and implications of population aging are examined in later chapters.

Indicators of population aging

Although the age composition of a population may be affected by changes in mortality, fertility, and net external migration, careful measures of the extent of these effects were slow to

10

be developed.[1] Indeed, their perfection awaited the development
of the concept of a *stable population,* a concept suggested by
Leonard Euler in 1760 and later anticipated by Laplace and
Quetelet (Coale and Demeny, Chapter 1; Keyfitz, 1976; Lotka,
1907, 1925; also, Unsigned, 1976). However, it was not fully ar-
ticulated until 1907 by A. J. Lotka, who along with F. R. Sharpe
demonstrated it in 1911 (Dublin et al., pp. 241–56; Lotka, 1925,
pp. 109–20). Associated with this work were improvements in
measures of fertility and mortality, development of measures of
intrinsic rates of natural increase, isolation of determinants of age
structures, and circumstances underlying waves in population
movements (Coale, 1972; Keyfitz, 1968, 1976; Shryock et al.;
United Nations, 1956, 1968; also Kuczynski, 1928, 1931). Improvements in measures of population aging and growth are reported in
periodic issues of *Population Index* and *Population.*

   Of special importance to this chapter is the fact that in a closed
population – one subject to neither emigration nor immigration –
the age structure of a population is determined by its fertility and
mortality behavior. In the words of Ansley J. Coale, leading
American demographer:

> the age composition of a population that neither gains nor
> loses by migration is determined by the sequence of fertil-
> ity and mortality risks at each age to which it has been
> subject. Its overall birth rate, death rate, and rate of in-
> crease at each moment are determined by the current age
> composition and the current age schedules of fertility
> . . .[Two] arbitrarily chosen age distributions no matter
> how different, subject to identical sequences . . . of fer-
> tility and mortality, ultimately generate populations with
> the same age composition. Age distributions gradually
> "forget" the past. (Coale, 1972, p. 3)[2]

Gross reproduction and age composition

The age composition of a population is determined predominantly by its Gross Reproduction Rate, particularly in countries with the reduced mortality characteristic of modern popula-

Table 2.1. *Female age structure and natural increase*

Rate of natural increase, %	% Population 0–35 years old
3.0	72.93
2.0	64.81
1.0	55.54
0.5	50.64
0	45.66
− 0.5	40.70
− 1.0	35.87

tions. For, given a high, rather than a low, fertility rate and hence a high rate of natural increase, the proportion of the population in the lower age categories is maintained at a relatively high level after the population has become stable and the number of persons in each age group is growing at the same rate. Conversely, given a low fertility rate in a stable population, the proportion of the population in lower age categories remains relatively low (see United Nations, 1954, 1956, 1968).

This fertility effect is illustrated in Tables 2.1 and 2.2.[3] Table 2.1 is based upon a model of stable female population with a life expectancy at birth of 75 years and a Gross Reproduction Rate yielding rates of natural increase ranging from 3 percent to `1 percent (see Coale and Demeny, p. 70). The fraction of this stable population less than 35 years of age decreases as the rate of natural increase is reduced. Similarly, in the parallel stable population described in Table 2.2 (Coale and Demney, p. 118), the fraction of the population under 35 years of age decreases as the assumed Gross Reproduction Rate is decreased. In each table, of course, stable conditions compatible with a life expectancy of 75 years and the designated fertility conditions underlie each of the reported age structures.

Variation in fertility owing to variation in the Gross Reproduction Rate or to irregularities in the age structure of a population gives rise temporarily to variation in the annual number of births

Table 2.2 *Gross reproduction and female age structure*

Gross reproduction rate, %	% Population 0–35 years old
3.0	78.49
2.00	67.72
1.25	52.39
1.00	44.69
0.80	37.20

Source: Ansley J. Coale and Paul Demeny, *Regional Model Life Tables and Stable Populations,* Princeton: Princeton University Press, 1966, pp. 70, 118.

(Easterlin, 1966, 1973; Fulop; Hall; Wachter; Easterlin et al.). In time, however, if mortality is invariable and the Gross Reproduction Rate becomes constant and remains so, the age structure will evolve until it takes on a stable form compatible with underlying fertility and mortality conditions (e.g., see actual cases depicted in United Nations, 1968, Chapter 1). Of course, changes in a population's age structure originating in and echoing past irregularities in this population's age structure may give rise to problems if suitable adjustments are not made to these irregularities (e.g., see Easterlin, 1966, 1973). The need for such adjustment diminishes, albeit slowly, if the age structure gradually takes on a stable form compatible with constant age-specific fertility and mortality.

Life expectancy and age composition

Although the evolution and final form of the age structure of a stable population is dominated by the Gross Reproduction Rate, it is conditioned by the ruling level and pattern of mortality (Coale, 1972, Chapter 5 and p. 213).[4] Thus, a decline in mortality of the very young affects the age composition much as does an increase in fertility (Coale, 1972, p. 213). In and before the early nineteenth century, high infant and child mortality sometimes eliminated close to half or more of the members of a newly born cohort before they had completed five years of life; it could thus affect the relative number of persons under 10 years of age, as did a low Gross Reproduction Rate. Smallness of the relative number of young children may have been a source of economic advantage to parents in the past in the event that these children could not be effectively employed (Spengler, 1968).

In and after the late nineteenth century, especially in high-mortality underdeveloped countries, increase in life expectancy could result in a significant increase in the relative number of persons under 10 years of age. For example, in a stable population, given a Gross Reproduction Rate of 2.5 and an initial life expectancy of 25 years, an increase in this life expectancy to 45 years would produce an increase of about 18 percent in the relative number of those aged 0–9; an increase from 25 to 60 in life expectancy would lead to an increase of about 27 percent in the fraction aged 0–9 (based on stable population tables in Coale and Demeny, pp. 74–106; see also Brotman, Keyfitz and Flieger, and on past mortality trends, United Nations, 1962, 1971, 1973).

Increase in longevity at higher ages may slightly increase the relative number of older persons in a stable population. An increase in life expectancy from 50 to 70.2 years may augment the fraction of a stable population 75 and over from 3.38 to 6.06 percent (United Nations, 1968, p. 182). Given a life expectancy of around 90 and a Gross Reproduction Rate at around the replacement level, about one-third of the population would be 60 and over compared with about 22 percent with a life expectancy of about 70 (United Nations, 1956, p. 29).

Coale (1959, pp. 36–41) shows that the Gross Reproduction Rate could dominate the age structure of a population even if man were immortal. Thus, although the proportion over 60 years of age would approach 100 percent if the Gross Reproduction Rate approximated unity, the proportion over 60 would approach only 41.4 percent if this rate were 1.5. Moreover, if the Gross Reproduction Rate were 3, "the proportion over 60 would become only 9.1 percent." In short, "when fertility is high, even immortality would produce only a moderate proportion of aged persons."

Immigration and age composition

Immigration can temporarily modify the age composition of an immigrant-receiving country if the age structure of the immigrant stream differs from that of the immigrant-receiving country. Under comparable conditions, emigration can effect a country's age composition. As Keyfitz (1968, p. 94) points out, however, "Non-sustained migration has only a transient effect on the age distribution of a population, so long as the migratory movements do not affect the prevailing patterns of fertility and mortality." During periods of heavy relative immigration into the United States, the age composition of the latter's population was tilted slightly though temporarily toward the age composition of the immigrant stream. Today, of course, the foreign-born population in the United States is much older than the native population (U.S. Bureau of the Census, Nov. 1975, pp. 12–13). Despite legal restrictions limiting the absolute number of new entrants, migration may become increasingly important in the population growth of countries that maintain low rates of fertility.

Internal migration produces and tends temporarily to sustain interregional differences in age structure, for relatively young persons are both attracted to economically promising areas and disposed to emigrate from unpromising areas. Population aging is more pronounced in rural regions (e.g., in France and the United States) and in areas attractive to older persons (e.g., Florida) (see Paillat; U.S. Bureau of the Census, 1973). Should net emigration persist, a region's fertility declines and eventually accentuates the aging associated with the selective outmigration of those under 65.

Pre-1950 trends in population aging

Among the determinants of population aging, a very gradual decline in fertility and natality became manifest in some Western countries in the nineteenth century, first in France and the United States (Spengler, 1938). During the last quarter of the nineteenth century, population aging became apparent in northwest Europe and Australia and New Zealand; later the decline

Table 2.3. *Percent of population 65 and over*

Country	%	Year	%	Year	%	Year	%	Year
Canada	—	—	5.07	(1901)	5.55	(1931)	7.76	(1951)
United States	—	—	4.07	(1900)	5.41	(1930)	8.14	(1950)
Brazil	—	—	2.11	(1900)	—	—	2.46	(1950)
Austria	3.92	(1869)	4.98	(1900)	6.77	(1927)	10.57	(1951)
Belgium	5.87	(1845)	6.18	(1900)	7.59	(1930)	10.69	(1947)
Denmark	5.45	(1850)	6.66	(1901)	7.52	(1935)	8.38	(1945)
France	6.47	(1851)	8.20	(1901)	9.35	(1931)	11.80	(1950)
Germany	4.72	(1880)	4.88	(1900)	7.36	(1933)	9.27	(1951)
Great Britain	4.64	(1851)	4.69	(1901)	7.40	(1931)	10.83	(1950)
Netherlands	4.75	(1849)	6.01	(1899)	6.21	(1930)	7.73	(1950)
Norway	5.75	(1855)	7.91	(1900)	8.29	(1930)	9.62	(1950)
Sweden	4.78	(1850)	8.37	(1900)	9.20	(1930)	10.31	(1950)
Switzerland	5.11	(1860)	5.84	(1900)	6.87	(1920)	9.62	(1950)
Australia	—	—	4.29	(1911)	6.49	(1933)	8.04	(1947)
New Zealand	2.96	(1891)	2.06	(1901)	6.56	(1936)	9.57	(1951)

Source: United Nations, 1956, Table III, pp. 94–168. The figures in parentheses accompanying the age fraction indicate the year to which the fraction relates.

spread to southern and eastern Europe (United Nations, 1971, 1973). Elsewhere there was little or no change. After World War I, however, the natality decline became more intense and widespread (United Nations, 1971, 1973). Moreover, Kuczynski found that although crude natality still exceeded crude mortality in western and northern Europe, the net reproduction rate had descended below 1.0, and the population was no longer replacing itself in the countries covered or in several countries of eastern Europe (Kuczynski, 1928, Chapter 3–4, and 1931, especially Chapter 5; also, Dublin et al., Chapter 12).

With its net reproduction rate below 1.0, a stable population would include relatively more older persons (persons over 59 or over 64) than would a corresponding stationary population with a net reproduction rate of 1.0, and still more than a stable population with a net reproduction rate slightly above 1.0 (Dublin et al., pp. 244–8). In general, with a lower rather than a higher net reproduction rate, the aged proportion of a population would be

Table 2.4. *Sex and age structure for France and the United Kingdom*

France

	Men			Women		
Year	0–14	15–64	65 and over	0–14	15–64	65 and over
1896	26[a]	66	8	25.5[a]	65.5	9
1911	26	66	8	25	66	9
1921	24	68	8	21.5	68.5	10
1926	24	68	8	22	68	10
1936	26	65	9	24	65	11
1946	23.5	67.5	9	20.5	67	12.5

United Kingdom

1891	35.9	59.5	4.6	33.7	60.9	5.4
1911	31.8	63.0	5.1	29.9	63.8	6.3
1921	29.5	65.1	5.4	26.6	66.7	6.7
1926	27.6	66.5	5.9	24.9	67.9	7.2
1936	23.9	68.6	7.4	21.6	69.4	8.9
1946	22.2	68.8	9.0	20.0	68.6	11.4

[a] Percent of population.
Source: Annuaire statistique retrospectif de la France (Paris, 1966), as reported in Carrè, Dubois, and Malinvaud, p. 43 and Feinstein, pp. T 123–4.

higher. A downward drift in the net reproduction rate would therefore lead to an increase in the average age of a stable population.

Data for selected years presented in Table 2.3 reveal a general upward drift in the relative number of persons 65 or more years old in more developed countries between 1900 and 1950. That this drift was already under way in 1900 is evident from the percentage in the first column of the table. There was little or no change in less developed countries (e.g., see Brazil), and less change in countries in which fertility declined less significantly (e.g., Netherlands). Table 2.4 provides more detailed age structure data for the United Kingdom and France which further indicate the pattern of population aging in these countries in the first half of the twentieth century. For France, Carré et al. argue that these changes were in response to the downward trend in the birthrate up to World War II, wartime reductions in births in 1915–18 and 1933–45, war-related deaths primarily among adult males, and migratory movements that increased the proportion of adults who were of working age.

Concern about possible consequences of population aging[5] accompanied concern in various countries that the population would decline absolutely as implied by the descent of net reproduction rates below the replacement level (Dublin et al.; Glass, Chapter 8; Spengler, 1978; Thompson and Whelpton). Concomitants of population aging are treated in detail in later chapters. In the section "Current prospect" (below, this chapter), we indicate some of the changes in age structure that would occur should fertility settle near or slightly below the replacement level.

Limits to aging trend

Population aging has continued since 1950, and most projections indicate that the elderly population will expand in size throughout the remainder of the twentieth century (Unsigned, 1975, 1977). Table 2.5 illustrates the growth in the proportion of the population 65 and over in the industrialized countries and estimates the size of this age cohort to 1985. For most of these countries, the fraction of the population aged 65 and over rises by 2 to 4 percentage points during this period.

The future course of population aging will likely be dominated by the course of fertility, for, as indicated below, prospective changes in migration and mortality will probably be of limited long-run significance to the age structure in advanced countries. Fertility is somewhat below the replacement level in Canada, the United States, and a number of European countries (e.g., Austria, Belgium, Denmark, both Germanies, Luxembourg, Sweden, Switzerland, United Kingdom) (see United Nations, *Demographic Yearbook, 1975, 1976*). As a result, a relatively high proportion of the population seems destined to be in the 65-and-over category. However, as actual population decline threatens to

Table 2.5. *Proportion of population 65 and over*

	Actual						Projected	
	1951	1956	1959	1965	1970	1975	1980	1985
Belgium	11.1	11.6	11.7	12.5	13.3	14.2	14.7	13.4
Canada				7.6	7.8	8.0	8.4	
Denmark	9.1	9.9	10.3	11.4	12.1	13.0	13.6	13.7
Finland				7.9	8.9	10.3	11.4	11.4
France	11.4	11.6	11.6^a	12.0	12.8	13.3	13.3	11.7
Germany	9.3	9.9	10.4	11.9	13.3	14.2	14.4	12.6
Ireland	10.7	10.9	10.8^b	11.2^c	11.2^d	11.3^d	11.5^f	11.4^g
Italy	8.1	8.7	8.8^h	9.7	10.6	11.7	12.7	12.0
Japan				6.3	7.0	7.9	8.9	9.5
Netherlands	7.8	8.4	8.8	9.5	10.1	10.6	10.9	10.8
Norway	9.6	10.2	10.6	11.9	12.8	13.4	13.8	14.0
Sweden	10.2	11.0	11.5	12.6	13.6	14.7	15.6	15.9
United Kingdom	10.9	11.3	11.5^h	12.0	12.8	13.5	13.9	13.5

^{a} 1960. ^{b} 1961. ^{c} 1966. ^{d} 1971. ^{e} 1976. ^{f} 1981. ^{g} 1986. ^{h} 1958.
Source: "Old Age Pensions: Level, Adjustment and Coverage," *The OECD Observer*, Sept. 1975, pp. 19–24.

materialize, fertility-favoring measures may be introduced (e.g., as in France; Spengler, 1938), and population growth stablized around or slightly above the replacement level. It is upon the outcome of such action that the age composition of a population may eventually depend. The outcome, of course, is uncertain, at least in the United States, where structural and institutional changes appear to be favoring childlessness and lower fertility (e.g., see Bumpass, pp. 67–9; DeJong and Sell, pp. 129–42). Although births are likely to fluctuate owing to echo effects of past fluctuations and to variations in fertility, it is not likely that fertility will settle much above the replacement level given lifetime births now expected per 1,000 wives and current net reproduction rates.

A slight increase in overall life expectancy at birth for most national populations is achievable through increasing the life expectancy of racial and other groups whose life expectancy is below that of groups with relatively low mortality. Given such an increase, however, these groups will encounter the forces restraining increase in the life expectancy of the more favorably situated groups, for man's age is limited to not much above 100 years (Le Bras, also his bibliography), considering current conditions and relevant knowledge.

The impact of migration on age structures in the future is likely to be small and transitory. Migration is unlikely to be sufficient in volume, continuous enough, and characterized by persistent enough form and fertility patterns to modify permanently the age composition of an immigrant-receiving country. Of course, waves of immigration may introduce transitory humps into age distributions (e.g., see Keyfitz and Flieger, pp. 13–15, 89, 162–3; also U.S. Bureau of the Census, Nov. 1975, pp. 12–13).

Even if we assume that man's life span is unlikely to undergo significant change, it may be assumed that man in the future will realize a somewhat larger fraction of his representative life span or potential longevity than he has in the past. Although a few individuals have attained more than 100 years of age, the length of a life span representative of a significant number of individuals can hardly be fixed much above 100 years. The presence of a few authentic centenarians, or an increase in their number, is prospectively of little significance, for the probability of a person aged 65 surviving to age 100 is very low – for example, less than 1 –3 in 1,000 in England and Wales (Metropolitan Life, 1971).[6] Of significance, however, may be an increase in the fraction of those over 65 who are over 75.

Today life expectancy at birth in countries currently characterized by most favorable expectations is at least 2½ times of that in areas where conditions are unfavorable or what it was in ancient, medieval, and early modern times when conditions affecting mortality were very unfavorable. By the early 1970s, expectation of life at birth in Sweden and Norway had attained 72.11 and 71.32 years among males and 77.51 and 77.6 years among females. Comparable expectations in Denmark were nearly as high. In ancient and medieval times and in some present-day underdeveloped countries (e.g., in Africa), life expectancy at birth has been as low as near 30, if not lower (see United Nations, 1962, 1975, pp. 80–1, 1976, pp. 524–6; also Blacker, pp. 107–28, and Brass, 1968, Chapter 4). Increase in life expectancy at birth, especially since the eighteenth century, has been accomplished principally through control of what Henschen calls "infectious diseases" (Dublin et al., Chapter 8; Henschen, pp. 1–163).

If we divide the causes of death somewhat as do Preston et al., we may distinguish between deaths (other than those due to accident or injury) that result from an initial invasion of the human body by other living organisms and deaths whose "origin is organ malfunction due to malformation, to cell mutation, or to deterioration which, in the present state of knowledge, seems predominantly a function of age" (Preston et al., Chapter 1, especially page 4; also U.S. Department of Health, Education and Welfare, pp. 5 –13). In a population characterized by a male life expectancy of around 35 years, close to 58 percent of newborns tend ultimately to succumb to diseases that may be attributed largely to the invasion of the human body by other living organisms (e.g., respiratory, TB, other infectious and parasitic diseases, influenza, pneumonia, bronchitis, diarrheal disease, and diseases of infancy). However, given virtual control of these diseases and reduction to about 8.5 percent of deaths attributable to them, one may expect a male life expectancy at birth of 70–4 years. Comparable improvement would take place in female life expectancy (Preston et al., pp. 2–7). Accompanying this decline in mortality due to control of the diseases would be an increase from about 9.26 to about 67.14 percent in the causes of death due to neoplasms and cardiovascular disease alone (Preston et al., pp. 2–3). Increase in life expectancy at birth and later years now depends largely upon the degree to which death due to neoplasms and cardiovascular diseases can be postponed or prevented.

According to a recent study, male life expectancy at age 45 could be increased by about 8 years, and at age 65 by about 7 years, if mortality due to diseases of the heart, malignant neoplasms, and cerebrovascular diseases were reduced by one-half. Comparable increase would take place in female life expectancy.

So great an improvement is not soon to be anticipated, however. Although it is possible that mortality could be reduced in the future by 5 or perhaps 10 percent, "it would require a major breakthrough in research to effect a reduction of as much as one-fourth in the number of deaths from any one cause" (Metropolitan Life, 1975, pp. 8–9). Improvements in life style and living environment could, of course, contribute to some reduction in mortality (Metropolitan Life, 1977, pp. 5–9). However, given the nature of the causes of mortality today, especially among older individuals (U.S. Department of Health, Education and Welfare; Busse and Pfeiffer, Chapters 2, 7, 12), attempts to reduce mortality further encounter difficulties much greater than those overcome in the course of reducing mortality so notably in the past one hundred years.

Two sets of changes may, however, facilitate increase in life expectancy, especially at more advanced years. First, since mortality is affected directly and indirectly by environmental factors and life styles, improvement in these conditions can reduce mortality and extend life, particularly if improvements reduce the impact of several or more possible causes of death (Strehler; Tanka et al.; Keyfitz, 1977). For example, in the United States environmental factors contribute greatly to socioeconomic, sexual, and racial mortality differences; thus correction of these factors can increase realized life expectancy appreciably (Kitigawa). Presumably such correction along with improvement in the treatment of diseases has contributed notably to the continuing increase in life expectancy, even that of persons of advanced age (Brotman, Depoid).

Second, a new approach to the nature of diseases mainly responsible for mortality among older persons may result in life extension. Thus, as Lewis Thomas observes, "what is new in medicine is the general awareness" that problems "posed by the senile dementias, arthritis, cancer, and so on" are "biological problems" and are "ultimately solvable." Attention is now being directed to changes in biological properties associated with aging, to the cumulative effect of the aging of individual cells, to entropic processes and changes at the functional level, and so on

(Curtis, Cutler, Kurtzman and Prillit, Le Bras, Shock, Strehler). "It is highly probable," Sheppard and Rix (Chapter 4) conclude, that current research and discoveries, together with "greater application of current and new medical practices, and adoption by individuals of life styles conducive to better health and longer life, will produce a critical mass bound to bring about a biomedical revolution." In the U.S. Bureau of the Census population projection of July 1977, male and female life expectancies as of 2050 were put at 71.8 and 81 years, respectively, rather than at 1972 estimate levels, namely, 69.9 and 78 (U.S. Bureau of the Census, Oct. 1975).

Even if the life-extending effects of efforts to reduce mortality further prove very limited, especially among those already experiencing high life expectancy, these efforts may produce a useful by-product. This by-product would be a notable increase in man's continuing effective use of his faculties in and beyond his fifties and sixties. Although the incidence of illness and/or disability is higher among older persons (Busse and Pfeiffer, Chapter 7; Metropolitan Life, 1974, 1977), it may prove subject to appreciable reduction. As a result, the potentially productive fraction of the population would be increased. Such increase is essential because increase in life expectancy at advanced years (e.g., above age 65) can increase problems associated with *population* aging. It can do this if the productive and functional capacities of the representative individual undergoing life extension at advanced age fail to keep pace with this extension. For then the burden of supporting the older population incident on the population of productive age will increase. It is quite likely, however, that the causal factors underlying extension of the life of older persons also contribute to improvement of the health of older members of the labor force and thus augment their productivity as well as their disposition to remain in the labor force rather than to retire.

Current prospect

The United States is used as an example to illustrate the effect of prolonged low fertility on the age structure of an industrialized nation. As noted earlier, the United States along with other developed countries has already experienced considerable population aging. The continuation of fertility rates at or below the replacement level will further augment the relative size of older cohorts. Alternative projections of the U.S. population indicate the ensuing age structure changes as a nation approaches a stationary state.

In Table 2.6 (derived from U.S. Bureau of the Census, July 1977) we present three projections of the U.S. population to illustrate how population aging may affect dependency relations within a population. Series II is based upon the assumption that fertility settles at the replacement level, but with net legal immigration running 400,000 per year. Series IIX is based upon the same assumption, but with zero net legal immigration.[7] Series III is based upon the assumption that the fertility rate settles at 1.7 or 0.4 below the replacement level, but with net legal immigration running 400,000 per year. With age-specific mortality essentially given, fertility levels govern the outcomes.

Whether what is called the "current prospect" will materialize is uncertain. Whereas U.S. fertility was at the 1.76 level, below the 2.1 replacement level, in 1976, lifetime births expected per wife 18–24 years old[8] suggested that fertility might rise slightly above replacement.[9] Moreover, in keeping with R. A. Easterlin's (also Keyfitz, 1968) and similar theories, not only may fluctuations in economic conditions contribute to fluctuations in fertility, but, as Wachter suggests, an upswing in the rate of growth of real wages "could cause a new 'baby boom,'" though he does not actually foresee such a boom. Given the wide distribution of fertility below the replacement level in advanced countries, however (United Nations, 1975; DeJong and Sell), the series included in Table 2.6 serves to illustrate the prospective impact of population aging upon the relative economic status of dependents.

We may divide the populations in the three series into three roughly conventional categories: young dependents under 18 years of age, those of working age, normally 18–64, though conceivably as low as 18–54, and those generally retired from the

Table 2.6. *Population projections for the United States (millions),*
1976–2050

Age	1976	1985	2000	2025	2050
Series II					
Total	215.1	232.9	260.4	295.7	315.6
0–17	65.2	62.3	69.0	72.5	76.5
18–64	127.0	143.3	159.6	172.3	183.6
65 and over	22.9	27.3	31.8	50.9	55.5
18–64/total	0.590	0.615	0.613	0.583	0.582
65 and over/total	0.107	0.117	0.122	0.172	0.176
Median age	29.0	31.5	35.5	37.6	37.8
Series IIX					
Total	215.1	228.9	248.4	267.4	269.4
0–17	65.2	60.8	64.9	64.3	64.2
18–64	127.0	140.8	152.1	154.5	155.5
65 and over	22.9	27.2	31.5	48.6	49.8
18–64/total	0.590	0.615	0.612	0.578	0.577
65 and over/total	0.107	0.119	0.127	0.182	0.185
Median age	29.0	31.7	36.0	38.4	38.6
Series III					
Total	215.1	228.9	245.9	251.9	231.0
0–17	65.2	58.3	56.9	49.4	43.8
18–64	127.0	143.3	157.2	151.6	134.9
65 and over	22.9	27.3	31.8	50.9	52.3
18–64/total	0.590	62.6	0.639	0.602	0.584
65 and over/total	0.107	0.119	0.129	0.202	0.226
Median age	29.0	32.0	37.3	42.4	43.7

Source: U.S. Bureau of Census, *Current Population Reports,* Series
P-25, No. 704, "Projections of the Population of the United States:
1977–2050," U.S. Government Printing Office, Washington, D.C.,
1977, Tables 8–12, D-2. Series II assumes fertility at 2.1 and immigration at 400,000 per year; Series IIX assumes fertility at 2.1 and no immigration; Series III assumes fertility at 1.7 and annual immigration of
400,000.

work force, usually those over 64 years of age, though conceivably some or most of those over 54 years of age.

Reading the table from left to right reveals striking changes.
First, the ratio of those 18–64 to the rest of the population remains in the neighborhood of 0.6; that is, about three-fifths of the

population remains of working age, or about 50 percent more than are defined as of normal dependent age. Second, the age composition of the population of dependent age changes, with the fraction under 18 declining and that over 64 rising. Third, the ratio of those over 64 to those 18–64, upon whom depends the support of the retired fraction, increases particularly when the population is stationary (i.e., IIX) or decreasing (i.e., III) Fourth, given that the cost per dependent of supporting older dependents exceeds the corresponding cost of supporting young dependents, the cost per worker of supporting dependents rises as a population approaches stationarity, and even more after fertility descends below the replacement level and a population begins to decline (see Series III).

Withdrawal from the labor force before the attainment of age 64 will accentuate the economically adverse trends described in the preceding paragraph. On the other hand, entry into the labor force prior to age 18, if without adverse effect upon human capital formation, and delay of withdrawal from the labor force until after age 64, will decelerate these economically adverse trends. In general, however, the per worker burdensomeness of the support of retirees, given the level at which a society elects to support older persons who have withdrawn from the labor force, depends mainly upon the size of the fraction of those aged 55–64 who remain in the labor force. Although some persons under 55 presently withdraw from the labor force, currently their number is not relatively large, nor is the number of those over 64 who remain in the labor force.

In sum, phenomena discussed in this section are dominated by the degree to which a population ages, a process mainly governed by the level of fertility as has been shown in earlier sections and as had been assumed in the several series presented in Table 2.6. Meanwhile, however, the degree of comfort with which a population is willing and able to support its nonworking components, especially older persons who have withdrawn from the labor force, is conditioned to a large degree by the relative number of those aged 55–64 remaining in the labor force and in some degree by the number of those over 64 who do not withdraw from the labor force.[10]

Given the growing awareness that many diseases pose biological problems (Thomas) and the current efforts to prevent disease and to extend life expectancy, especially at advanced years,the burden of supporting the aged incident upon the labor force could increase unless the average active working life is increased commensurately. For example, should a minimum preventable portion of major causes of death be eliminated by the year 2000, the number of social security beneficiaries would be 9.23 percent higher than it would be given a continuance of current mortality. As a result the tax rate required to support beneficiaries would be 13.55 percent higher than under present conditions. This increase might be offset in some measure by reduction in costs of disease care (see Gori and Richter; also Depoid, on recent increase in life expectancy at advanced ages in several European countries). Although the limit to man's life span has not been determined (Le Bras), Fowles's suggestion that within 50 years "the average life-span may be about 800 years" does not appear tenable, given man's environments and modes of conduct.

3

Population aging and dependency

The major concern in this chapter is to sample and review literature of the past four decades relating to the significance of
changes in age structure owing to population aging (Cowgill),
especially with reference to their impact on dependency and the
economic state of older dependents. However, the impact of
these changes in age structure associated with decline in the rate
of population growth must be distinguished analytically from the
impact of decline in the rate of population growth as such (e.g.,
see Sauvy, 1948). The nature of the relationship between decline
in the rate of population growth and increase in the relative
number of older persons was illustrated broadly in Tables 2.1 and
2.2, and in greater detail in Table 2.6.

Population aging alters the age structure of the dependent population and therewith the means through which support is transferred to dependents from the individuals and institutions with
whom this support originates. For example, given expectation of
life at birth of 70.2 years and a Gross Reproduction Rate of 2,
persons under 15 and over 59 in a stable population will constitute
45.3 percent of the population, with only 17.6 percent being 60 or
more years of age. If, however, the Gross Reproduction Rate
should settle in the neighborhood of the replacement level, about
40 percent of the population will be under 15 and over 59, and

about one-half of these will be 60 or more years old (United Nations, 1956, p. 27; also United Nations, 1973). Should nondependent age in our example be defined as 18–64 instead of 15–59, a parallel change in the age structure of dependents would occur (e.g., see tables in Coale and Demeny).

The impact of alteration in the age structure of the dependent population upon the support of this population has been modified by socioeconomic changes over the past 50 to 75 years. Old age has come to be recognized as a distinct period of life – a period likely to be marked by poverty should the family and complementary institutions prove incapable of supplying adequate support (e.g., see Hareven). Although greater provision for support of the aged became available from outside the family, it was not always adequate (e.g., see Hurff; Webber, 1955). Relatively more persons attained the age of 60 or 65 and lived longer upon attaining this age than was the case earlier in the present century, though not always with the assurance of a corresponding increase in worklife or sustained support (e.g., see Corson and McConnell). Moreover, with the replacement of gold and monetary standards by what J. R. Hicks (p. 391) has called a "labor standard," the real earning power of income sources other than labor became subject to erosion through inflation – a change that affected adversely various income sources of the aged (Spengler, 1956). Although political organization on the part of the aged might, of course, restrain upward price movements (Reder, also *The Annals*), the long-term objective of the American labor movement amounts to a strengthening of the "labor standard" (Neufeld). Moreover, given inflation, only indexing could prevent early retirement from being a financial disaster, according to the Science Council of Canada (p. 33). The question of how to overcome problems of inflation and intergenerational transfer thus is made more difficult by population aging.

Interest in retirement and related problems on the part of the International Labor Organization contributed to growing interest in demographic aspects of these problems on the part of the

United Nations, an interest manifested in *The Aging of Popula-tions and Its Economic and Social Implications* (1956), Chapter 3). It is found that:

> aging brings about a change in the very nature of the trans-fers by the working members of the population to the non-working groups. The general trend has been an in-creasing substitution of social contributions for the bur-dens freely accepted within the framework of the family. Hence in a population that has aged, the support of the non-working members becomes more difficult because it is less readily accepted. The psychological effects of this change in the nature of economic transfers are among the most important consequences of the process of aging. (p. 81)

"The family," as J. C. Weldon remarks, "is no longer remotely able to cope with anything like the proportion of problems it once handled" (p. 578). He adds:

> The state increasingly displaces or complements family structures in providing intergenerational transfers . . . Governments . . . search for a redistributional process their successors will respect out of similar self interest. The process that allows continuity across generations is to compute current transfers by giving equal weight to (for example) pensionable years now being lived and those still to be lived. The state thus relies on the source of continuity that supports family transfers. (p. 559)[1]

Recognition of population aging prior to 1950

Marked attention was not directed to changes in age structure until the present century. Indeed, despite a growing awareness in the late nineteenth and early twentieth century that in some countries or regions natality and natural increase were declining – since the early 1800s in France – it was effects of de-cline in the rate of population growth rather than effects of changes in the age structure (see Table 2.3, in Chapter 2) that initially commanded attention or aroused concern. In France, for example, especially after the Franco-Prussian War (1870–1), concern was expressed that there were too few young adults and potential conscripts. Little attention was directed to effects associated with changes in the age structure as such (Spengler, 1938, Chapters 6, 11) until in and after the 1940s (e.g., see Daric; Sauvy, 1948). Again in 1895, Edwin Cannan (Cannan, 1933, pp. 108–24) predicted that the population of England and Wales would be nearly stationary in 1941, but he made no reference to the changing age structure, though six years later he did indicate that England and Wales would no longer be able to supply many emigrants, presumably young, to population-short Australia, New Zealand, and Canada (Cannan, pp. 125–35). The significance of manpower of military age, stressed in pre-1914 France, was stressed by Daric (pp. 41–2) in 1948 and noted in 1950 by Britain's Royal Commission on Population (Vol. 3, paragraph 212).

With the development of population projections, however, implications of population aging (as distinguished from slowing down or cessation of population growth) were noted. For example, in 1933 Thompson and Whelpton (1933, Chapter 4), having estimated that by 1980 the fraction of the population over 64 (5.4 percent in 1930) would have risen to between 12.1 and 13.3 percent, pointed to the consequences of an increase in the relative number of elders (pp. 163–71). They indicated that the prospective age changes would permit a slight increase in the potentially productive fraction of the population provided older workers retained their productive powers and could find employment, and that business organization remained progressive. It was possible, however, that

> the increasing proportion of those in the older productive ages may create some very urgent problems in employment and dependency unless the economic organization allows them to produce in accord with their capacity. A marked reduction in the actual productiveness of the one-fourth of the population which will soon be found in

the 45-to-64 age group could not but prove a very serious matter. (p. 170)

Moreover, they continued, "the problem of old-age pensions" would become much greater, as would that of old age dependency (pp. 165–6, 170).

R. E. Chaddock wrote in similar vein (pp. 190–3), saying that it was "impossible to ignore longer the problem of jobs for older workers" and that "institutions and agencies for the care of the aged, the burden of old age pensions, and the costs of dependency will increase rapidly." The National Resources Committee (1938, p. 31, p. 166 on health) indicated the need to keep older persons in the labor force and to avoid too early retirement because the resulting pension costs might become too burdensome. Concern occasionally was expressed not only that the absence of population growth might slow income growth, but also that the burden of military and related pensions would increase as aging made for a more rapid growth in the numbers of older persons than of members of the labor force (Spengler, 1950).

It was emphasized that if the fraction of the labor force over, say, 44 increased, maintenance of productivity per worker depended upon making effective use of workers 45 and over. John Durand (pp. 64–5) in 1948 pointed out that "the decline of self-employment and the advance of technology are almost certain to continue their relentless force pushing the aged out of the labor market." Spengler (1948) presented evidence in support of the view that prospective changes in age composition need not make for decline in output per capita. Much of the thrust of the New York State Joint Legislative Committee's report, *Birthdays Don't Count,* was designed to overcome barriers in the way of effective employment of older workers.

In the appendix to the "Report of the Economics Committee" (see Vol. III of the *Papers of the Royal Commission on Population*), it was pointed out that according to various projections of the population of England and Wales, the proportion of the population of working age (i.e., 15–65) would move below the 1950 level, but "not to so low a level as prevailed throughout nearly the whole of the Victorian era." In the Commission's *Report*

(Chapter 11 on "age balance"), the hope was expressed that "the average level of fitness now associated with age 65 may come to characterize age 68, or even 70" and thus prevent a decline in the ratio of producers to consumers. It was noted, however, that "the pension arrangements of the National Insurance Act of 1946" gave "a substantial inducement to retire" to males on reaching the age of 65 and to females on reaching the age of 60. This effect of pension systems has been noticed frequently over the past two decades (e.g., Munnell, pp. 73–6). As indicated below, the Commission's *Report* points also to fiscal and other problems affected by the prospective decline in both the ratio of the work force to the population and the relative number of young persons.

Increases in the cost of support programs for the elderly

With the development and expansion of public pension or social security systems, concern developed that the ratio of the working population to the retired population would decline to levels incompatible with the adequate support of the retired population, especially the population of pensionable age. This danger was stressed by the Royal Commission on Population (*Report,* Chapter 11), which found the most satisfactory solution in the prolongation of man's working life through removal of physical and institutional influences conducive to early withdrawal from the labor force. Premature retirement and limitations upon the employment of older persons limited the work force and produced forces that tended to produce an imbalance between consumption and production, a deficit in the balance of payments, and an increase in the cost of pensions (*Report,* pp. 112–16).

Essentially similar views were expressed by PEP (Political and Economic Planning) in its report, *Population Policy in Great Britain:*

> Clearly, as Lord Keynes suggested, there is danger that an increasing ratio of retired dependent people to productive workers will reduce the buoyancy of State revenue while adding to the cost of social services. Above all, there is danger that output per head will decline. (p. 84)

Increasingly it was recognized that early retirement rather than age structure itself made the advent of a stationary or near-stationary population a potential source of economic problems (e.g., see Clark, 1977a, b; Rejda and Shepler; Turchi). For example, according to the U.S. Bureau of the Census, the potential U.S. stationary population, with a median age of 38.9 years, would consist 18.98 percent of persons 65 and over, 57.66 percent of persons 18–64, and 23.66 percent of persons under 18; 20.78 percent would be under 16. The ratio of the population of working age to that 65 and over thus would approximate only 3 to 1 instead of 5 to 1 or higher over the next 25 years (see also Ryder). Of course, a 3-to-1 ratio might make tolerable a pension system under which the average pension approximated 60 percent of average earnings, though at a much higher tax rate than required at a 5-to-1 ratio.

However, should retirement prior to age 65 increase, the tax burden might become unbearable. For example, given a stationary population and universal retirement at age 55, the ratio of contributors (e.g., persons 18–54) to pension funds to number of beneficiaries (e.g., persons over 54) would approximate only 1.53 to 1. The resulting tax burden probably would prove intolerable despite the associated reduction in the cost of supporting those under 18. Of special interest are Munnell's estimates (p. 77) that under the American social security system the tax per worker required to provide $1.00 of benefits per retiree amounted to 40 cents given retirement at age 55, compared with 18 cents given retirement at 65 and 13 cents given retirement at age 68.

Presumably W. B. Reddaway (p. 29) had in mind an age composition resembling that of a stationary population when he dismissed "the 'increased pension' bogey as quantitatively negligible, so far as it rests on demographic factors; its real basis is the general desire to improve the provision made for the elderly by raising the real value of the pension." He pointed out, of course, that when a population was growing, each generation was greater, and that when "the active population" belonged to "a bigger generation," there were more people to share the cost of pensions (p. 28).

W. A. B. Hopkin, noting that "a change in age-distribution exerts its principal economic effects via the change in the relative numbers of producers and consumers in the population," said that "as a general principle it would seen reasonable to avoid as far as possible arrangements which will tend to lower the ratio of 'producers' (adjusted for levels of productivity) to 'consumers' (adjusted for levels of expenditure)." He recommended that the pension age under the old age pensions system be raised two years, enough to offset the prospective increase in the proportion of old people (cf. Sauvy, 1948, p. 121, on the advantage of increasing retirement age from 60 to 65). He pointed also to the danger of committing a government "to provide a retirement pension at a definite age laid down years or even decades in advance" of time for retirement, and argued that it was desirable that the age at which a retirement pension might be claimed be declared variable (Hopkin, pp. 32–6).

Alfred Sauvy (1948, pp. 115–24; also 1969, pp. 303–19) in 1948 examined the ways in which population aging decreased the ratio of persons of working age to those of retirement age, tended to slow down increase in output per worker, and by increasing the cost per worker of providing support for the aged contributed to family limitation and to inflationary policies especially incident upon the incomes of older persons. The cost of supporting older persons was augmented by the comparative inability of persons over 50 to find employment as well as by making age 60 instead of age 65 "the dividing line between working and retirement." These reactions to aging, especially successive currency devaluations, were particularly evident in France, "which entered the aging process well before other countries" (p. 117).

> An increase in the number of old persons entails an additional burden on the adult population, to the full extent to which old age implies inactivity. Indeed, whatever the legal source of income of an old person (direct support by his children, retired pay or old age pension, annuities, income from capital, etc.), such income is a charge upon the production of adult persons. (p. 117)

The same point has been made by Daric (p. 38; see also Spengler, 1978a).

This burden was destined to increase both in France and elsewhere in western Europe, Sauvy noted (see also Bourgeois-Pichat), as the ratio of persons of productive age to those of retirement age decreased with population aging. If the average pension income of an old man were fixed as by current convention at 60 percent of an adult's income, the cost incident on the working population would rise because productivity could not be increased adequately; for the spirit of enterprise would grow weaker as a population aged, and willingness to accept risk would be replaced by "the desire for security." Then no longer would the incentive to create and produce to contribute to the growth of average output be strong, as it is under classic capitalism. Indeed, Sauvy reported, hostility to collectivism of sorts was developing in France and elsewhere.

At the present time, particularly in France, a reaction against social security is taking shape. Social contributions have become extremely heavy (about 35%) and producers are offering resistance against which the Government is so impotent that at times it actually helps the resistance to become vocal. (p. 119)

In the United States support for social security is diminishing also, according to Eldred.

Of greater concern than the advent of a stationary population is the prospect of a decline in numbers presaged by the descent of fertility below the replacement level in a number of advanced countries, and an increase in early withdrawal from the labor force due in part to the development of national and private pension and social security systems. Illustrative of the impact of a decline in population owing to natural decrease is Series III in Table 2.6. There the ratio of the population 18–64 to that 65 and over approximates 2.9, in contrast to about 3.5 in a stationary population (see Series IIX in Table 2.6) and about 5 to 1 prior to the development of the impact of below-replacement fertility (U.S. Bureau of the Census, 1977). A consequence of this decline is a reduction in the number of contributors to pension and social security funds relative to the number of beneficiaries of these funds. Increase in early retirement (e.g., see Bixby; also Reimers's critique of retirement age measurement) on the part of male members of the labor force intensifies, as was noted earlier, the decline in the ratio of contributors to beneficiaries and produces an imbalance between claims on funds and the rate at which these claims can be met.

Illustrative of this potential imbalance dependent upon changes in age structure and retirement behavior is the American social security system. Whereas in 1950 there were only six beneficiaries for every one hundred workers, the number of beneficiaries per one hundred workers had risen to thirty by 1975 and is expected to rise to forty-five by 2030 (see *Reports* of the Advisory Council on Social Security, pp. 120–2). Also illustrative are underfunded and undersupported industrial, municipal, and state pension funds with large unfunded liabilities and too little economic growth to permit easy meeting of these liabilities out of expanding gross revenue (see A. F. Ehrbar, Faltermayer, also Skolnik).

Failure to cope adequately with pension and related problems has come about in part through neglect of the nature of intergenerational transfers of income – the fact that they are instances of debt finance and of the shifting of real costs to future generations (Browning). As a result of this neglect of the nature of the relationship, the burden imposed by the provision of pensions has been overlooked or underestimated. First, too little attention has been given to the fact that the goods and services consumed by pensioners and other inactive retirees must be produced by the active, productive population contemporary with these retirees. Therefore, how much can be made available for the support of the retired population is conditioned by the size of the active population, its average productivity, and its acquiescence in the taxes, corporate costs, and so on, destined to finance the real costs of supporting the retired (Spengler, 1978a). Second, in the past, each cohort or generation has been larger than its predecessor and so has sometimes made the burden of supporting the retired more tolerable. In addition, municipalities and other bodies responsible for the support of municipal and similar pensioners have tended to grow and make only partially funded pension systems workable. In the future, however, successive cohorts will be either unchanged or smaller in size and hence less capable than their predecessors of supplying the goods and services demanded by pensioners.[2] Similarly, various municipalities and other bodies responsible for the payment of pensions have ceased to grow, thereby making more burdensome the cost of meeting pension commitments as they become due (e.g., see Stein, Gujarati, Muny).

It is sometimes argued that the increase in the cost of supporting dependents aged 65 and over is wholly or nearly offset by decrease in the cost of supporting dependents under age 18.[3] For example, each of the several populations described in Table 2.6 is comprised of about 60 percent of persons aged 18–64 and 40 percent of persons under 18 and over 64. At issue (see Kelley, Yung-Ping Chen and Kwang-Win Chu) is the degree to which the net monetary cost per year of dependency under age 18 approximates that per year of dependency in and above the 65th year (see Hogan). Sauvy (1969, pp. 310–11) reports the support costs of a person under 18 to be lower than that of a person over 64 – 27 percent lower in 1950. Robert Clark's estimates also indicate that the yearly net public cost of supporting a dependent over 64 exceeds that of supporting one under 18 (Clark, 1977a). Moreover, the psychic cost associated with the support of old dependents tends to exceed that associated with young dependents. Furthermore, some of the investment in young dependents is likely to increase the quality of the labor force and its average productive capacity (e.g., see Leibenstein, Clark and Spengler).

Given a population that is stable and stationary or declining slightly, the only effective means of reducing the cost per employed worker of supporting a tolerable pension system is elevation of the age of retirement to 65 or higher (Kreps, 1977, also 1976; Lampman; Spengler, 1978a). Such a policy entails keeping most of those aged 55–68 in the labor force – an objective that can be hindered by barriers to the employment of older workers (Kreps, 1977; Best and Stern) – for then the ratio of workers to elder retirees will be compatible with the goal of providing a retiree with an adequate pension (perhaps 60 to 70 percent of what he earned annually in his later years). Even then, a retiree's relative income position may be reduced through erosion of his real income by inflation and through his nonparticipation in the increase in average income owing to technological progress. Basing a retiree's pension actuarially upon the number of years he worked, together with his earning rates and the age at which he elects to retire, should provide adequate incentive to deferment of retirement until a suitable pension is realizable.

Samuelson has called attention to the significance of the growth rate of a population for the support of older persons of dependent age. He made several inquiries into the existence of an *optimum growth rate for population* when natural resources are not assumed to be limiting and the conventional *optimum level of population* is not at issue (e.g., Oct. 1975a, pp. 531–8). Earlier Samuelson, 1958, p. 473; see also Samuelson, Oct. 1975b, pp. 539–44) he pointed out that under specified conditions the aged could live better under a growing rather than a stationary population because the retired then would be "outnumbered by workers more than in the ratio of the work span to the retirement span." Later (1975a) Samuelson derived "the conditions for an optimum intermediate population *growth rate*" and proved "as a serendipity theorem, that under laissez-faire private savings would *just* suffice to support this growth rate if biological and cultural factors happened to mandate it" (p. 531). Given this intermediate rate of population growth which depended upon the parameters of the problem, "the disadvantages of further growth were cancelled by the advantages. At such a point we should have the optimal rate of population growth, at one which maximizes per capita life time utility of consumption" (1976, p. 516). Given that rate, moreover, "it would turn out to be the case that voluntary life-cycle personal savings would just suffice to support equilibrium without recourse to social security alterations of life-cycle consumption patterns" (p. 516). In response to a critique by Deardorff of Samuelson's 1975 paper, Samuelson, in his reply (1976), took into account possibilities to which Deardorff called attention, among them that, in keeping with neoclassical growth theory, economies could benefit, under specified conditions, from low or negative population growth patterns (p. 516).

Unfortunately, even given attainment of an optimum rate of population growth, maintenance of that rate would prove extremely difficult if at all possible. The demographic policy maker is limited by the age-structural and environmental constraints that may characterize populations and by limitations upon corrective measures available to policy makers.

Age structure changes and the responsiveness of the labor force

The flexibility of an economy is conditioned ceteris paribus not only directly by the rate of population growth but also by the character of population age structures associated with the behavior of fertility and mortality. According to the *Report* (pp. 118– 21) of The Royal Commission on Population, "change in age balance impinges on the welfare or efficiency of the working population." It could affect the flexibility of the economic system by altering "the rates of inflow of new workers to the labour force and of outflow by retirement," thereby limiting the growth of expanding industries and "the mobility of the productive system." Change in the age distribution and decline in the proportion of the labor force made up of young men and women could also reduce the flexibility of the economic system, for younger workers are more adaptable and exceed their elders in physical strength and energy. Perhaps more important would be reduction of "a worker's chance of promotion to a better job" by the change in age balance under way. There would be less pressure to promote young men; only the most exceptional of the younger people would be promoted, and "many good older men (or women) will have to be passed over" – whence "a powerful sense of frustration may arise" among younger workers and their discontent "reinforce the demand for the early retirement of older workers."

Decline in the absolute size of the group of young men (e.g., between 15 and 40) could be unfavorable on military grounds. For it is "from these alone that the Defense Forces can be recruited" (p. 120).

Decline in the relative number of young people could also have adverse social effects. For whereas older people excel "in experience, patience, in wisdom and breadth of view," the young are "noted for energy, enterprise, enthusiasm, the capacity to learn new things, to adapt themselves, to innovate" (pp. 120–1). Possibly a society in which the relative number of young people diminished "would become dangerously unprogressive, falling behind other communities not only in technical efficiency and economic welfare but in intellectual and artistic achievement as well" (p. 121). (For an examination of the relationship between age and creativity, see Page; Roe, 1965, 1972; Sweezy and Owens).

Sauvy (1948, pp. 116–17) described the age composition of an aging population and its labor force as inflexible, in part because of "demographic stagnation."

> Owing to demographic stagnation, no sizeable new businesses are started, so that enterprising young men must enter an inflexible, slow-moving machine, without any hope of promotion to posts of higher responsibility until relatively late in life. (1948, p. 17; 1969, p. 315)

Sauvy pointed also to the restrictive impact of a shortage of manual workers, usually younger people, that could affect adversely industries such as coal mining and those dependent on coal (p. 117). Sauvy (1969, p. 319) also notes that in an aging population under modern technologically progressive conditions, men tend "to be more and more behind their times."

Stassart (pp. 167–8, 170) does not distinguish sharply between constraints on the structural flexibility of economies due to the absence of population growth and those due to population aging. Given these two sources of inflexibility, however, it is more difficult to maintain a satisfactory balance between the primary, secondary, and tertiary sectors of an economy.

Changes in the relative numbers of persons in some age groups compared with the relative numbers of persons in other age groups may affect vertical or horizontal mobility within a population and thereby condition its adaptability to changes in the economic conditions confronting a population. Such changes in age structure may be examined either while they are in process or as they appear in a stable population characterized by a given age structure that is subject to hypothetical change traceable mainly or entirely to change in fertility (Spengler, 1978b).

Five age ratios may be chosen tentatively to illustrate the significance of changes in age structure:

(a) The ratio of those of what may be called age of entry into the labor force to those of what may be called age of departure from the labor force.

(b) The ratio of those of age of entry into the labor force to those or working age and hence (presumably) in the labor force.

(c) The ratio of those of age 50–9 and in the labor force to those of age 25–34 and in the labor force.

(d) The ratio of those in the relatively low age categories – 18 to 30 or 34 – compared with those in the older age categories – over 45 or 50.

(e) The ratio of those of voting age who are under 45 to those of voting age who are 45 or more years old – an indicator of the likely impact of younger versus older voters upon economic and social policies.

These ratios do not bear directly upon potential per capita productivity as does the relative number of persons of productive age in a population, but they may affect average productivity. Ratios (a), (b), and (c) may affect upward mobility, opportunity, and ease of finding employment, whereas ratio (d) is likely to affect a population's capacity for invention, innovation, and so on. Ratio (e) conditions the distribution of political power between the relatively younger and the relatively older electorate and thereby may affect the security of older members of a population, the proneness of a government to resort to inflationary finance, and so on.

The economic significance of these ratios is conditioned by (1) a population's institutional structure, its flexibility, and its adaptability to change, and (2) the stability of a given set of age ratios. For example, given a population long stationary, its economy becomes relatively adjusted to the fixity of these ratios, with the result that adverse effects initially associated with the advent of particular ratios may be accommodated or compensated for in various ways. Accordingly, given change in these ratios, the compensatory impact of adjustments and accommodations may be reduced or intensified in comparison with their impact under stationary-population conditions, at least initially until compensatory adjustments have been made.

Given a population that is approximately stationary and corresponding values for ratios (a) and (b), the flow of workers into the labor force will tend to balance the outflow due to retirement, mortality, and disability. There is no need to expand the economy in order to absorb a variable or constant increment in the annual flow of workers into the labor force. Such need arises, however, when successive cohorts are larger (though in varying degree), and the derived demand for labor is not always easily adjusted to variable increase in the size of the population of working age. As a result, unemployment is much more likely to be associated with relatively high than with relatively low values for ratios (a) and (b), particularly if the economy is not very flexible owing to trade-union, governmental, and other disincentives to expansion on the part of potential employers.

Although relatively low values for ratios (a) and (b) make the maintenance of employment easier, they may make more difficult the adaptation of an economy to changes in the composition of output and in the occupational and industrial composition of the labor force. If what may be called the unattached or uncommitted "Mobile Category" of the labor force is relatively small as when a population is stationary and its members of working age are not increasing, it is difficult to maintain an optimum distribution of the population of working age among industries and occupations. Within the "Mobile Category" and not yet committed to particular employments we may include (1) those persons who are replacing persons withdrawing from the labor force; (2) unemployed persons displaced from previously held employment; (3) those who, though employed, are dissatisfied and on the verge of transference from their current employment; and (4) the annual increment, if any, in the population of working age. Of the members of components (1), (2), and (3), most will be required to replace persons who have withdrawn from the labor force; not many will be available to man new or expanding occupations, with the result that there will be upward pressure against some wages and salaries (Spengler, 1972). If, however, a population is growing and component (4) is positive, its members may help staff expanding industries and occupations and thus facilitate the adjustment of occupational and industrial composition to changes in final demand and technological and occupational structure.

Given low mortality and a stationary or slowly growing population, ratio (c), or a corresponding ratio of relatively young to relatively old members of the labor force, is unfavorable to promotion and upward mobility. Then the available relative number of preferred positions, for which aspirations to and expectation of attainment increase with age, is much smaller than the relative number of self-elected aspirants. We may, for expositive convenience, compare the number of persons in their thirties with those in their fifties in a stationary population. For example, the ratio of those 50–4 to those 30–4 in the 1974 life table of U.S. white population approximated 0.94. In the ultimate U.S. stationary population, the ratio of those 55–64 to those 30–9 is projected as 0.89. In contrast, the ratio of those aged 55 to those aged 35 in the 1900–2 life table population approximated 0.58. As a result of the then higher mortality, survivors had much better chances of attaining favorable situations in 1900–2 than they do today; their chances were further improved by growth of population and the number of favorable situations.

Keyfitz employed a model to estimate the degree to which the rate of vertical mobility declines when a growing population becomes stationary.

> Change from the 2% annual increase of the United States a few years ago to its prospective stationary condition implies a delay in reaching the middle positions of the average factory or office of 4½ years. (p. 335)

The advent of stationarity of population thus reduces the rate of promotion and limits the degree to which improvement in a situation is possible. Although mortality contributes to upward mobility by producing vacancies in a hierarchial structure, the net effect of mortality on vertical mobility is less than that of the combined effects of population growth, premature retirement, and net migration (pp. 339–40, 346–7).[4]

Given the increasing competition of older persons for preferred situations in a stationary population and the comparative scarcity of young members of the labor force, the character of the situations open to the latter is likely to improve relative to that of the situations aspired to by older persons. This may occur despite the fact that "the aging of laborers . . . is likely to intensify efforts of older established workers to keep the better jobs for themselves" (Thompson, p. 300). There may also be, of course, greater incentive for older persons to create situations comparable to those that formerly existed but have been crowded out or neglected by today's large corporations and conglomerates, which find small undertakings insufficiently profitable.

Fear of policy formation becoming too dominated by corporate and other institutional gerontocracies may lead to the establishment of conventions requiring corporate and similar ruling bodies to be composed of a significant number of persons aged under 50 as well as persons in their fifties and beyond their fifties.[5] Under these conditions, the creativity supposedly associated with younger corporate leadership may be realized even though some corporate leaders are in and beyond their sixties.

Ratio (d) is significant insofar as smallness of the ratio of relatively young to relatively old persons is unfavorable to (1) discovery, invention, and innovation and (2) willingness to adopt new methods and products.

Sweezy and Owens (p. 49; see also Lehman) conclude that although youth is important in knowledge of theoretical subjects such as physics and in activities such as athletics, it is less important in experimental research and in activities in which experience is a significant factor (e.g., business, politics). There is no justification "for fears that slow or zero population growth would have a stultifying effect on scientific creative activity." The authors add that "over the whole range of creative activities fears that a stationary population will bring stagnation seem unjustified" (p.49).

Leibenstein suggests that the

rate at which a population transmits acquired characteristics to subsequent generations will depend in part on the growth rate of the population and its age structure . . . . To the extent that entrants into the work force are of higher quality (i.e., higher education and acquired skills, etc.) than those that leave through retirement or death, the average quality of the labor force improves more rapidly if the rate of population growth is higher (other things equal) rather than lower. (p. 188)

Of course, even if a population is stationary, the quality of the population improves over time if younger members of later cohorts are better trained than correspondingly young members of earlier (and now older) cohorts. The rate of improvement is higher, however, if, under the given conditions, successive cohorts are larger.

Ratio (e) is important insofar as the tastes, aspirations, political orientations, and view of the present vis-à-vis the future, change with an individual's age. As a result, the composition of a population's tastes, aspirations, political orientations, and stress upon the present relative to the future may change with its age composition. As a population ages, therefore, its concerns and efforts to realize and guard these concerns through political means change accordingly. That such change may prove considerable is suggested by a comparison of the age composition of a prospective stationary American population with that of the U.S. population as of 1976. This comparison indicates that whereas in 1976 55.5 percent of those of voting age (i.e., 18 and over) were 18–44 years of age, this fraction will decline to 44.7 percent should the population become stationary early in the next century. The fraction of the population 18 and over that is 65 and over will increase

	1976	Stationary
Percent under 18	30.3	23.36
Percent aged 18–44	38.7	34.26
Percent aged 45 and over	31.0	42.38
Total	100.0	100.00
Median age	29.0	38.9

from about 15 percent in 1976 to about 25 percent when the population becomes stationary.

The change described indicates that the age composition of the voting population will be increasingly tilted toward support of the concerns of the older population, particularly if in their late forties individuals begin to adopt or favor concerns of older persons. Insofar as this outcome materializes, political opposition increases to inflationary policies, to policies that deny older persons a share in the fruits of technical progress, and to other policies that adversely affect the situation of older persons (Spengler, 1978b; *The Annals*). Upon retiring and having their incomes appreciably reduced, older workers will have greater incentive to call on the state for economic assistance.

4

Economic status of the elderly

The economic well-being of the elderly has been the focus of considerable public debate during the past two decades in most developed countries. The standard of living attainable by the aged differs from country to country and is determined in part by the national per capita income, government transfers to the elderly, and the propensity and ability of older persons to continue to work. The international commitment to the income support of the elderly through social security systems is noted in Chapter 8, whereas the following discussion outlines the absolute and relative economic position of older Americans through an examination of currently available data and research assessing the economic status of the aged.[1, 2] This analysis should be considered as illustrative of worldwide changes in the sources and patterns of income of the elderly. Although the American experience is not fully comparable to that of other nations, this examination does indicate the effects of a maturing national pension system and the decline in labor-force participation of the elderly. Of course, many problems such as inflation transcend institutional frameworks and international boundaries.

Income of the aged
The number of individuals 65 and over with incomes below the Social Security Administration's poverty level[3] de-

clined from 5.5 million in 1959 to 3.3 million in 1976, a reduction in the proportion of the nation's elderly below this poverty index from 35.2 to 15.0 percent. The decline in the poverty rate of the aged families was even more pronounced, falling from 27 to 8 percent during this period (U.S. Bureau of the Census Series P-60, No. 106, p. 21; also No. 107, p. 20). The 1976 figures, however, represent increases in both the number of older persons below the poverty level and the incidence of poverty when compared to 1974 data. The rate of decline in the incidence of poverty among the aged has been accelerated by the expansion in coverage and liberalization of benefits in both public and private pension systems as well as the initiation of additional income transfer programs such as Supplemental Security Income (SSI).

Even this relatively significant reduction understates the actual increase in consumable resources of older persons because of the simultaneous expansion of in-kind benefit programs over the last two decades. Hearings before the House Committee on Aging revealed 47 major federal programs intended for the benefit of the elderly in the areas of employment, health care, housing, income maintenance, social service programs, training and research, and transportation (U.S. House). Marilyn Moon estimates that in-kind transfers to the aged average more than 10 percent of the size of the mean current money income for aged families. Rising real wages during worklife have also contributed to the increasing income of successive aged cohorts.

Since 1965 the median income of families in which the head of the household is 65 years old or older has more than doubled, increasing from $3,514 in 1965 to $8,721 in 1976, representing an increase in real income of approximately 38 percent. The relative income position of the aged also showed gradual improvement during that time. For example, the ratio of median income of families whose head is 65 years old or over to the median income of all families rose from 49.3 percent in 1965 to 58.3 percent in 1976. However, this measure of relative economic status lies only slightly above its 1950 level of 57.3 percent (U.S. Bureau of the Census, Series P-60, No. 107; P-23, No. 59). Theodore Torda traces the decline in the relative income of the elderly during the early 1960s and its subsequent rise. He finds that between 1965 and 1971 "all categories of the elderly (families, unrelated, individuals, male and female) enjoyed growth rates in real income above the national average" (p. 10). (Also see Palmore.)

This measure of the relative income of the elderly may overstate the degree of their disadvantage due to the difference in family size. A comparison of the per person income of families with heads 65 and over with the per person income of all families reveals that in 1974 the per person income of the older families was only about 18 percent below the corresponding figure for all families (U.S. Bureau of the Census, Series P-23, No. 59, p. 53).

James Schulz (1976, pp. 11–16) notes the need to recognize age differences of the elderly. Thus, one useful comparison is to examine the differences in the levels of income of individuals just prior to age 65 and those over age 65. Such a comparison would more nearly capture the relative decline in income associated with aging at the end of worklife. In 1976, a family whose head was aged 55–64 had a median income of $16,118, whereas the median level for families 65 and over was only $8,721 or an income ratio for these groups of 54 percent (U.S. Bureau of the Census, 1977, Series P-60, No. 107). Susan Grad, employing data from the 1972 Survey of the Status of the Elderly, reports that the median income of all units aged 60–1 was $6,993 in 1971. The comparative figure for those 62–4 was $6,388, whereas units 65 –7 had a median income of only $4,450. Further aging was associated with a continued decline in this income measure to $3,503 for those 68–72 and $2,480 for those 73 and over.

These comparative age groups do not represent one group of workers on the verge of retirement and another group in the immediate postretirement years, for many individuals aged 55–64 have already withdrawn from the labor force, whereas a significant proportion of families whose head is past 65 continue to have labor earnings. For example, in 1971, 49 percent of married couples aged 65 and older received earnings, whereas 18 percent of nonmarried persons had labor income (Grad, p. 25). Schulz

(1976, pp. 11–13), using data from the 1968 Survey of the Aged, reports that earnings and work effort substantially contribute to the income levels of older families.

For any individual worker, the decline in income at retirement may represent a form of relative impoverishment. The reduction in income associated with the termination of earnings provides the rationale for retirement income programs, which – whether collective or individual, public or private – attempt to replace lost earnings. A frequently used measure of the adequacy of retirement income is the replacement ratio, that is retirement income as a percent of preretirement earnings during the final year of work.

Disposable income in the last working year can be used as a standard to calculate the severity of income reduction occurring upon retirement. Alicia Munnell (1977a, p. 59) calculates the replacement rate necessary to maintain preretirement disposable income by adjusting gross preretirement income by federal and state income tax, OASDHI tax, and any decline in expenditures resulting from retirement. These replacement rates, depicted in Table 4.1, range from 80 percent for a worker with preretirement income of $4,000 to 66 percent if income prior to retirement was $15,000. As income rises, lower replacement rates are needed to maintain disposable income primarily because of the progressive federal income tax. In the following sections of this study, the probability of achieving this relative income standard is assessed in light of the contributions of the various sources of retirement income.

The income of families whose head is over age 65 has generally been more unequally distributed than the income for younger families. Mary Henson (pp. 182–7) shows that from 1947 to 1964 Gini coefficients for older families were always larger than similar measures of income inequality for families whose head was less than 65 years of age.[4, 5] Using census data, Herman Brotman illustrates the distribution of young and old families by income class in 1975, revealing that a higher proportion of the elderly are in the lower income brackets. Table 4.2 indicates that almost one quarter of families with an aged head have incomes of less than $5,000,

Table 4.1. *Retirement income equivalent to preretirement income for married couples retiring January 1976, selected income levels*

Preretirement income (dollars)	Preretirement tax payment (dollars)			Reduction in expenses at retirement[b] (dollars)	Equivalent retirement income[c]	
	Federal income	OASDHI	State and local income[a]		(dollars)	Percent of preretirement income (dollars)
4,000	28	234	4	544	3,190	80
6,000	330	351	43	816	4,460	74
8,000	679	468	89	1,088	5,676	71
10,000	1,059	585	139	1,360	6,857	69
15,000	2,002	824	262	2,040	9,872	66

[a] In 1974 state and local income tax receipts were 13.1 percent of federal income tax receipts. This percentage probably rose in 1975 because federal taxes were decreased whereas state taxes increased. Therefore, the percentage of preretirement income needed to maintain living standards is probably slightly overstated.
[b] Consumption requirements for a two-person husband–wife family after retirement are 86.4 percent of those for a like family before retirement (aged 55 to 64). Savings are therefore estimated at 13.6 percent of preretirement income.
[c] Assumes that retirement income is not subject to tax. If retirement income is subject to taxation, a larger preretirement disposable income would be needed to yield the equivalent retirement income.

Source: Munnell, 1977a, p 59.

Table 4.2. *Distribution of money income in 1975 by age group (percentage)*

	Families by age of head		Unrelated individuals	
	14–64	65 and over	14–64	65 and over
Under 2,000	2.3	1.3	14.6	13.2
2,000–4,999	7.8	22.3	25.4	59.4
5,000–9,999	18.3	37.7	31.9	20.1
10,000–14,999	23.0	18.8	17.5	4.5
15,000–24,999	33.1	13.9	8.8	2.0
25,000 and over	15.5	6.2	1.9	0.7
Median income ($)	14,698	8,057	6,460	3,311

Source: Brotman, computed from Table 2, p. 24.

whereas 60 percent were below $10,000 compared to median income of $14,698 for families aged 14–64.

Moon argues that an assessment of the economic welfare of the aged must measure the ability of the older family to purchase and consume goods and services. Thus, economic well-being is not determined just by current money income but should also include in-kind government transfers, value of government expenditures and tax considerations, intrafamily transfers, annuitized flow of wealth, and value of nonmarket time. In addition, earnings should be adjusted for the number of working years remaining relative to life expectancy and future pension income. Employing the Survey of Economic Opportunity from 1966–7, she estimates that the median value rises from $2,396 when only current income is included to $3,879 for her final measure of economic welfare. The broad measure of welfare produces a decline in the percentage of elderly families under $2,000 from 40.7 to 14.4 percent (p. 68).

The expanded measure of economic well-being reduces the Gini coefficient of distribution by 0.55 percentage points. There is also a significant reranking of family units, as approximately 30 percent of the families in the bottom two quintiles of current income are transferred into the highest 60 percent of the distribution of economic welfare. Moon argues that this measure of economic welfare captures the flow of consumable resources that a family can expect to maintain over its remaining lifetime; thus, it "underscores the permanent low resource position faced by a substantial minority of the population" (p. 112).

Income sources and their importance

Social security is the most prevalent source of income for aged individuals. In 1974, over 90 percent of all families whose head was 65 years old or older was receiving social security benefits. Approximately 70 percent of the aged were receiving income either from private pension, annuities, or other forms of privately attained "unearned" income (U.S. Bureau of the Census, 1976, Series P-60, No. 102, p. 9). The 1970 Survey of Newly Entitled Beneficiaries (SNEB) conducted by the Social Security Administration found that 32 percent of their sample of married men and their wives were receiving private pension benefits, whereas an additional 12 percent had benefits from other public retirement plans. The incidence of pension coverage was significantly lower for the nonmarried aged; 18 percent of the unrelated individuals received benefits from private pensions, and 8 percent had additional public retirement benefits (SSA, p. 20). The SNEB showed that 55 percent of the married couples and a somewhat smaller percentage of individuals were able to supplement their living standard with income from accumulated assets. The elderly may also be expected to generate a flow of expendable funds by drawing down their stock of wealth. In addition to these sources of income, approximately half of all aged families continue to depend on earnings to maintain consumption patterns during the "retirement" years.

Of considerable significance is the relative importance of each of these sources to a family's total income in late life. The share of aggregate income represented by social security benefits declines sharply with the rising income of beneficiaries. SNEB data indicate that for the lowest income groups–those with approximately $1,000 in annual income – social security benefits account for over 80 percent of total income; however, this proportion drops to less than 20 percent for high-income groups. This decline occurs because of the progressivity of the benefit structure, a maximum benefit, and the fact that individuals with social security benefits at or near the maximum are more likely to have additional sources of income. In 1971, social security benefits represented more than half of the annual income of 44 percent of married couples and 65 percent of nonmarried persons who receive these payments (Grad, p. 5).

The proportion of income derived from other public pensions and private pensions rises steeply with increases in the level of total income. Private pensions represented only 1 percent of the total income of married men and their wives with annual incomes between $500 and $1,499; however, these benefits comprised 15 percent of aggregate income for those in the $9,500 to $12,499 income group. Asset income followed a similar pattern, increasing from 4 percent of the total for the lowest income groups to 16 percent for high-income couples. Earnings accounted for a greater proportion of total income as the income of the beneficiaries increased (SSA, p. 40).

Moon's analysis of income sources by age of family reveals a significant shift in the composition of family income with age increases. Table 4.3 illustrates that earnings decline steadily as a percentage of income, falling from 92 percent for families aged 41 –55 to less than 30 percent for those 75 years and older. Property income and social security increase in relative importance; however, mean income falls continuously with age.

Replacement rates by income sources

A variety of factors influence the percentage of preretirement income a worker receives in the form of retirement benefits from a public or private pension – the individual's work history, earnings level, age of retirement, marital status, and so on. Whereas social security benefits provide the base of retirement income for most of the elderly, some workers are able to supplement this through private-pension benefits and asset income in an effort to maintain their preretirement standard of living. The

Table 4.3. *Components of income by age of head, 1972*

Age of family head	Mean income ($)	Sources of income (as percent of total)					
		Earnings (%)	Property income (%)	Social security (%)	Welfare, public assistance (%)	Remaining transfers (%)	Other income (%)
41–55	14,155.19	92.26	2.99	1.39	0.55	2.18	0.91
56–61	12,087.97	87.57	5.44	2.41	0.62	2.86	1.44
62–64	9841.29	76.64	7.65	7.65	0.77	4.00	3.35
65–69	7432.93	49.95	12.78	24.01	1.11	4.91	7.54
70–74	5895.25	31.56	18.35	35.76	1.63	5.88	7.46
75–79	5237.44	26.30	17.65	40.03	1.83	7.17	7.14
80–99	4566.42	22.85	22.70	39.06	2.88	6.50	6.03

Source: Moon, 1977, p. 6. Calculated from Current Population Survey computer tapes for 1972.

poorest of the elderly are also eligible for welfare and SSI benefits. Thus, any analysis of retirement income in relation to pre-retirement consumption standards must include each of these sources, as well as consideration of the ability of the elderly to attain coverage under these pension systems and to accumulate assets for retirement.

The social security system provides almost universal coverage to the elderly. In Table 4.4, Munnell (1977a, p. 26) illustrates replacement rates from social security benefits for three hypothetical earnings histories, two retirement ages, and presence of spouse for workers who retired in January 1976 using the benefit formula in effect in June 1976. The proportion of income replaced for the worker with a history of low earnings ($3,439 in 1975) ranges from 99.4 percent for the individual who retires at age 65 whose spouse is also 65 and over to 53.0 percent for a worker who retires at age 62 without a spouse or whose spouse is less than 62. Thus, a low-income worker with an aged spouse would have a social security benefit equal to his preretirement earnings. These replacement rates refer to family benefits with the wife accepting the spouse benefit; however, benefits are compared only to the primary earner's salary. Therefore, these ratios overstate the social security replacement ratio when benefits are compared to family earnings. In addition, an individual's benefits may be reduced through further labor-force activity because of the earnings test.[6] Schulz (1978b) reviews these and other factors that limit an individual's ability to achieve these seemingly high rates of income replacement from social security. He concludes that actual replacement rates will usually be considerably below those based on the hypothetical earnings histories.

As the earnings record of a worker rises, the social security replacement rate falls rapidly. The proportion of preretirement income received in retirement from social security benefits is almost one-third less for the worker whose taxable earnings were equal to the median in each year ($8,255 in 1975) compared to the low-earnings worker. For example, the replacement rate from social security benefits for the single worker with a history of

Table 4.4. *Replacement rates and family benefit as a percent of primary insurance amount, by type of beneficiary, June 1976[a]*

| Type of beneficiary | Family benefit as percent PIA (%) | Replacement rates[b] for three earning levels | | |
		Low[c] ($3,439 in 1975)	Median[d] ($8,244 in 1975)	Maximum[e] ($14,100 in 1975)
Male worker				
Aged 65	100.0	0.663	0.462	0.330
Aged 62	80.0	0.530	0.369	0.264
Male worker aged 65 with wife				
Aged 65	150.0	0.994	0.693	0.495
Aged 62	137.5	0.911	0.635	0.453
Male worker aged 62 with wife				
Aged 65	130.0	0.862	0.600	0.429
Aged 62	117.5	0.779	0.543	0.387
Widow aged 65; spouse retired at				
Age 65	100.0	0.663	0.462	0.330
Age 62	82.5	0.547	0.381	0.272
Widow aged 62; spouse retired at				
Age 65	82.9	0.549	0.383	0.273
Age 62	82.5	0.547	0.381	0.272
Widow aged 60	71.5	0.474	0.330	0.236

[a] Assumes worker retired Jan. 1, 1976.
[b] The ratio of the PIA at award (June of year) to monthly taxable earnings in the year just before retirement. The wage and price assumptions are the same as the intermediate asumptions used in the *1976 Annual report o the Board of Trustees of the Federal Old Age and Survivors Insurance and Disability Insurance Trust Funds,* H. Doc. 94-505, 94:2 Washington, D.C.: U.S. Government Printing Office, 1976), 4 percent annual increase in prices and 5.75 percent annual increase in wages.
[c] Assumes wages before 1975 followed the trend of the median wage in past years.
[d] Assumes taxable earnings equal to the median in each year.
[e] Assumes income equal to the maximum taxable amount each year.
Source: Alicia H. Munnell, *The Future of Social Security,* Washington, D.C.: The Brookings Institution, 1977, p. 26.

median earnings retiring at age 65 was 46.2 percent. The replacement rate is reduced further, to 33 percent, for a single worker retiring at age 65 whose earnings were equal to the maximum taxable each year. Each class of high-income workers has similar reductions in the replacement ratio. The rate of earnings replacement would continue to decline with higher earnings histories because no additional benefit is given for earnings above the tax ceiling, and in no case would such a worker have a replacement rate of over 50 percent. Schulz et al. (1974) examine the adequacy of replacement rates in the United States and find them considerably below the rates that exist in the western European countries (also see Horlick and Haanes-Olsen).

To have social security benefits supplemented by a private pension, not only must workers have been employed by a firm with a retirement-benefit program, but they also must have remained with a particular company or within a multiemployer system for a length of time sufficient to insure these benefits. In private-pension systems, benefits and replacements rates vary from plan to plan. Within any particular plan, the proportion of earnings replaced is a function of length of service and, frequently, of salary status. Peter Henle found that in 1972 the median replacement rate in a small sample of pension plans was 21 percent for the average earner with twenty years of experience and 28 percent with thirty years of service.

SNEB data provide information on the pension – earnings ratio for newly entitled beneficiaries who receive private-pension benefits from their longest job. The median replacement rate was 25 percent for all beneficiaries, with male low earners (those with annual earnings of less than $5,000) receiving benefits having the highest replacement rates – a median ratio of 30 percent. This ratio declines to 23 percent for the next income group and then gradually rises to 28 percent for those with annual earnings of over $15,000. Pension earnings rates follow a similar pattern for females except that highest replacement rates are received by the highest earners (Kolodrubetz, p. 26). Pension benefits of this magnitude combined with social security benefits would enable low- and middle-income workers to approach or in some cases exceed their preretirement disposable earnings. However, it is the low- to middle-income worker who is least likely to receive a private pension and thus must depend solely on social security for his retirement income.

In addition to pension benefits, some individuals are able to provide supplementary retirement income by dissaving during late life and by using asset income for consumption expenditures. The ability of a worker to accumulate assets during worklife is, in part, a function of the size of his annual earnings and of whether his earnings were interrupted by periods of unemployment or disability. Individuals with low retirement income have, on average, only minimal income from assets. Only 20 percent of those in the SNEB sample with annual incomes of between $500 and $1,499 received any income at all from assets. As retirement income increased, both the likelihood of having asset income and its proportion of total income rose (SSA, p. 40). The annuitized flow of income from assets will depend on the age at which the individual retires and begins to dissave.

Information on the ability of workers to accumulate assets is contained in The Retirement History Study (RHS) conducted by the Social Security Administration on individuals 58–63 as they entered retirement. Sally Sherman reports that in 1969, 19 percent of those included in the RHS survey had estimated net worth reported to be negative or equal to zero; the net worth of another 30 percent was estimated to be less than $10,000. The asset picture is even more unfavorable if nonfarm home equity is excluded. The median value of net worth less nonfarm home equity was $2,382 with 30 percent of the persons surveyed having no net worth or a negative value (Sherman). Peter Diamond reviews various data sets pertaining to the accumulated wealth of the aged. He concludes that, "Inadequate savings appears to be a phenomenon which is widespread, not confined to the bottom of the income distribution" (p. 286).

In summary, retirees with an aged spouse who had a lifetime record of low earnings are able, with social security benefits, to maintain their relatively low incomes into the retirement years. For other classes of retirees, social security benefits *alone* are not sufficient to enable a continuation of preretirement disposable earnings, and private pensions hold the promise that beneficiaries can replace a significant proportion of their preretirement income.

Only long-term employees can achieve the relatively high replacement rates from pensions that enable median- and perhaps high-income workers to receive high rates of income replacement, and, further, private savings appear to be a significant factor for income replacement only for those with high earnings histories.

Retirees who attain maximum pension-earnings replacement rates from private pensions may be able, for several income brackets, to approach a continuation of preretirement disposable income in the first years of retirement. Except for the lowest income groups, however, workers who rely solely on social security benefits will experience significant income reductions in retirement. Therefore, private pensions play a significant role in providing income maintenance for the elderly, and it is only those retirees receiving these pension benefits in addition to social security benefits who are able to continue preretirement consumption levels during the retirement period. Social security traditionally has not been intended to be the *sole* source of income of the elderly, but to work in conjunction with private pensions and individual savings. Thus, it should not be surprising that in order for individuals to achieve high absolute or relative retirement income, they must supplement social security benefits with other forms of income replacement.

Inflation and the income of the aged

Considerable difficulties arise in the estimation of whether a demographic group gains or loses in terms of real and relative income in response to inflation. However, Arthur Okun concluded that the "retired aged are the only major specific demographic group of Americans that I can confidently identify as income losers" (p. 14). Andrew Brimmer found that the proportion of national income accruing to aged families declined more during the latter part of the 1960s with yearly price increases of over 3 percent than between 1961 and 1964 when prices rose by 1.5 percent annually. However, in his analysis of consumer expenditures and the income of the elderly, Theodore Torda does not find support for the thesis that the elderly suffer greater losses due to inflation. In addition, we have earlier noted the rise in the relative income of the elderly during recent inflationary years.

Schulz (1976, pp. 30–2) lists the following five principal ways that the aged or any other group can be affected adversely by unanticipated inflation:

(1) Assets that do not adjust with inflation depreciate in value.
(2) Transfer payments may adjust only with a lag.
(3) Earnings may lag behind prices.
(4) Real tax burden may rise.
(5) Elderly persons may allocate their budget differently from others; thus CPI-adjusted benefits may not fully compensate for increased prices.

Examination of these factors should enable the determination of whether the real income and wealth position of the elderly suffers relative to other groups during inflationary periods.

G. L. Bach and James Stephenson find that the portfolios of the elderly imply that in the presence of unanticipated inflation, the largest decline in wealth of any age group is for the elderly. Most government transfers are now adjusted at least annually for price changes; however, few private pension plans automatically increase benefits with inflation (Tilove, Hodgens). Considering the importance of social security as an income source for the elderly, the indexing of these benefits for changes in the consumer price index significantly reduces the argument that the elderly live on fixed incomes and are therefore most likely to be harmed by inflation. Items (3) and (4) would appear to be less important for the aged than the remainder of the population because fewer of the elderly are working, and many do not pay income taxes. Increases in property taxes caused by rising prices may, however, significantly affect the tax burden of the elderly.

The consumer price index is compiled by the Bureau of Labor Statistics to represent the expenditure patterns of a middle-income worker with a wife and two children. This index is used to determine changes in government benefits and may result in the elderly being undercompensated or overcompensated for inflation if their buying habits are markedly different from those of younger families.[7] Robinson Hollister and John Palmer have concluded, however, that the cost of living has not risen faster for the elderly poor than for other age groups. Torda reweighted the market baskets of goods used to determine the consumer price index by substituting the expenditure patterns of the elderly. He found that cost of living to aged retirees rose by 2 percent more than it did for urban wage workers from 1960 to 1972. However, this was offset by the introduction of Medicare. More recently, Thomas Borzilleri estimated that from 1970–7 prices for older persons rose 4 percent faster than for the population in general.

Further population aging and economic status of the elderly

The absolute and relative welfare of the older population during the next half century will be determined by their own productive capacity, labor-force participation, demographic characteristics, and the willingness of those remaining in the labor force to provide benefits to the elderly. In this section, we briefly examine probable changes in these factors and discuss the ensuing impact on the welfare of the elderly.

Productive or earnings capacity of an individual is a function of the marketable skills that the individual possesses. Health status and degree of educational attainment are important factors governing obtainable wage offers. Expected future improvements in health and mortality reductions, previously examined, should enable increased labor-force participation, whereas the extension of life among males and females 65 and over should extend the integrity of the family for several additional years (U.S. Bureau of the Census, Series P-23, No. 57, 1975). These tendencies could increase lifetime earnings, thus augmenting welfare during late life.

Further mortality reduction will, however, increase the number of the oldest segment of the elderly population (e.g., over 75 or over 85 years of age). These individuals will have been out of the labor force for a longer period of time and, as shown in Table 4.3, have lower income than those 65–74. In addition, the widening differential between male and female life expectancy implies an increase in the number of elderly widows, typically the poorest of the aged population.

Rising educational attainment should improve the labor-market position of the elderly into the twenty-first century. Table 4.5 indicates the significant improvement in degree of education for older cohorts that will occur by the year 2000. The relative educational status of the elderly should also be improved from its 1975 level when the ratio of average length of schooling of those over 64 to individuals 25 and older was 73 percent (U.S. Bureau of the Census, Series P-23, No. 59). The observed negative relationship between age and education is attributable to the increased opportunities for investment in human capital that have become available to each new cohort of youths and the history of immigration that has generated a larger proportion of foreign-born persons with less formal education among the older cohorts.

The pattern of rising educational attainment may have ended as enrollment rates have declined during the 1970s, reversing the long-term trend of continuous increases in the enrollment patterns of successive cohorts. Forecasts of the tendency for future cohorts of youths to complete high school and enroll in college are subject to considerable error; however, it seems unlikely that the increase in educational attainment will resume its previous growth rate. Richard Freeman projects that enrollment rates will gradually rise during the 1980s, but in 1990 will still be below the levels of the late 1960s. The result of this cessation of growth in educational attainment is that younger workers in the next century will have only slightly greater amounts of formal education than the elderly. The ratio of educational attainment for those over 64 to individuals 25 and over is expected to increase to 94 percent by 1990, whereas the percentage of high school graduates 65 and over will be only about one-third less than the rate for the entire population (U.S. Bureau of the Census, Series P-23, No. 59). This shift in relative educational status may have important

Table 4.5.   *Educational status of the elderly*

Age	1970	2000[a]
Median years of schooling completed		
55–64	10.6	12.5
65–74	8.8	12.3
75+	8.5	12.1[b]
Percent of cohort that are high school graduates		
55–64	40.4	71.5
65–74	29.2	61.7
75+	24.1	54.2[b]

[a] The projections for 2000 assume that no additional education is completed after 1970 and that differential mortality rates do not influence the measures of educational attainment for the cohort. Thus, the estimates may somewhat underestimate the educational attainment of these cohorts in 2000.
[b] Only population aged 75–84 is represented in these figures.
Source: U.S. Bureau of the Census, *Census of Population: 1970* Subject Reports, Final Report PC(2)-5B, "Educational Attainment," Washington, D.C.: U.S. Government Printing Office, 1973, Table 1.

implications for the ability of older workers to compete in the labor market.

Despite the expected improvements in health and educational attainment, the labor-force participation of older men is forecast to continue to decline. Howard Fullerton and Paul Flaim estimate that the participation rate of men 65 and over will fall from 21.7 percent in 1975 to 16.8 percent in 1990, whereas the market activity rate for males 55–64 will drop from 75.7 percent to 69.9 percent. Less fluctuation is anticipated in the rates for older women, with women 65 and older expected to reduce their labor-force participation, whereas those 55–64 will slightly increase their market activity rates.

Measures of the well-being of the average elderly family are also sensitive to demographic characteristics of the aged population. Assuming replacement level fertility and annual net immigration of 400,000, the proportion of the population aged 65 and over increases from 10.8 percent in 1977 to 17.6 percent in 2050. During this same period, the proportion of those 65 and over who are over age 84 rises from 8.7 to 17.2 percent, with most of the increase coming between 2025 and 2050. In addition, the number of aged females is estimated to be 33.4 million in 2050, exceeding the number of men 65 and over by 50 percent (U.S. Bureau of the Census, Series P-25, No. 704, 1977). The increase in the groups that are typically the poorest of the aged may necessitate increased expenditures per aged person throughout the next century.

The economic status of the elderly is significantly dependent on the level of public transfers. Much of the improvement in the relative income position noted earlier in this chapter was due to increases in social security benefits and other governmental programs. The willingness of future generations of working-age cohorts to support continued improvements in payments to the elderly is a function of the tax rate necessary to finance these programs. Population aging increases the number of elderly eligible for such benefits relative to the number of working-age persons, necessitating higher tax rates to finance equivalent benefits. Thus, further improvements in the relative economic position of the elderly can be expected to be moderated by population aging.

5

Age and economic activities:
life-cycle patterns

Analysis of the relationship between age and economic activities may be approached from the standpoint of the individual undergoing aging or from that of the manner in which the behavior of the older segment of the population differs from that of the younger segment. The former approach reveals how the economic behavior of an individual changes as he grows older. The latter approach directs attention to the collective economic behavior of older segments of a population, contrasts their behavior with that of younger segments of the population, and inquires into macroeconomic effects of population aging. In this chapter we deal with the former or *life-cycle* approach; in other chapters we deal with economic behavior characteristics of older segments of populations. Although the life-cycle approach concentrates upon stages in the life of an individual and the interrelation of these stages, information yielded by the life-cycle approach contributes to an understanding of the group behavior and characteristics of older segments of a population – that is, to macroeconomic aspects of population aging.

Economic stages of human development

During their lives, individuals pass through a series of economic, social, and physiological stages that both influence and reflect their consumption and labor-supply activities (Brennan et al.; Woytinsky). The economics of aging includes explicit recognition of effects associated with change in functional capacity as an individual matures and declines, together with its significance for the social framework of a population (e.g., see Botwinick). Moreover, income transfers and tax liabilities which constitute a significant proportion of lifetime income usually vary with age. Furthermore, the reallocation of resources over the life cycle, as required by governmental regulation or other arrangements, may significantly alter an individual's utilization of his remaining assets (e.g., on wealth see Shorrocks). The political system may therefore significantly influence allocation of an individual's resources over his life cycle, in part also because political concerns are likely to change with age (Eisele).

The concept of stage or life cycle serves the economist in several ways (see Kreps, 1971, 1977). It allows him to divide an individual's life or a long period of his life into component subperiods and determine how man's changes in economic situation or status are correlated with his passage from one subperiod to the next. It also allows the economist to determine how man's economic behavior in one subperiod reflects memory of the past and/or influences his activity or fortune in one or more succeeding periods. Division of man's life and the aging process into its temporal parts also facilitates inquiry into the impact of aging upon the nature and content of his economic activities and decisions. Life-cycle analysis requires the analyst to take into account the impact of aging upon memory of the past, expectations concerning the future, change in economic status, and interaction between an individual's economic life cycle and other of his life cycles such as family and occupational (e.g., see Glick, 1947, 1955, 1977; Glick and Norton; Glick and Parke; Oppenheimer; Young), as well as changes in the basis of family support (Treas).

The concept of cycle may be applicable to institutions as well as to individual and economic phenomena (e.g., on mobility see Yee and Van Arsdol) when the passage of time is accompanied by a somewhat orderly sequence of change as distinguished from a secular trend or approach to a limit. For example, according to some scholars (e.g., see Bernstein, Weaver), regulatory agencies subject to evolution may undergo change somewhat cyclical in character. Such change, however, is less subject to the influence of memory, expectations, and aging than is change at the level of the individual or that of institutions (e.g., the family) dominated by individuals.

The concept of stage or cycle commonly has been used to describe the course of development of a society or of the life of a group or an individual. An individual's behavior, along with his ascribed status, has long been associated with his temporal stage or period, of which, according to Shakespeare (see Rylands) there were three – youth, manhood, and a final period. Classification and subdivision of life into descriptive stages facilitates discussion and understanding of man's economic and other behavior insofar as this behavior is correlated with a particular stage in life. Classification can do this, however, only if the content and application of a life-cycle concept reflects its empirical base closely. Otherwise it may be misleading, as when a concept such as stage is defined in essentially ideological rather than empirical terms. For example, in the early 1920s, G. Stanley Hall, under the influence of Darwinian biology, described "adolescence" as lasting until age 25 or 30 and "senescence" (which he lumped with "old age") as beginning at age 40 or 45, thereby limiting the important intervening period of "maturity" to between 10 and 20 years (Jordan, p. 21).

Correlation between man's age and his behavior is subject to variation inasmuch as man's behavior is not rigorously time-bound, and the limits to conventional temporal stages are subject to variations with individuals and over time. Moreover, how man behaves economically and how he fares are conditioned by the "spatio-temporal framework" he occupies as well as by the application he makes of the inputs of time at his disposal, inputs that have alternative uses (see Becker, 1965). Furthermore, because man is "a time conscious creature" living in a present that lies between "memory" of the past and "expectation" as to the future, his use of time as an input is dominated by his view of the future, which is not yet real, and the prospects it embodies (on time generally see Fraser, pp. xviii, 3, 6, 589).[1]

Although the life cycle is the product of aging at the individual level, an increase in the relative number of aged in a society may produce a group effect and thus accentuate the response of the autonomous individual to the process of aging. Such a group effect is essentially a twentieth-century phenomenon along with the decline in fertility that mainly underlies population aging. It may also condition the impact of institutions that can affect the comparative length of the stages composing the life cycle (Best and Stern, Ryder et al.).

While population aging was of little concern to nineteenth-century economists, the economic significance of individual aging commanded some attention. As early as 1834 John Rae (pp. 53–4) in effect noted a relationship between length of life and the propensity to save, a connection later emphasized by Gustav Cassel (pp. 242–6), who associated the tendency to dissave with shortness of length of life and lowness of the interest rate, though to the neglect of the "estate motive," the propensity to accumulate wealth for heirs (e.g., Mayer, p. 28).[2] While Eugene von Böhm-Bawerk's emphasis (pp. 255–6) upon futurity had indicated to the significance of length of life for capital formation, it remained for Irving Fisher (Chapter 5), as James Tobin has pointed out (p. 231), to relate saving and dissaving to the personal life cycle. With the explicit identification of the role of uncertainty in economic affairs, it became possible to assess the impact upon consumption decisions of change in life expectancy and the distribution of lifetime uncertainty (Levhari and Mirman).

The life of the representative individual usually is divided into three economically significant stages: (1) the period preceding entry into the labor force; (2) the period in the labor force, usually running from age 18 or slightly lower, to the late fifties and sixties; and (3) the period of retirement, usually beginning in the late fifties or in the sixties and continuing to death. Individuals in the first and third periods are mainly dependents, in the first with claims chiefly upon parents and the polity and in the third upon responsible agents of the economy and polity. Decisions determining activities within the first stage are made largely by an individual's parents and preceptors; within the second stage they are made mainly by individuals situated therein, and within the third stage by retired persons or those responsible for them. The length of each stage is conditioned by life expectancy, the state of an individual's health and economic prospects, and by the structure and character of the society and economy within which he finds himself. For example, between 1890 and 1940 participation in the labor force on the part of those under 14 virtually came to an end, whereas that of persons 14–17 declined greatly (Long, pp. 28–9, 208–15; Jordan, pp. 8–10, also Hareven). Meanwhile, there was much less inclination on the part of older workers attaining retirement age to withdraw from the labor force than there is at present (Long, pp. 76–7, 159–63).

As noted above, as he passes from infancy to extreme old age, the individual moves through three seccessive stages, the boundaries of which have varied over time and among individuals. Today the initial stage normally ends at age 16–18, whereas around 1900 it often ended several years earlier. Moreover, whereas formerly the second stage generally continued to age 65 and for many beyond 65, today it often ends in the early sixties or late fifties. Entry into the final and essentially residual stage, therefore, is determined by the circumstances that in the individual case set upper boundaries to the second stage. The critical stage, therefore, is the second or intermediate stage, determinants of which, for the representative individual, fix the upper boundary of the first stage and the lower boundary of the third stage.

Determination of stage limits, together with activities within each stage, is governed both by convention and other extra-individual influences and by the intervention of the individual's autonomous decision-making power. At least four factors determine an individual's decision-making power – his capacity to act in the present in such a way as to make the future more attractive. These factors are his age, his stock of human capital, his control over facilities or property, and his socioeconomic status. Whereas an individual's age and stock of human capital increase during the first stage, his decision-making power is greatly limited by lack of facilities and appropriate status. Upon the individual's passage into the second stage, all four determinants increase, normally attaining peak values, the aggregate effect of which is to fix a plateau or upper limit to the individual's capacity to shape his future advantageously. Passage through time beyond his plateau tends to be accompanied by adverse effects associated with aging, together with diminution in his stocks of human capital and facilities as well as his socioeconomic status. One effect is a partial replacement of aggressive forward-looking decision making by rearguard action suited to resist decline in faculties and status and to a slowdown both in the rate of this decline and in that of human capital (see Colberg and Windham).

An individual's capacity for making decisions conducive to the improvement of his long-run future tends to rise from a relatively low level in the first stage of his life, to peak in the second stage, and thereafter to decline unless partially cushioned by the acquisition (along with others in the same stage) of organized political power. This capacity varies greatly from individual to individual; however, it varies with the relative condition of many governed by external circumstances and that of a minority affected in a marked degree by their future-shaping decision-making powers.

Increase in life expectancy at birth, together with improvements in health care and increase in average output, has facilitated extension of the boundaries of dependency over the past half century. It has also made possible extension of the boundaries of active working age, though this possibility has not been generally realized, given the opportunity to retire and still have support in the form of a pension (Boskin, Carp, Patton).

For purposes of illustration we may contrast life expectancy and survivorship among white males in the United States in 1900 –2 and 1974. Of major importance is difference in life expectancy at later years – for example, age 15, at which the margin of *relative* superiority of the 1974 cohort over the 1900 cohort was not

Table 5.1. *Life expectancy and survivorship among white males,*
1900–2 and 1974

	1900–2		1974	
Age	Life expectancy	Survivors	Life expectancy	Survivors
0	48.23	100,000	68.9	100,000
15	46.25	78,037	55.6	97,588
50	20.76	57,274	24.0	86,578
60	14.35	46,452	16.5	77,734
70	9.03	30,460	10.6	56,737
85	3.81	5,252	4.9	14,912

Source: Vital Statistics of the United States, 1974, Life Tables, Vol. II,
Section 5, Rockville, Md.: U.S. Department of Health, Eduction, and
Welfare, Public Health Service, 1976.

quite half as large as it was at birth. Indeed, given allowance for
improvement in the life expectancy of the surviving members of
the 1900–2 cohort during its lifetime, the margin of superiority of
the 1974 cohort over the 1900–2 cohort would be even less than
is suggested by the values for 1900 and 1974 (see Table 5.1). The
scope for realizable improvement is greater, of course, when mortality is relatively high and still susceptible to appreciable reduction. Even so, as will be indicated, life expectancy and an individual's estimate of it, help to shape his general expectations and
his tentative organization of activities in his remaining years. Life
expectancy also influences the environment of man's opportunity. For example, a survivor to age 50 of the 1900 cohort of
100,000 individuals faced the competition of only 57,274 cohort
members, compared to 86,578 offering competition under comparable conditions in 1974. Moreover, this increase in number of
competitors is not cushioned by population growth. In a stationary population, growth of output per capita corresponds closely
to growth of overall demand per capita (Keyfitz), thus limiting
opportunities accessible to survivors at age 50 compared to a
growing population.

Age, productivity, work capacity, and job performance

As an individual moves into and through the middle stage of his life – the stage when he is most likely to be enrolled in the labor force – his productive powers and his capacity to work and fulfill the requirements of his vocation or job move upward to a peak, level off, and eventually undergo some decline. This movement reflects changes in the state of his human capital, his physical and mental powers, and his expectations about the near and the more removed future.

In general, underlying the economic concomitants of aging at both the aggregate population or macroeconomic level and the autonomous individual level are mainly the physical and psychological effects associated with the process of individual aging, together with the diminution of an individual's anticipated life expectancy and his view of his future prospects as he grows older. The macroeconomic significance of population aging turns, of course, on the size and changes in the size of the fraction of the population describable as old (e.g., over 60, 65, or 70), together with the degree to which aging is likely to affect a population's productive power, investment behavior, consumption patterns, and political along with politically affected behavior (Eisele).[3]

Psychologist A. T. Welford has found that many age-related variations in ability are due primarily to changes in the nervous system which result in two effects: slowed timing of perception and response, and diminished capacity of the mind for short-term retention of information. "Aging . . . holds a magnifying glass to human performance so that many facets present but scarcely noticeable in the twenties have become important by the time we reach the sixties" (Welford, p. 1).[4] The importance of these decrements in job performance depends on whether the tasks assigned actually require peak-capacity performance on the part of individuals, and on the extent to which job experience and training may offset possible effects of physiological decline.

Aging is important, of course, not only because of its effect upon the productivity of individuals (Davis, Donahue, Schwab and Heneman, Welford) but also because of the significance of productivity for the earnings for workers and hence for such earnings-related behavior as consumption, savings, and labor supply.

Some studies have indicated, however, that the effect of age on productivity is insignificant before age 60 (Birren) or before 50 (Thorndike, p. 55, said that thereafter abilities requiring energy and speed declined about 1 to 2 percent per year until age 75), and that chronological age alone is a poor indicator of work performance. Although individual differences in performance increase with age, persons with high levels of competence appear to lose little or no ground as long as they continue to work at challenging tasks (Shock). Capacity for reasoning and judgment does not suffer impairment with age because slowing of comprehension is counterbalanced by increase in depth of knowledge (McFarland and O'Doherty). As a result of the compensatory character of these factors, Ross McFarland has proposed the use of functional rather than chronological age in the determination of a mandatory retirement age (see also McFarland and O'Doherty).

Technological progress may adversely affect an older worker. The introduction of new technologies and the expansion of knowledge in an occupation may render a portion of an older worker's human capital obsolete. This vintage effect can eliminate much of the value of the experience of senior workers relative to that of younger employees. The combination of decrements in learning ability and obsolescence of human capital implies that training costs are likely to be higher for older workers, particularly those with lower-than-average education and skills (Belbin). However, evidence from a study of 2,200 workers in four industries ". . . contradicts the notion that older workers cannot learn or cannot be trained. The findings imply that age, by itself, is not a reliable or useful criterion for determining the suitability of workers for training" (BLS Bulletin No. 1368, p. 6). Of course, given a stationary or near-stationary population such as may eventually be associated with population aging, the resulting scarcity of labor will be favorable to the continuing employment of older workers.

When the components of job performance are analyzed separately, studies continue to support the general thesis that only small changes in an individual's ability to perform in the work place are associated with age. In a series of studies, the Bureau of Labor Statistics examined age changes in average productivity in different occupations. Among office workers, no decline is observed (BLS Bulletin No. 1273); with mail sorters, a slight decrease has been noted after age 60 (Walker). For factory workers in the footwear, furniture, and clothing industries, the decline in productivity after age 45 is more noticeable; however, the variation within an age group is usually larger than the productivity differences between cohorts (BLS Bulletin Nos. 1203, 1223). These findings suggest that shifts in the occupational distribution away from manual tasks may enhance the relative position of the elderly in the labor market.

In all occupations individual performance varies over the distribution of employees. The age-specific distributions of productivity overlap, with older workers frequently being more productive than younger ones. Older employees have steadier, more consistent working patterns on the job (Walker, pp. 298–300; BLS Bulletin No. 1273, p. 15), and there is no apparent age variation in accuracy (BLS Bulletin No. 1273, p. 16; Clay; De la Mare and Sheppard; Welford). There is little variation with age in the attendance patterns (Mack; Kossoris; Spengler, 1948, pp. 111–14). Even among production workers where physical stamina is an important qualification, attendance rates do not vary consistently with age. Job changes become less frequent with age, with older workers much less likely to quit or be fired (Bancroft and Garfinkle, Mack). Work injuries do not increase with age, although the types of accidents involving older workers are somewhat different, and work injuries result in longer periods of disability for the older employee (Kossoris, McFarland and O'Doherty). In summary, "a comprehensive review of available medical and psychological evidences reveals no support for the broad age lines which have been drawn on the basis of claimed physical requirements" (U.S. Department of Labor, 1965, p. 9). Matilda Riley and Anne Foner (pp. 426–33) provide a summary of these studies reviewing the relationship between age and job performance.

Spengler (see Kreps, 1971) draws a distinction between the physical and mental requirements of employment and one's capacity to meet such requirements. In calling attention to the "disparity between man's physical withdrawal from worklife in his later years and his prior expulsion from work by society's contemporary institutional restrictions," he points out that throughout most of worklife, one's ability far exceeds the demands of one's job. The individual's capacity curve, which eventually starts to decline with age, will in time intersect the requirements curve. But even then, work performance can be extended through job redesign or worker retraining.

Kreps (1977) noted that the age – productivity profile would be expected to vary substantially between occupations, the differences being determined by patterns of investment in human capital and the physical and mental requirements of the job. The age – earnings profile may deviate from the age – productivity profile because of seniority rules, job tenure, and wages based on longevity of service (Lazear, Leigh).

Age earnings profiles: saving

Whereas a consistent relationship between age and productivity is difficult to detect even within an occupation, correlation of the behavior of earnings with age is more readily observable. Average earnings profiles constructed from cross-sectional data typically follow the same general pattern for most occupations. Immediately after entry into the labor force, annual earnings are low, the income of each successive age group being higher, with an earnings peak usually achieved by 45- to 54-year-olds. Persons in the last decade of worklife typically have lower average earnings than those in the preceding age group, although they do not necessarily earn less than they did when they themselves were younger (Spengler, pp. 105–7; Becker and Chiswick; Kreps, 1971, Chapter 8, 1976a, p. 275, 1976b). Patterns of the relationship between age and income by occupational groups indicate roughly equivalent cross-sectional profiles, although the age at which average income peaks varies with education and occupation. In general, the higher the level of education and/or skill level of the job, the later the age at which income is maximized (Becker, 1964; Hanoch; Kreps and Pursell).

Houthakker observed that "in a growing economy every individual may expect an upward trend in his own earnings superimposed on the cross-sectional pattern for a given year" (p. 27). Lacking adequate longitudinal data to examine lifetime earning patterns, Herman Miller (1966) and Becker (1964) combined several cross-sectional data sets to observe a cohort during its worklife. Kreps (1976a) extended the analysis to include the years 1939, 1949, 1959, and 1969. These studies show that the average earnings of a cohort continue to rise until age 65 in contradiction to the cross-sectional data (see also Colberg and Windham, pp. 34, 36). Nancy Ruggles and Richard Ruggles employed the Longitudinal Employee–Employer Data file developed by the Social Security Administration to estimate the age–earnings profiles of individual birth cohorts. Using data from 1957–69, they find, "In relating the age–earnings profiles to the earnings patterns of specific birth cohorts, the leveling off and decline in average earnings shown by the cross-sectional age–earnings profile is in marked contrast with the continued rise in earnings exhibited by every birth cohort up to the point of retirement at age 65" (p. 129).[5]

Distinguishing between that portion of the increase attributable to the worker's added experience and that portion due to economic growth, Miller finds that the relative significance of the two sources shifts during the worker's lifetime. For college graduates, for example, experience contributes heavily to the rise in earnings during the male's thirties, but much less to any increase accruing in subsequent decades of worklife. During the male's fifties, moreover, experience has a negative impact on earnings for college graduates as well as males of less education; except for the impact of economic growth, all incomes would drop during the last decade of work. Miller also notes that "the impact of growth appears to be greater for young men than for those past the prime working years" (p. 384). Yoram Ben-Porath (1966) points to a bias in Miller's growth effect; it gives rise to an upward bias in the estimates of the gain due to growth and implies that the growth effect will decline with age.

Consumption and saving

Saving varies with age, mainly in response to variations in an individual's earnings and in his essentially nondiscretionary expenditures, which are dominated by household and family formation (Kreps, 1971, Parts I, III, cf. Nagatani), but somewhat subject to life-cycle influences (Creedy, Clark). Saving tends to be augmented as well by conditions contributing to increase in worklife. Improvement in health has such an effect. For example, Reimers finds "the stability of the conditional mean retirement age in the face of Social Security pensions" to depend "on the effects of improved health on ability to work until an advanced age." Moreover, extension of life also extends what Glick (1977) calls the "empty nest period" – the length of time ensuing between the marriage of the last child and the death of one spouse – and thus makes wives freer to find employment. Prevention of discrimination against older workers, thereby guarding their earning capacity, could also prolong their participation in the labor force, given the finding of Ghez and Becker (p. xv) that "people retire at old age when their productivity is low" (and presumably their earnings). Conversely, factors that increase the comparative cost of hiring older workers discourage their employment (Science Council of Canada, p. 34) and reduce their lifetime saving capacity.

Saving as well as consumption is subject to life-cycle influence (Lydall, Thurow). Modigliani finds that a life-cycle model provides the best explanation of the dynamics of saving and capital formation (Modigliani and Ando, 1957; Ando and Modigliani, 1963; also Landesberger).

The point of departure of the life cycle model is the hypothesis that consumption and saving decisions of households at each point of time reflect a more or less conscious attempt at achieving the preferred distribution of consumption over the life cycle, subject to the constraint imposed by the resources accruing to the household over its life time. (Modigliani, 1966, p. 162)

Because "on the average, earning power tends to dry up well before the termination of life . . . the preferred allocation of resources over life will typically call for a rate of consumption, after this drying up, on a scale commensurate with earlier consumption." Households must, "on the average, save in the earlier part of life in order to accumulate a stock of wealth . . . which will eventually be used to support consumption through dissaving in the later part of life" (Modigliani, 1966, p. 163; also 1970).

Given a household behaving optimally over its life cycle, "the ultimate goal is to derive for each household an optimal plan of consumption, capital accumulation, work, leisure, and an optimal bequest" (Blinder, 1974, p. 27). Then given certainty,

(a) the level of consumption at any point of time depends on the present value of the entire life time earnings; and

(b) the proportionate rate change of the marginal utility of consumption at any point of time is equal to the difference between the subjective discount rate and the objective discount rate. (Nagatani, p. 344; also Yaari)

Given uncertainty, the central message of life-cycle theory – "that the lifetime pattern of consumption is independent of the lifetime pattern of earnings" – cannot be literally true, Blinder (1976) finds. Presumably, increase in life expectancy, especially in life expectancy at age of entry into the labor force, tends to reduce uncertainty insofar as it is associated with age of withdrawal from the labor force or with age of death.

Life-cycle models

The economic status of the elderly is not merely the result of chance occurrences but is essentially the outgrowth of resource-allocation choices over the life cycle, concerning education, on-the-job training, work, consumption, and, as already indicated, saving and investment. Over the last two decades, life-cycle models have been employed to examine these decisions of individuals over their lifetimes. In these models, each person is hypothesized to maximize his lifetime utility given personal characteristics, wealth, and preferences by optimally allocating his personal resources over his life.

With the development of macroeconomic models of the economy following World War II, economists became concerned with the specification of the aggregate consumption function. Modigliani and Brumberg (1954) and Milton Friedman (1957) shifted the focus from income in the year of consumption to include considerations of future income stream or wealth position of the consumer as determinants of consumption. Men were seen as "forward-looking animals" who plan their consumption decisions for the whole lifetime based on the perfectly known present value of future income. Hours of work, leisure, and earnings were exogenously determined with earnings hypothesized to follow a parabolic profile. The derived rate of consumption was independent of income with total consumption over the lifetime equal to total income. Ando and Modigliani (1963) found empirical support for consumption as being a function of present income and the last period's wealth (see also Modigliani, 1970). Although consumption and savings were modeled as subject to individual choice, personal income and wealth were not. Martin Feldstein (1974, 1976) and Alicia Munnell (1974) used aggregate life-cycle consumption functions of the Ando-Modigliani variety to introduce the promise of social security benefits as an independent variable influencing savings, consumption, and labor supply during the lifetime of a worker. This approach has been extended by Munnell (1976) to examine effects of private pensions on savings and by Feldstein (1976) to show how pensions might reduce or increase personal saving and how the social security system reduces saving. The controversy concerning this latter point is examined in Chapter 8 as more recent research casts doubt on the savings-reduction effect of social security systems (Esposito, Burkhauser and Turner).

Along with the growth of literature relating to aggregate consumption functions (see Mayer, 1972), recent years have witnessed the development of microeconomic decision models that require workers to make decisions with regard to the allocation of their time to work, consumption, and investment in human capital. The human-capital approach calls for examination of the choice between investment in human capital in the form of education or on-the-job training and market work as a key to explanation of variations in wage and earning patterns. The human-capital problem as formulated by Becker (1964) consisted of a comparison of the costs of education in the form of forgone earnings and other expenditures in any period with the resulting returns to investment in the form of higher productivity. The simple model thus formulated shows net earnings over the lifetime to be determined by the path of investment in human capital. The earnings profile over the working life of the individual would be an increasing function because investments in human capital are decreasing. The more closely an individual approaches the end of his life, the more difficult it becomes to recover costs of new investments, with the result that as age increases, less investment is undertaken, and net earnings more closely approximate potential earnings.

Since its first application to life-cycle earnings, the model has been made more realistic in a number of ways. Becker and Chiswick (1966) modified the model by making the cost of the investment in human capital proportional to earnings potential in the period. The fraction of earnings potential forgone in investment in any period is exactly equal to the fraction of human-capital stock invested in the accumulation of more human capital; thus if the investment rate is known over the lifetime, the earnings profile is known. Thomas Johnson (1970) employed a specific investment function and introduced a depreciation of the human-capital parameter to predict earnings. Human-capital models of this type produce earnings paths very similar to those found empirically from cross-sectional data, that is, an earnings path that increases until age 45 or 50, and then decreases. Ben-Porath's theoretical analysis (1967) provided a method of determining a unique investment function over the lifetime as a result of choice behavior. He assumed individuals maximize present value of disposable earnings given that one must combine a portion of the human-capital stock with market inputs to produce additional human capital. Out of this optimizing behavior comes a unique proportion of earnings forgone in investment over the life cycle. Jacob Mincer and Mark Blaug provide partial reviews of this literature, whereas Sherwin Rosen provides a review of the empirical work done in this area.

More general models of choice allow individual choice between investment in human capital, work, and household production or leisure in a utility-maximizing framework. Such models of allocation of human resources have been proposed by James Heckman, Ali Sadik and Johnson, Blinder and Yoram Weiss, Ghez and Becker, and Frank Stafford and Paula Stephan. These models provide the links between income and consumption and leisure that are in some part missing in previous work. The earnings profile generated in these models has a concave shape as it rises to a peak and then declines afterward. The decline toward the end of the working life occurs because of both the increasing value of leisure and the depreciation of the human-capital stock (Heckman). The consumption profile depends upon the values of the interest rate and the time-preference rate for its slope. Saving and dissaving are used by the consumer to spread his consumption optimally over the lifetime, again similarly to the macroeconomic consumption model.

In the three-activity life-cycle model, profiles of consumption, earnings, hours of work, and assets depend for their shape and level on individual parameters such as initial stocks of assets and human capital, rates of time preference, depreciation rates of human capital and market parameters, the interest rate on bonds, and the rate of return to investment in human capital. A system is offered that can incorporate the complex interactions of savings and variable retirement age, obsolesence of skills and assets, education and retirement age, and so on. Aging is a complex process involving the deterioration of the human capital stock and changing valuations of income and leisure. To understand the effects of pensions, social security, the earnings test, compulsory retirement, Medicare, and other economic incentives or disincentives, models must be adopted that include the amount of work, consumption, and on-the-job training as the result of individual choice. In addition, attention has been called to the difficulties attendant upon attempts to estimate the optimal consumption levels at any point in time (Irvine) and upon efforts to estimate the impact of the advent of zero population growth upon aggregate consumption (Espenshade).

It should be noted that the pattern of the representative life cycle as of the representative family cycle is conditioned by vital,[6] technological, and related conditons lying outside the cycle as such. In India, for example, the family cycle differs somewhat from that characteristic in the United States and hence must affect economic behavior accordingly (Collver). In the United States the family life cycle and labor force behavior are strongly related (Peterson). In France (and presumabley elsewhere) the cycle of habitation, and the age structures of population and housing are interrelated (Le Bras and Chesnais). Although aging may have, or is believed to have, an adverse effect upon an individual's productive and related powers after he has reached a certain age, this supposed effect has not been introduced as a cyclical determinant other than as an unfavorable concomitant of a too-low rate of population growth (Leibenstein, Stassart, Rosen and Irde). After all, activities of individuals may be slow to be affected by age (Rae, Poitrenaud and Moreaux).

D. L. Bosworth estimates the rate of obsolescence of technical knowledge at well over 10 percent in the post-war period, a rate double at least one other estimate. He does not, however, estimate the rate at which a worker can learn new technologies and thus minimizes the impact of technical obsolescence upon his total skill as a workman.

6

Labor supply of the elderly

Applying labor supply models to older workers

Questions concerning the supply of labor by an individual have been fertile ground for economic researchers since Adam Smith (Spengler). The standard presentation of individual labor-supply decision making evolved through, among other studies, a paper by Lionel Robbins, John Hicks's explication of income-substitution effects in *Value and Capital,* and a family-context framework formulated by Marvin Kosters. This analysis presents an individual with a constrained maximization problem where, subject to a resource constraint, he attempts to maximize his utility function which includes income and leisure. (Graphic expositions can be found in Fleisher, pp. 38–51, and Rees, pp. 22–4; for a formal presentation, see Henderson and Quandt, pp. 29–37.) Becker provided a framework for examining the allocation of time between market work and home production (i.e., value is placed on hours away from market activity because of the home-produced goods that are generated). More recently, Heckman and Sadik and Johnson, have expanded the time-allocation model to include home production, market work, and investment in human capital over the life cycle.

The most appropriate framework in which to examine the retirement decisions in late life is the life-cycle concept. Many of the factors that influence the withdrawal from the labor force are

85

a function of prior economic decisions. Thus, retirement should be viewed as one of the many resource-allocation decisions that an individual faces throughout life; however, only the most recent theoretical and empirical research has formulated the labor-supply choices of older workers in the life-cycle framework. Empirical studies of labor supply have increased rapidly over the past two decades with the availability of more extensive micro data sets. Glen Cain and Harold Watts provide an excellent bibliography and review of many of these studies. Unfortunately, many economists have limited their empirical analysis to individuals less than 65 years of age and, in some cases, less than 55 years old. In the remainder of this section, we outline a series of factors that may preclude the adequate explanation of the labor-supply decisions of older individuals using only the same variables that perform reasonably well for workers 25 to 54. This is done in conjunction with our review of the empirical and theoretical studies that have concentrated on the labor-market activity of the elderly.

**Labor supply, retirement, and inconsistencies
in the literature**
The dependent variable in estimates of labor supply is intended to capture the market response of individuals to changes in other factors. One of the difficulties in reviewing studies of labor-force participation of the elderly is the variation in the use of a measure of labor supply or retirement. A particular problem arises when the expected influence of factors is contradictory between the alternative indicators of participation. The following have been employed in various studies as the individual labor-response variable: termination of a particular career (Barfield and Morgan), extent of earnings, hours of work (Quinn, Bowen and Finegan), receipt of pension benefits (Vroman), individual's perception of retirement status, labor-force participation rates (Bowen and Finegan, Quinn), annual work rates, and expectations of retiring (Parnes et al.). Using aggregate data, labor-force participation rates (Bowen and Finegan, Tella, Dernberg and

Strand) and receipt of pension benefits (Pechman et al., Campbell and Campbell) are the primary measures of labor-market activity.

Clearly, it is possible for a person to be counted as retired by some of these measures but not others. For example, military personnel can retire from the service (termination of a career) and begin receiving pension benefits, yet still work 40 hours a week for another employer. Thus, the reader must be cautious when comparing studies of labor supply of older individuals.

The elderly are not a homogeneous group as measured by a variety of socioeconomic factors including age. Therefore, social or economic conditions may influence those, say, 55–64 years old differently from those over 65. Early retirement prior to age 65 may be caused by a different set of factors from the withdrawal from the labor force at or after age 65. In addition, the significance of explanatory variables may depend on whether one is examining individual labor-supply decisions or long-term trends in economic aggregates. In fact, some of the aggregates may move in the opposite direction. Cordelia Reimers shows the possibility of average retirement age – as measured by permanent withdrawal from the labor force – rising while participation rates are falling.

Despite the diversity of indicators employed to measure labor supply of the elderly, a historical examination of most of these measures reveals decreased labor force activity coupled with increased acceptance of pension benefits for older males in most industrialized countries (Unsigned). Table 6.1 illustrates that in the United States the labor-force participation for males 65 years and over fell from 46.8 percent in 1948 to 20.3 percent in 1976, whereas the market-activity rate for men 55–64 dropped from 89.5 to 74.5 percent during this period. Participation rates for older females have only recently begun to decline slightly. Prior to the mid-1960s, this measure of labor supply had risen significantly for females ages 55–64 in conjunction with the overall increase in the market work of women. Table 6.2 indicates a similar decline for older males in France. Thus, it is the large and continuing decline in labor supply of older males that most studies

Table 6.1. *U.S. Civilian labor-force participation rates for older workers by sex, 1948–76 (percent)*

Year	Male 55–64	Male 65 and over	Female 55–64	Female 65 and over
1948	89.5	46.8	24.3	9.1
1949	87.5	47.0	25.3	9.6
1950	86.9	45.8	27.0	9.7
1951	87.2	44.9	27.6	8.9
1952	87.5	42.6	28.7	9.1
1953	87.9	41.6	29.1	10.0
1954	88.7	40.5	30.1	9.3
1955	87.9	39.6	32.5	10.6
1956	88.5	40.0	34.9	10.8
1957	87.5	37.5	34.5	10.5
1958	87.8	35.6	35.2	10.3
1959	87.4	34.2	36.6	10.2
1960	86.8	33.1	37.2	10.8
1961	87.3	31.7	37.9	10.7
1962	86.2	30.3	38.7	9.9
1963	86.2	28.4	39.7	9.6
1964	85.6	28.0	40.2	10.1
1965	84.6	27.9	41.1	10.0
1966	84.5	27.5	41.8	9.6
1967	84.4	27.1	42.8	9.6
1968	84.3	27.3	42.4	9.6
1969	83.4	27.2	43.1	9.9
1970	83.0	26.8	43.0	9.7
1971	82.2	25.5	42.9	9.5
1972	80.5	24.4	42.1	9.3
1973	78.3	22.8	41.1	8.9
1974	77.4	22.4	40.7	8.2
1975	75.8	21.7	41.0	8.3
1976	74.5	20.3	41.1	8.2

Source: U.S. Department of Labor, *1977 Employment and Training Report of the President,* Washington, D.C.: U.S. Government Printing Office, 1977, Table A-4, pp. 142–3.

have attempted to explain. Moreover, it appears that following withdrawal from the labor force few retirees are interested in returning to market work unless family income declines significantly (Motley).

Table 6.2. *Labor-force participation rates of French males, 1901–68 (percent)*

Year	25–54	55–64	65 and over
1901	96	88	60
1906	96	87	60
1911	96	86.5	60
1921	96.5	89	61
1926	96.5	86	55.5
1931	96.5	85	53.5
1936	95.5	79	47.5
1946	96	81.5	48
1954	96	76.5	34.5
1962	96	76.5	25
1968	96	71.5	16

Source: J. J. Carré, P. Doubois, and E. Malinvaud, *French Economic Growth,* Stanford: Stanford University Press, 1975, p. 47.

Data sources

A limited number of data sets from the United States have emerged as the principal sources of information for use in examining the labor supply of the elderly. Table 6.3 lists these surveys and briefly describes the sample population while providing a source for further documentation. The following review of the empirical literature will refer to these surveys as the data source for most of the research.

Factors influencing the labor supply of the elderly

In this section and the following one, and in the following chapter, the primary individual and economy characteristics that influence the labor supply decision of the elderly are reviewed. We have divided these influences into the following categories: pension-related, health status, aggregate economy characteristics, other financial, individual and family characteristics, and job-related. The pension-related effects, which are analyzed in the remainder of this chapter, include social security benefits, the earnings test, age of eligibility, private pensions, and compulsory

Table 6.3. *Data sources employed for labor-supply analysis of the elderly*

Survey	Population surveyed	Frequency and scope	Description source
Retirement History Survey	Men 58–63 Women 58–63 (without spouse)	Every two years beginning in 1969 with 11,153 cases – 1969, 1971 tapes now available	Irelan, 1972
National Longitudinal Survey	Men 44–59	Periodic surveys since 1966, 5,020 cases initially	U.S. Department of Labor, Monograph No. 15
Survey of Newly Entitled Beneficiaries	Workers initially awarded benefits, primarily individuals aged 62–65	Samples selected monthly, July 1968– June 1970	U.S. Social Security Administration, 1973
Michigan Income Dynamics Panel	5,000 households	Eight years 1968–75, approximately 20 per cent 55 years and older	Morgan, 1974; *A Panel Study of Income Dynamics*, 1972
1967 Survey of Economic Opportunity	30,000 households	1967 survey with 6,100 cases having at least one member aged 65 and older	
United Automobile Workers	UAW workers aged 58–61 in 1966	1,123 interviewed in 1967, and 943 in 1969–70	Barfield, 1970; Barfield and Morgan, 1969
Louis Harris Survey	Individuals 55 years and older	2,797 persons 65 or older; 486 persons 55–64	Harris, 1975

retirement. Other factors that influence the labor supply of the aged are discussed in the next chapter. While the scope of the review is international, most of the research concerning labor-supply decisions of the elderly has employed U.S. data. Unless otherwise specified, the studies examined below are based on data collected in the United States.

After reviewing the retirement literature, Colin Campbell, Rosemary Campbell, and Michael Boskin conclude that two competing hypotheses exist concerning primary influences on retirement. "On the one hand, a group of studies suggest that the Social Security System plays a relatively passive and minor role, the major reason for retirement being poor health. On the other, evidence . . . suggests that Social Security induces – or enables – elderly men to withdraw from the labor force" (Boskin, p. 4). Campbell and Campbell attribute the former group of studies to researchers in the U.S. Social Security Administration and the second category to "economists outside the Social Security System" (p. 369).

Our interpretation of the relevant research does not indicate the dichotomy of findings that Boskin and Campbell and Campbell charge. In fact, there are an increasing number of studies finding that together pension systems – benefits and labor-force restrictions – and health status are the most significant factors that influence the labor-supply decision of older workers. There may also be interactive effects between health of an individual and the availability of pension benefits. In the following review of these and other factors that influence labor supply, we provide the reader with the measure of labor supply as well as the source of data employed in each study.

Pension-related incentives

Social security and other pension benefits provide non-wage income to the elderly and therefore would be expected to have an unambiguously negative effect on the labor-supply decision. The receipt of these benefits is, however, in many instances contingent on the total or partial withdrawal from the labor force by the beneficiary (i.e., earnings test and compulsory retirement). Munnell argues that "Social Security's influence has been three-fold, including a pure income effect, the impact of the retirement test, and its influence in general attitudes toward the appropriate retirement age" (p. 19). The impact of the social security system on the development of private pensions should surely be added to this list.

Whereas most researchers prior to the mid-1970s concentrated on the annual flow of pension benefits, Feldstein and Munnell introduced the concept of social security wealth (i.e., present value of expected social security benefits) into the resource allocation decisions of individuals. R. C. L. Hemming and Richard Burkhauser argue that an individual accepts a pension in order to maximize full lifetime wealth. Thus, it is the lifetime present value of benefits, not the annual flow, that is the determining factor of labor-force withdrawal. The retirement decision should be governed by the characteristics of the pension formula that determines the discounted value of the benefits to an individual from an additional year of work along with the other personal and financial factors that influence labor-supply decisions.

Social security benefits

Most examinations of the labor-supply decisions of individuals in older cohorts have found that eligibility for social security benefits has lowered market-activity rates, especially over the last two and one-half decades. Prior to this time, benefits may have been so small as to have had only a negligible effect on participation. Examining trends in U.S. labor-force participation from 1890 to 1950, Clarence Long noted a significant and continuing pattern of reduced market work during this period, when public and private pensions were virtually nonexistent. During this period, the labor-force participation rate of males 65 and over declined from 70 to 42.5 percent, a decline of about 5 percentage points per decade. Long concludes that prior to 1950 ". . . Social Security and pensions were far from being the main force (though they doubtless helped) in bringing about the withdrawal of elderly persons from the labor market'' (p. 163).

The expansion in coverage and level of benefits since 1950 apparently has resulted in social security benefits playing a major role in determining the proportion of older individuals in the labor force. Margaret Gordon hypothesizes that the ratio of retirement benefits to earnings is the more important variable, rather than the absolute level of benefits. She reports a significant inverse correlation ($-.83$) between labor-force participation of men aged 65 and over and average benefits as a percentage of average earnings in fourteen industrial nations for 1950 (Gordon, 1963b; see also Gordon, 1963a). Pechman et al., employing 1960 aggregate data from nineteen countries in a multivariate regression, reported that increases in the ratio of average social security benefits as a percentage of average manufacturing earnings produced lower labor-force participation rates for older cohorts. Their analysis indicates that a rise of one percentage point in per capita social security benefits relative to average earnings would reduce the rate of labor-force participation of men 65 years old and over by approximately four-tenths of 1 percent (p. 130). Supporting this hypothesis, Lowell Gallaway (1971) found a strongly significant negative correlation between state labor-force participation rates in the United States of males 65 and over in 1959, with the ratio of annual social security benefits to median earnings of male members of the experienced civilian labor force.

Bowen and Finegan, in their study of labor-force participation, used an "other income" variable (OI), which included social security benefits and private pension benefits, as well as asset income. They recognized the potential bias that occurs owing to the fact that pension benefits are often contingent on partial withdrawal from market activity. Thus, the OI-participation profile is not a pure income effect of nonlabor income on participation decisions. They estimate that increases in social security benefits and other nonlabor income reduced labor-force participation rates of males over 64 by 9.8 percentage points between 1948 and 1965. During this period, average annual real social security benefits in 1959 dollars increased from $378 to $1,000, whereas the fraction of all males 65 and over receiving retirement benefits from social security rose from 14 to 76 percent. The interrelated rise of average benefits and expansion in coverage produced the drop in labor-force activity. Although they agree with Long that social security probably had little effect prior to 1950, Bowen and Finegan conclude that their results leave "little doubt that rising levels of other income – and particularly the increase in social security benefits and coverage – have played a major role in reducing the participation of older males during the postwar years" (p. 357).

Periodically, SSA has conducted surveys of older cohorts to assess their economic well-being and rationale for labor-force withdrawal. These surveys have indicated an increasing tendency of retirees to respond that desire for leisure or retirement and the availability of pension income is the primary determinant of their withdrawal from the labor force. Wentworth reported that in 1941–2 only about 5 percent of beneficiaries responded that they had filed for benefits because they wished to do so. She concluded that the ". . . fact that only 3–6 percent of the beneficiaries retired voluntarily in order to enjoy leisure is significant in evaluating the part old-age insurance benefits have played in influencing aged workers to leave the labor market" (p. 18). In his analysis of the 1963 survey of the aged, Palmore found that 19 percent of the males who retired at age 65 and 11 percent of those retiring between the ages of 62 and 64 gave a preference for leisure as the cause for their withdrawing from the labor force. In summary, he found that although most men retire involuntarily, voluntary retirements are increasing. Virginia Reno (1976b) reported that approximately 20 percent of the nonemployed men awarded benefits in the latter part of 1968 gave eligibility for social security benefits or that they wanted to retire as the most important reason for leaving their last job. Thirty-one percent responded affirmatively to the question "Did you leave your last job because you wanted to start getting social security or a pension?"[1] Data from the RHS indicate that for male retirees in 1973 who were employed in 1969, 31 percent of those aged 62–63 and over 40 percent of those aged 64–67 had left their jobs to draw pension benefits or voluntary work reductions (Bixby, p. 15).

Bowen and Finegan also estimated the individual response to changes in other income using the 1/1,000 sample of the 1960 U.S. Census. The expected negative correlation was found; however, a reversal of this relationship is found in both the analysis of labor-force participation and hours of work at the highest income levels – over $5,000 for older males. Bowen and Finegan argue that this twist is the result of the personal characteristics of the men in the top other-income bracket, the kinds of work open to them, and the fact that older persons with continuing high earnings opportunities and large amounts of other income from non-OASDI sources will be less likely to be induced to withdraw from the labor market by the social security earnings test than are less affluent older men (Bowen and Finegan, p. 313).

Boskin employed a sample of families whose head was aged 61–65 in the first year selected from the Panel Study of Income Dynamics for the period 1968 through 1972. His estimates, based on a sample size of only 131, indicate that an increase in social security benefits raises the annual probability of retirement. A rise in annual social security benefits from $3,000 to $4,000 for a couple increases the annual probability of retirement from 7.5 to 16 percent. The effect of a change in benefits generates a response seven times as large as that from asset income. Boskin justified this result by explaining: "Social Security benefits are guaranteed for the remainder of one's life and are indexed against inflation. Further, to the extent bequests are planned, personal wealth may be transferred to one's heirs, whereas Social Security benefits cannot. Also, income from assets includes the imputed income to owner-occupied housing; the elderly may be reluctant to borrow against their equity for fear of living so long as to have to vacate the house and pay capital gains taxes" (p. 13). He concludes with the assessment that the social security system – expansion of coverage, increases in benefits, and earnings tests – has increased annual probability of retirement 40 percent and therefore ". . .

Social Security has been the prime mover in the acceleration of retirement" (p. 19).

Data from the first wave of the Retirement History Survey (RHS) composed of 11,153 persons aged 59–63 were used by Quinn to examine the primary determinants of early retirement. Using zero, one values for health limitation, eligibility for social security, eligibility for private pension, and presence of dependents, he found that eligibility for social security benefits was the second most influential variable with current eligibility reducing the probability of labor-force participation by 15 to 20 percentage points. Existence of benefits exerted a greater influence on those reporting some form of health limitation. In his analysis of hours of work, Quinn also finds a reduction in hours per week for those eligible for social security benefits. Because he does not incorporate the earnings test directly into his estimate, Quinn believes that the social security coefficients probably reflect labor-supply adjustment to avoid the tax. The magnitudes of these coefficients are small, leading Quinn to conclude that ". . . work reductions (as opposed to complete labor force withdrawal) do not seem to be a widespread phenomenon among those below 65" (p. 180). In a subsequent study, Quinn (forthcoming) finds that self-employed workers are more likely to reduce hours as they age than wage and salary employees.

Burkhauser examines labor-force participation decisions of males aged 60–64. Seeking to explain the rise in early retirement, he estimates labor-force participation as a function of the present value of social security benefits at age 62, proportion of men 62–64 receiving benefits, and the participation rate of men 55–59. His analysis indicates that the social security variables account for 8.8 percentage points of the 15-percentage-point decline in the participation rate of men aged 60–64 since 1957. The derivation of the cost of living adjustment and the payment of a Supplemental Security Income benefit for the poorest of the elderly combine to encourage early acceptance of social security benefits because they tend to offset the actuarial reduction imposed on the early acceptance of social security benefits (Tolley and Burkhauser).

Earnings test

Pension benefits that are subject to an earnings test[2] require that as earnings rise, the benefit be reduced. Such tests may apply only to income above a certain percentage of past earnings or, as in the United States, a fixed ceiling for all pensioners. Above this ceiling, the benefit is reduced with additional earnings. For the United States, the 1979 ceiling was $4,500 per year with benefits being reduced one dollar for every two dollars in earnings above the ceiling. Tolley and Burkhauser argue that the real marginal tax rate is well above the 50 percent reduction in benefits. They note that for a married worker earning the median wage over his lifetime who reached 65 in 1974, the annual social security benefit would be $4,704. If he were to continue to work, his gross earnings would be $7,723. This would be reduced by a marginal federal income tax rate of 17 percent and social security payroll tax of 5.85 percent. When combined with the reduction in benefits, the implied marginal tax rate is 72.85 percent.

In his examination of the U.K. retirement system. G. P. Marshall argues that the tax and benefit formulas of the national pension are similar to a negative-income-tax framework. During the first five years of retirement, benefits are reduced by 50 percent for earnings within a band of £35 to £39 per week and 100 percent for earnings greater than £39 per week. The total effect of the benefit combined with the earnings test will necessarily be a decline in work effort.

Wayne Vroman outlines the theoretical implications of this tax that should include an income and substitution effect on hours of work with the sign of the final adjustment ambiguous. He raises the possibility that leisure may not be a normal good for those who are involuntarily retired – still in the labor force but consuming more leisure than desired. Therefore, "the predictions of a negative income effect on labor supply are weakened" (p. 7). His results indicate that the 1965 amendments in the United States raising the earnings ceiling caused a small increase in the proportion of beneficiaries who had covered earnings. K. G. Sander, however, reported that workers did not distinguish for labor supply decisions between the 100 percent tax on earnings that existed prior to 1960 and the subsequent 50 percent tax rate. Boskin finds a much greater impact of the earnings tests. He estimates that a decrease in the implicit tax on earnings from its current 50 percent to one-third would decrease the annual probability of retirement by one-half for the typical worker.

Gallaway (1965) argued that labor-force participation rates should be unaffected by an earnings test because of the untaxed portion of earnings. Thus, workers might reduce hours but would never totally withdraw from the labor force. Bowen and Finegan point out that one method of reducing labor-supply effort is to reduce the number of weeks worked per year. If this occurs, the labor-force participation rate on any given survey week would be lower because of the earnings test; however, annual work rates should be unaffected. Bowen and Finegan provide two findings to support the contention that the earnings test lowers labor-force participation. First, their adjusted participation rate by age declines continuously after 65 until the age of 71 when this activity rate stands at 31.5 percent. It increases to 34.4 percent for men aged 72 when the earnings test is eliminated, and rises to 35.2 percent for those 73 years old before beginning to decline again. Second, their regressions for hours of work by older men indicate that men aged 67 do not work significantly longer than men 64 years old. "The fact that there is no significant difference in hours worked which remains after allowing for the income effect, advancing age, and other control variables, certainly suggests that part-year participation has been the more common method of adjusting labor input" (p. 284).

Despite these findings, response to the earnings test in the form of reduced hours may be responsible for the increasing tendency of males over 65 to engage in part-time work. The proportion of employed males who were voluntarily part-time rose from 20 percent in 1957 to 42 percent in 1974 (Campbell and Campbell). Pechman et al. (p. 127) noted the related observation that the incidence of part-time work increased with age in 1962. Only 10 percent of the men aged 62–64 usually held part-time jobs, com-

Table 6.4. *Persons with work experience in 1976 who were employed at part-time jobs (percent)*

Age	60–61	62–64	65–69	70 and over
Men	6.7	11.6	38.3	54.0
Women	31.4	32.3	56.1	68.0

Source: U.S. Department of Labor, "Work Experience of the Population in 1976," Bureau of Labor Statistics, Special Labor Force Report, No. 201, 1977, Table B-1, p. 12.

pared to 16 percent for those aged 65–72. The age-related rise in part-time employment was even more significant in 1976. As shown in Table 6.4, men over 64 were more than three times as likely to be part-time employees as those aged 62–64.

Burkhauser and Turner (forthcoming) illustrate that the decline in labor-force participation of the elderly due to the earnings test will reduce social welfare. To some extent this will be moderated by increased hours of work by younger workers. Marshall Colberg questions the desirability of the retirement test and notes that it reduces national output and decreases tax revenues.

Age of eligibility

The pensionable age as defined by social security may have an influence beyond that of merely providing the lure of benefits. Private companies may use this age in determining the normal age for full benefits in their pension system. Societal pressures may be exerted such that individuals believe that they are expected to retire at that age. Therefore, "OASDI may also encourage retirement because it sets the pattern for private and for state and local government retirement plans and, more generally, because it conditions both employer and employee attitudes toward 'normal' retirement age" (Pechman et al., p. 123). Thus, it is important to note the extent to which the actual retirement age has come to approach eligibility age for full benefits. More than one-third of the nations responding to a survey stated that the average exact age of initial receipt of benefits was either the same or within one year of the normal pensionable age (Kreps, p. 31). Whether the current normal retirement ages (see Tracy) will continue to be financially acceptable given the prospective decline in the ratio of workers to pensioners is questionable (Clark and Spengler, forthcoming).

Private pension benefits
   In a single-period context, the availability of private and other public pension benefits should lower labor-market activity through the income effect. Feldstein and Munnell argue that the promise of pension benefits will induce earlier retirement in a life-cycle model. Hemming illustrates that the response to an increase in the replacement rate from a pension may not be so certain. In his model, the individual delays retirement until the present value of net wage income plus accrued pension benefits from postponing retirement are equal to the present value of pension benefits being lost by the continuation of work. In this framework, increases in the replacement rate are ambiguous; however, with declining wages, higher pension benefits will always lower the retirement age. Increases in benefits that are not wage-related will induce earlier withdrawal from the labor force. Thus, the labor-supply response to changes in pension benefits will depend on the manner in which these benefits are determined. Hemming's argument, which would also explain an individual's response to social security benefits, is that at each point the individual acts so as to maximize lifetime wealth. (Also see Burkhauser.)
   Barfield and Morgan (1969) and Barfield (1970), analyzing a sample of auto workers, and Parnes et al., using the National Longitudinal Survey (NLS), found that pension income was significantly associated with the retirement decision. The studies of the auto workers provide evidence for a threshold effect of retirement income – $4,000 in 1967 and $5,000 in 1969. They report that "for the great majority of the sample, only one variable – the postretirement/preretirement income ratio – was found influential

. . . the average propensity-to-retire score rising smoothly and swiftly across the five groups'' (Barfield, p. 25). This variable, which includes both social security and private pension income, accounted for 37 percent of the variance in the propensity to retire.

Burkhauser's analysis indicates that the present value of pension benefits was a significant factor determining retirement for these workers. He calculates the present value of an auto worker accepting an early pension as compared to the value of deferring benefits until age 65. The greater the difference in the value of an early pension over the normal pension taken when the beneficiary reaches 65, the higher the probability of accepting an early pension. Burkhauser's theoretical model also illustrates the importance of considering other market opportunities that confront an individual when deciding whether to accept a pension and retire from a particular job. The greater the difference between the wage in the present occupation and the higher the value of the worker's time to other firms, the less likely he is to take an early pension by retiring from the present job. These effects indicate that: "A worker will take a pension at the point in time where it maximizes his full wealth. It is the lifetime present discounted value of the pension which is looked at, not yearly payments" (p. 31).

Parnes et al. find additional support for the threshold effect by noting that the propensity of workers expecting to retire early is over 65 percent for those with an expected monthly pension income of $300 or more, whereas it is only 47 percent when benefits are expected to fall between $1 and $299. The Survey of Newly Entitled Beneficiaries (SNEB) between July 1968 and June 1970 revealed that of the nonworking men claiming reduced benefits, the proportion who responded that they were willing to retire when they did increased from 15 percent when annual retirement benefits were less than $1,000 to 75 percent of those with $5,000 or more of pension income (Reno, 1976b). Quinn's analysis of the RHS data indicated that the influence of private pension benefits is less than that of social security. The influence of pension eligibility was found to fall mostly on those with health limitations.

Compulsory retirement

A review of the influence of private pensions on the labor supply would be deficient unless the resulting imposition of compulsory retirement age is recognized. A 1961 survey of firms employing 50 or more workers showed that those plants without pension plans rarely had compulsory retirement provisions, whereas only 25 percent of the employers with pension systems did not have mandatory retirement clauses (Slavick). Four out of five newly entitled beneficiaries in the SNEB of late 1969 with compulsory-retirement policies on their most recent job indicated that they were covered by a pension plan (Reno, 1976a). Dorothy Kittner reported that in 1974 approximately 10.4 million workers or almost 45 percent of the covered workers were in plans with mandatory-retirement provisions. One-fifth of these workers were in plans that also provided for forced early retirement before age 65. Thus, it seems that the existence of compulsory retirement is closely related to participation in a pension plan. Schulz, reviewing the economic arguments for mandatory-retirement policies, finds the following justifications being given for compulsory retirement: increased productivity to business, impersonal screening device for removal of older workers, increasing health problems, and inflexibility of work assignment due to work rules, seniority, and pay scales (also see Macdonald). Current research attempts to explain mandatory retirement within the framework of lifetime contracts that imply that during final working years wages are greater than the value of the marginal product of older workers.

Reno (1976a) reports that 36 percent of the men in the SNEB sample stated their most recent job had a mandatory retirement age. Of this group, 14 percent retired before the mandatory age and 9 percent at the compulsory limit, whereas 12 percent were still employed and subject to a compulsory retirement on their current job. "Thus, the total proportion of newly entitled men in wage and salary jobs who might ultimately face mandatory retirement would fall between 9 percent . . . and 21 percent . . ." (Reno, 1976a, p. 58). Incidence of compulsory-retirement coverage is lower for women, 23 percent reporting coverage in their last job; however, 11 percent retired prior to the mandatory age. The incidence of compulsory retirement apparently has increased with the expansion of private-pension coverage. Surveys conducted by SSA in 1951 and 1963 indicate a rise from 11 to 21 percent in the proportion of men aged 65 or older on the beneficiary rolls who retired in the preceding five years because they reached the compulsory retirement age (Epstein and Murray). Bowen and Finegan estimate that compulsory-retirement policies produced a decrease of approximately 5 percentage points in the labor-force participation rate of males 65 and over. As might be expected, the effect of compulsory retirement is age-specific. Only 1 percent of the SNEB men aged 62, and 7 percent aged 63–64 gave mandatory termination as the most important reason for leaving their last job, whereas 36 percent of those 65 gave this reason (Reno, 1976b).

Retirement from a job or termination of a long-term career does not necessitate withdrawal from the labor force. However, retiring from one's current job generally entails loss of seniority and, with it, the elimination of protection from layoff. It may be more difficult for the older worker to find new employment, and the pension guidelines may prevent work related to previous employment – especially multiemployer pensions. The termination of seniority and loss of job-specific skills may imply a fall in the wage offers that older workers receive. This reduction in wage offers may induce withdrawal from the labor force or a decline in the number of hours worked.

The 1978 Amendments to the Age Discrimination in Employment Act raised the age of mandatory retirement in the private sector from 65 to 70 and completely eliminated the mandatory retirement of federal workers. Thus, in the future the importance of compulsory retirement in determining the labor supply of the elderly will be significantly reduced. Janice Halpern reviews some of the effects of this legislation on the employment of older workers.

Given the legal immunity to forced retirement before age 70

(e.g., in the United States) or before the upper sixties, the actual choice of year of retirement will depend in good part upon what the retiree plans to do with his time upon retiring, upon his health condition and expectations, and upon the degree to which the older retiree has easy access to relatively inexpensive forms of recreation and entertainment. Unfortunately, inadequate research has been made on this aspect of the retirement decision, though care of the aged is beginning to command considerable attention (e.g., see Kane and Kane).

Part-time or other flexible working arrangements apparently would attract older persons to work who no longer wanted full-time employment, particularly in the absence of an earnings test. Carol Leon and Robert Bednarzik found one of five employed women working part-time by choice in 1977, and Fred Best has stressed the need for more flexibility in life scheduling.

7

Personal and market characteristics affecting retirement

In the preceding chapter, the basic labor supply model was described as it relates to older workers. We focused our review on the impact of the public and private pension systems on the retirement decision. There are, however, a variety of personal and market characteristics that have been employed to examine labor-force withdrawal by the elderly. In this chapter, the effects of health impairments on the labor supply of older workers are analyzed in detail. In addition, a series of economy characteristics and other financial variables are reviewed. We conclude this section with our assessment of the factors influencing the retirement decision.

Health

Health impairments may reduce a worker's productivity and therefore, the market wage rate that he is offered. In addition, such impairments could be expected to increase the onerousness of work, thus affecting the individual's desire for nonmarket time. The likely result is that fewer individuals with health limitations would choose to be in the labor force than workers without ailments. Therefore, on an individual basis, health status can be expected to pay an important role in the retirement decision. However, for health to be a significant explanatory factor in the steady decline in the labor-force participation of older men, one must hypothesize a continuing depreciation of the health of the elderly.

A significant empirical problem is the lack of adequate objective data on the health status of individuals. The use of survey responses may be biased as the respondent attempts to provide a socially acceptable reason for retirement. Campbell and Campbell believe many SSA studies may have underestimated the influence of social security on retirement because of the interview technique. They argue that: "One would expect persons to give socially acceptable reasons for retirement and not to tell interviewers that they wanted to qualify for benefits or stop working. Self-interest is not considered a praiseworthy motive for personal conduct" (p. 373). Brennan et al. also urge caution in the use of interview health data to explain retirement behavior. In the following, we review studies that employ self-assessment of health as well as those that use work absences. In general, researchers examining the labor-supply decisions of the elderly find measures of health status to be a significant determinant of labor-force withdrawal.

A 1952 Current Population Survey of households with one or more persons aged 65 or over supports the assessment that health is a significant determinant of labor-force participation of the elderly (Dorfman, Steiner and Dorfman). In this data set, "about three-quarters of all those who retired voluntarily did so because of poor health. Retirement for reasons of health is noticeably more prevalent in manual than in nonmanual occupations" (Dorfman, 1954, p. 640). Brennan et al. (pp. 34–5) question the reliability of these conclusions because events recorded in the survey took place at many different times and because of the inability to sort out these different time periods, which distorts the composition of samples that lack a control group. In addition, the answers given to investigators may not be valid, especially in relation to the use of health as a reason for retirement. Finally, they argue that early retirement and involuntary unemployment result from interactions of demand and supply; however, only the supply side of the labor market is observed in this study.

A series of surveys by SSA has indicated that poor health is the primary reason given by individuals for their retirement (Wentworth), although the proportion of beneficiaries giving health as their reason for retirement fluctuated with economic conditions (Bixby, p. 9). The 1968 SNEB finds that 44 percent of the wage and salary male workers gave health as their main reason for leaving their last job. The percentage of nonworking men giving health as the main reason for leaving their last job declined with age from 57 percent of those 62 years of age to 48 percent of the 63- to 64-year-olds and only 21 percent of those aged 65 (Bixby). The RHS data indicate that 65 percent of male nonparticipants in the labor force responded that health was the primary reason for leaving their last job (Schwab), and that health is also the primary generator of early retirement for women (Sherman).

An examination of The National Health Survey by Bowen and Finegan revealed "that slightly more than one-half of the elderly men in the survey reported at least one chronic condition resulting in an activity limitation. Second, the data tell us that the overall participation rate for men with such a condition (21 percent) was less than half as high as the rate for men with no activity limitation (45 percent)" (p. 304). Barfield concluded that among auto workers, two measures of health status indicated that those in relatively worse condition were more likely to desire early retirement. Ethel Shanas et al. report that a 1962 survey of the United States, Great Britain, and Denmark indicated that the majority of males in these countries who left the labor force prior to the age of 64 did so for health-related reasons.

Results from the NLS of older men show that, ceteris paribus, men who expressed health problems in 1966 were twice as likely to have retired between 1966 and 1971 as men who were free of health impairments. "Since the health condition used in the analysis was that reported in 1966, one can be confident that the association reflects a truly causal influence rather than a post hoc rationalization" (Parnes et al., p. 191). Multiple classification analysis of the early-retirement behavior of men 60–64 in 1971 found that health-related limitations were a primary determinant of withdrawal from the labor force prior to age 65 (Bixby). Parnes et al. (p. 180) concluded that males in their fifties rarely withdrew from the labor force in the absence of a health limitation, and while it is more common for healthy men in their early sixties to retire, the proportion of early retirees without health problems is not large.

Quinn's econometric analysis of early retirement using the 1969 RHS data also indicates the importance of health status. "The existence of a health condition limiting the amount or kind of work is the dominant explanation of retirement status. It . . . predicts, *ceteris paribus,* probability decreases of between 26 and 36 percentage points" (Quinn, p. 145). In his hours-of-work equation, he estimates that health impairments produce significant reductions in market hours on the order of 5 to 20 percent. Burkhauser employs a dummy variable pertaining to the number of weeks of work lost due to sickness to capture the impact of ill health on pension acceptance. He states that this measure of health ". . . is not as subject to the criticism of bias due to a worker's need to present a socially acceptable excuse for retirement" (p. 19). Examining the UAW sample, ill-health is found to increase the likelihood of taking an early pension.

The consensus of research analyzing the effect of health impairments on the labor supply of older workers is that health problems reduce market effort. Boskin (1977) is virtually alone in his finding that health has no influence on labor-force participation. In fact, Boskin actually reports that the greater the number of hours ill, his health variable, the lower the probability of retirement. He acknowledges that this effect ". . . is not estimated very precisely" (p. 11).

Thus, the available research indicates that health is a significant factor in the decision of individuals to withdraw from the labor force. One should not, however, infer from this that poor health is one of the primary factors causing a long-run decline in the labor-force participation of older workers. Little reliable evidence has been presented that would indicate that the health of older people has deteriorated during the past century. "It is only a *change* of general health conditions over time which could account for the *change* in labor force participation of older people" (Brennan et al., p. 23).

Economy characteristics
Unemployment

Two hypotheses are put forward to explain the response of the labor force to short-run variations in the level of business activity. The added-worker hypothesis holds that when the primary earner of a family becomes unemployed, additional family members enter the labor force in an effort to maintain their income level; thus, the labor force would expand as unemployment rises. The opposing view is the discouraged-worker hypothesis, which states that unsuccessful job search induces workers to withdraw from the labor force. High unemployment decreases reemployment prospects; individuals become discouraged and cease looking. Therefore, the labor force varies inversely with changes in unemployment rates.

The basic theoretical constructs of these competing hypotheses have been known since at least the 1930s. Wladimir Woytinsky argued that the unemployment rate during the depression years was raised by the inflow of wives and children seeking to augment family income. Although he criticized Woytinsky's statistical methodology, Don Humphrey noted the possibility of discouraged workers withdrawing from the labor force. Bowen and Finegan were among the first to employ econometric techniques to estimate the response of the labor force to changes in the level of unemployment.

In their cross-sectional analysis of intercity differences in market-activity rates of age–sex groups, Bowen and Finegan find that the discouraged-worker effect is dominant. For males, the elasticities[1] of labor-force participation rates with changes in unemployment are considerably greater for the young and old than for men in the prime working ages. Table 7.1 illustrates that the relative labor-force participation response to changes in un-

Table 7.1. *Impact of unemployment on labor-force participation*

Population group	Net regression coefficient (absolute change in participation rate per 1 point change in unemployment rate)	Mean labor force participation rate	Relative change in participation rate per 1-point change in unemployment rate [(1) ÷ (2)/100]
	(1)	(2)	(3)
Males 25–54	−0.31	96.4	−0.32
Males 55–64	−1.27	85.0	−1.49
Males 65+	−1.34	36.7	−4.36
Married women 14–54	−0.94	34.1	−2.76
Married women 55–64	−0.93	26.0	−3.58
Married women 65+	−0.25	7.1	−3.52

Source: Bowen and Finegan, p. 343.

employment increases with aging for both men and married women. "The sizes of the net regression coefficient reveal the extraordinary sensitivity of the participation rates of older persons to levels of unemployment in local labor markets" (Bowen and Finegan, p. 324).

Cain (Appendix J) presents strong support for the Bowen and Finegan results, indicating that the labor-force activity of older men and women is negatively correlated to changes in the level of unemployment. Marc Rosenblum concludes that workers 55 and over have the highest rate of discouraged workers of any age group. The greater incidence of discouragement among older workers is consistent with life-cycle human-capital models because job search is clearly a form of investment in human capital.

Employing time-series data, Tella provides a model in which quarterly participation rates by age–sex group are regressed on the previous quarter's employment rate of that specific demographic group and on a time trend. His results are similar to the cross-sectional finding of Bowen and Finegan, that labor-force participation of older men and women is among the most responsive of any group to business fluctuations. Dernberg and Strand find support for both the discouraged-worker and the additional-worker hypothesis, with the discouraged effect dominant. Their results find males 65 and over most responsive to employment changes; however, they present evidence that adverse economic conditions may increase the rates and market activity of men 55–64.

Mincer (1966) criticized the methodology of both the cross-sectional and the time-series studies. Variations in the unemployment rates between cities in any one year may correspond to long-term structural differences rather than short-run cyclical variations. Potential migration from cities with high unemployment rates to cities with low rates implies possible changes in city aggregates even though no individuals leave the labor force. A possible negative bias is also introduced through the use of the labor-force participation rate as the dependent variable (which contains size of labor force in the numerator) and unemployment rate as an independent variable (which includes size of labor force in the denominator). Bowen and Finegan, as well as Mincer, criticize the methodology of the time-series studies and then present evidence of their own. Their findings are consistent with this literature. First, the discouraged-worker effect dominates, and, second, older workers tend to be most responsive to adverse economic fluctuations. Perry's analysis of the period 1949–76 confirms these findings over the most recent recessionary period.

Attempting to estimate the labor-supply response to unemployment changes, Quinn uses the spring 1970 unemployment rate and annual percent change in employment with the RHS data from 1969. He reports statistical support for the hypothesis that higher unemployment reduces participation. His estimates indicate that for white married men, participation probabilities are between 3 and 4 percent higher in low-unemployment cities.[2] The coefficients of employment changes had incorrect signs, which

Quinn attributed to a correlation between high-growth areas and
retirement communities (Miami, Fort Lauderdale, Phoenix, and
Tucson).

The response of older workers to changes in unemployment
may not be symmetrical. The decision to retire from one's job is
often irreversible, and "relatively few older workers who lose
their jobs and drop out of the labor force during a prolonged
recession are likely to reenter the labor market several years
later" (Bowen and Finegan, p. 320). Thus, over the business
cycle, older cohorts as a group may suffer a net loss in employment (Brennan et al., p. 19).

Older men and women have consistently been found to be the
most responsive demographic group to changing aggregate
economic conditions. Each of the studies reviewed reported that
the labor-force participation rate of the elderly was significantly
negatively correlated to the unemployment rate, and the elderly
were among the most sensitive to adverse economic fluctuations.
In addition, there is some evidence that the participation rate of
older cohorts is permanently lowered by a period of high unemployment.

Urbanization

Increasing urbanization may have contributed to the decline in market activity of the elderly, primarily because of the
declining number of farmers who have historically had high rates
of market participation. Noting that the proportion of the
employed work force who are farmers declined from 40 percent in
1900 to 4 percent in 1970, Munnell believes that increased urbanization is one of the long-term factors affecting the labor-force
participation of the aged. Gallaway finds that increased urbanization in states reduces the labor-force participation rate of the
aged. Bowen and Finegan believe the most important demographic change influencing the aggregate labor supply of older
workers to be change in residence. They "estimate that the
change in residential characteristics of males over 64 (taken by
itself) would have reduced their overall participation rate by 2.7
points between 1948 and 1965" (p. 354).

Labor-supply competition

Long attributes much of the decline in participation of elderly men to the growth of market labor supply of women. He presents two hypotheses: (1) younger, better trained women competing for jobs drive older men out of the labor force, and (2) older men may be retiring sooner because of the increased family well-being from working daughters and wives. Kreps argues that the large inflow of young workers during the 1950s and 1960s has produced employment responses to shorten the worklife of older workers. Brennan, et al. (pp. 43–58) provide estimates of supply-and-demand equations that indicate that the employment of females adversely affects the employment of males, most significantly the oldest men.

Other financial variables

Wage

The theoretical implication of wage changes in hours of market work is ambiguous, containing a negative income effect and positive substitution effect. Cain and Watts (pp. 332–7) summarize some of the recent estimates of labor-supply elasticities. These estimates, using similar data, have a high degree of variability and are quite sensitive to model specification (Da Vanzo et al.). Because of the availability of pension benefits and the acceptability of withdrawing from the labor force, one might expect older workers to be more responsive to wage changes than prime-age males.

Bowen and Finegan reported in their 1960 intercity regressions that they found no evidence of the expected positive correlation between earnings and the rate of labor-force participation of males 65 and over. They conclude that "it is best to assume that earnings per se has had a negligible impact" on the decline in market effort by aged men (p. 359). A similar result is found for married women aged 65 and over. However, for males and married women aged 55–64, a positive association between earnings and labor-force participation is found. Quinn finds no significant correlation between labor-force participation and the wage of an older worker. He concludes that for men "it appears that the respondent's own wage is not an important factor in the retirement decision" (p. 148). Women in the RHS seem to be more sensitive to wage changes, with the probability of labor-force participation of white women rising by 4.4 points with each dollar of wage increase (p. 150). Parnes et al. provide support for the hypothesis of wage inelastic supply of older men by failing to discover a significant correlation between average hourly earnings and the likelihood of declared retirement.

The influence of wage changes on hours of labor supply may be more pronounced. For all groups except nonwhite men, Quinn reports that his ". . . equations describe gently, but definitely backward bending labor supply curves" (p. 173). His conclusion is that the response of hours to wage changes is small. Parnes et al. find a significant but irregular association. Boskin (1973), using Survey of Economic Opportunity data of low-income families in 1967, simultaneously estimates labor-force participation and hours of work decisions. He finds that for elderly white husbands, wages produce a modest positive effect on participation; however, once the decision is made to enter the labor force, "wages exert virtually no influence on hours of work" (p. 168). Employing the same data, but only estimating the responsiveness of hours supplied, Robert Hall reports that husbands of retirement age, 60 and over, show substantial positive variation in hours of work as related systematically to wage changes. In his later article using longitudinal data, Boskin (1977) estimates a large positive relationship such that a $1,000 increase in net earnings (after tax and earnings test) lowers the probability of retirement by 60 percent. Burkhauser concludes that increased wages decrease the likelihood of accepting a pension. Thus, no consensus has emerged from this literature on the impact of wages on the number of hours of market work by older workers.

Spouse's earnings
For males, there seems to be only a small or no response to variation in the wage or earnings of their wives. For example, Boskin (1977) finds a small negative effect of wife's earnings on

the probability of the husband retiring, thus indicating that the nonmarket times of husbands and wives are complements in old age. The finding of little or no significant results may be due in part to treating this as an exogenous variable. The labor-supply decisions of family members should be treated in a simultaneous framework. To date, data limitations have precluded such analysis of older families. Most studies of nonaged families report that wives are more sensitive to spouses' earnings than are husbands. Quinn confirms this hypothesis for older couples in the RHS data.

Asset income
As discussed in the preceding chapter, the influence of nonwage income on the labor-supply decision is unambiguously negative and expected to be smaller in magnitude than the correlation with social security or private pension benefits. Within a life-cycle framework virtually all of the accumulated assets of the elderly are the result of past resource allocation decisions. Thus, larger stocks of wealth indicate a greater preference for market work. As a result, the inclusion of a wealth variable in a labor-supply equation may be more of a proxy for the lifetime wage than for differences in inherited wealth.

Quinn reports significant negative effects of asset income; however, his quantitative results are generally smaller than results of previous studies, suggesting that a rise in asset income from $1,000 to $3,000 would reduce the participation rate of married white males by 6.5 percentage points. Further increases have even smaller effects. Boskin (1977) estimates a greater response such that a $1,000 annual increase in asset income raises the probability of retirement by 15 percent.

Early studies lumped pension benefits with income from assets. Using this definition, Bowen and Finegan[3] and Hall report the expected significant negative relationships. However, Boskin (1973) estimates no effect on the participation of elderly white husbands and only insignificant influence on hours. For wives, he finds that income effects are small or absent. This is in sharp contrast to his 1977 findings. In addition, Barfield finds that income available from assets is essentially unrelated to the propensity to retire.

Occupation
     The ability of a worker to reduce work effort without severing the relationship with a long-time employer may depend on his occupation. In addition, desire to remain on the job is probably correlated with prestige and physical stress required by a particular job. Schwab reports for men in the RHS that a smaller proportion of professionals, farmers, and managers are out of the labor force compared to operatives, service workers, and laborers. Parnes et al. estimate that "the adjusted proportion of men expecting to retire early is 4 percentage points smaller for self-employed individuals than for private wage and salary workers" (p. 166). Sheldon, Pechman et al., Munnell, and Bowen and Finegan indicate that decline in self-employment has contributed to overall reductions in labor-force participation. Also self-employed and professional workers may be able to avoid the earnings test of social security because of their greater flexibility in work scheduling, thus increasing the attractiveness of remaining in the labor force.

     Ease of response on the part of older workers to situations that might induce retirement may lead some to defer such action as well as make it easier for unemployed older workers to reenter the work force. Thus, given high elasticity of substitution between different kinds of labor, especially when it is facilitated by pertinent training, adjustment is relatively easy to changes in the structure of demand (Dougherty, Humphrey and Moroney, Gallaway). Emphasis on firm-specific skills, on the other hand, makes reallocation of older workers a more difficult response to changes in the structure of demand (Davidson and Eaton). Flexible working conditions, the elasticity of substitution, and extent of specific training can be expected to vary across occupations and therefore to influence the employment prospects of the elderly.

Dan Jacobson (1972a,b) examined a sample of semiskilled British operatives aged 55–64 and noted their occupation by degree of strain. Men in the heavy-strain job categories were much more likely to be willing to retire at the pensionable age than workers in jobs with light or moderate strain. Quinn estimated the influence of low-autonomy work and undesirable working conditions in addition to strain. All but one of his race–marital status categories for men had the expected negative correlation with participation; however, only two were significant. The reverse was found for women, indicating that they were less likely to retire if they held strenuous jobs or jobs with bad working conditions.

Depreciation or growing obsolescence of one's stock of human capital will lower the potential wage and may place the older worker at a competitive disadvantage. If wages of older employees are somewhat rigid, the relative cost of training older workers would be higher compared to that of younger workers (Brennan et al., pp. 18–19). Thus, a more rapid rate of introduction of new technology may partially explain the decline in market activity of the elderly (Sheldon, p. 54). Dorfman reported in the 1952 CPS that ''aging was associated with a drift away from skilled occupation, it revealed a drift toward unskilled labor'' (p. 635).

In his human-capital model, Mincer (1974) outlines the importance of depreciation of a worker's capital stock; noting that declines in earnings occur when investment is outstripped by depreciation, he states the importance of these two variables. ''If retirement age is related to the time of onset of declining earning power, this analysis might well explain why persons with more schooling retire later in life, and yet have a somewhat shorter earnings span'' (p. 30).

Family and individual characteristics

Significant association between a variety of family and individual characteristics has been noted in the literature. Education increases expected wage and influences occupational choice.

Increases in the level of schooling raise the average retirement age and are usually associated with longer hours of work (Bowen and Finegan; Sherman; Boskin, 1977). Married men are more frequently in the labor force and retire later than single males, whereas the reverse holds for women (Quinn, Parnes, Bowen and Finegan). Black males are more apt to retire earlier and work fewer hours than white men; however, labor-force participation of black females is greater than that of white women. Responses to variables by race are usually in the same direction, though magnitudes may differ (Bowen and Finegan, Parnes, Hall).

A summing up

Our review indicates that the existence of pension income and health limitations of workers usually exert the dominant influences in labor-supply models of older workers. Recent debate has centered on which is the more significant factor in inducing retirement. There exists a strong interactive effect between these two variables. Quinn finds the social security effect is five times greater for those with some form of health impairment. He argues that: "Many people of early retirement age have health problems which are not serious enough to preclude work, but which are serious enough to make continued labor force participation less desirable. For these people who are *predisposed* to retire, social security eligibility is a very important factor, and in fact increases the probability of retirement by over 40 percentage points" (p. 213). Barfield emphasizes that it is the financial variables that form the framework within which other variables affect the retirement decision. Both of his studies of the UAW conclude that "people retire (or plan to retire) early when they feel financially able to do so" (Barfield, p. 31). Parnes et al. assert that early retirees fall into two groups, which may be governed by alternative factors. The first group is characterized by good health, sufficient financial resources, and a desire for additional nonmarket time. The other group consists of those with health problems.

The composition of retirees from a particular cohort may

change as they age. Parnes et al. believe that disadvantaged retirees with health problems form a larger percentage of total retirees while the cohort is in its late fifties than for men in their sixties. The SNEB data show that health declines with age as the most important reason for leaving a job. Of increasing importance in job termination was compulsory retirement, which was given by 36 percent of the 65-year-old respondents but only 3 percent of those 62–64 (Reno). Bixby concludes that "health emerges as the most common reason for premature retirement but declines in importance among those who retire closer to the institutionalized age of 65 when full Social Security benefits become available and the compulsory retirement policies of private pensions often go into effect" (p. 13).

Future research must distinguish among the socioeconomic factors that influence the retirement decision of individuals. We must also remain cognizant of the changing composition of a cohort as it ages. Studies of early retirees necessitate alternative model specifications compared to analysis of the over-65 retirees. The emergence of several longitudinal data sets should enhance our capability to examine the retirement process.

8

Pensions and the economy

Pension systems – public and private – have been among the fastest-growing economic institutions during the last thirty years in many of the industrialized countries. For the United States, the relatively young social security system has expanded to include approximately 90 percent of the labor force, and benefits have been dramatically improved. Private pension plans have been rapidly incorporated into the compensation package of most large companies and cover approximately half of the total U.S. work force. This chapter examines the economic impact of pension systems. The individual and aggregate responses to the social security program are the primary focus of the first section, and the ensuing parts will analyze the effects of private pensions.

The expansion of social security has significant implications for the behavior of individuals and the performance of the economy. In Chapter 6, the effect of pension benefits on the labor supply of the elderly was discussed. This chapter focuses on the labor-supply response of the remainder of the work force. In addition, the growth and development of social security and private pensions are highlighted. Issues concerning incidence of payroll taxes, rates of return to contributions, and the impact of pensions on savings are also examined.

Social security

Growth and development

Old age and survivors benefit programs had been established in 108 countries by the beginning of 1975. Some of the more mature plans are those of Germany (first legislation in 1889), the United Kingdom (1908), France (1910), Sweden (1913), and Italy (1919). The United States did not enact a national retirement program until 1935. Although each nation faces essentially the same problem of financing the income security of the elderly, considerable diversity exists among countries pertaining to taxes, eligibility conditions, level of benefits, and retirement age.

A report by the U.S. Social Security Administration (1975) briefly outlines the major characteristic of the social security programs throughout the world (also see OECD and Wilson). Almost all of the national pension programs are financed from at least two sources, with more than half of the countries requiring tripartite financing (i.e., employer and employee taxes combined with a government contribution usually from general revenues). Among those with bipartite financing, employer–employee contributions are the norm, and in most countries the tax rate on the employer is larger.

One of the most important eligibility standards is the age at which benefits are payable. The determination of the pensionable age has important cost implications for social security programs with lower ages requiring increased tax revenues. In recent years, the tendency has been to lower the age of entitlement for old age benefits (Unsigned). In 1975 Israel was the only remaining nation with a retirement age of 70 for entitlement to full benefits (also see Tracy).

Considerable variation exists in the proportion of national income that countries devote to expenditures on social security benefits. On the basis of a study of 22 countries that allocated 5 percent or more of national income to social security during 1949–57, Aaron (1967) concludes that a high percentage of the variations can be explained by economic and demographic factors along with the age of the system. "This would indicate that common determinants of the level of Social Security outlays are far more important than administrative or other differences peculiar to each country" (p. 21).

Social security programs are established parts of public welfare systems throughout the world. Although considerable diversity exists among the social security programs of the world, these national pension programs strive to attain similar objectives and face common problems. In this chapter, the U.S. program is used as an illustration of a mature national plan that must continue to provide retirement benefits to an aging population. The primary concern of our examination is the interaction between pension institutions and the national economy. In this regard, international research is analyzed and integrated into an assessment of the economic effects of social security programs.

The U.S. Social Security Act was enacted in 1935 to provide cash benefits to individuals whose income from earnings had been reduced by retirement. Early economic assessments of the social security system are provided by Paul Douglas and Seymour Harris. Arthur Altmeyer, Edwin Witte, and John Turnbull et al. discuss the growth and expansion of the system until the mid-1960s. Robert Myers (1975), Martin Feldstein (1975), Juanita Kreps, and Alicia Munnell (1977a,b) analyze the current program as it has developed and discuss the problems that are confronting this system. Marilyn Flowers and the U.S. Senate Special Committee on Aging review the issues relating to the treatment of women and dual-career families by the social security system. Sylva Gelber provides an international view of the treatment of women by social security systems.

In their review of the evolving social security program, Joseph Pechman et al. (pp. 56–66) examined the economic rationale of why a society would choose to inhibit the intertemporal allocation of resources by individuals. They argue that benefits must be provided to the aged poor and that the earnings-related program is preferable to a universal demogrant or a means-tested welfare program.[1] In addition, they argue that "there is widespread myopia with respect to retirement needs," and that imperfect information and uncertainty pertaining to family status, future employment and income streams, and inflation may prevent individuals from achieving their retirement-income goals. Thus, they conclude that "individual saving decisions cannot be relied on to provide a socially acceptable level of income for most of the aged" (Pechman et al., p. 64).[2]

Richard Musgrave outlines the need for a compulsory-retirement system in an economy where, for humanitarian reasons, the elderly will not be permitted to live in severe poverty. In this situation, a forced-savings system is a method of requiring individuals to finance partially the income transfer program that will provide benefits to them in their old age; otherwise the prudent worker who saved for his own retirement would also be forced to provide benefits to those who did not save. Feldstein (1977a) adds the potential high cost of private choice to the above-mentioned myopia and necessity of welfare programs for the elderly to the rationale for a compulsory social-insurance program for those who would not purchase private insurance. He also favors mandating social security coverage because of capital market imperfections that prevent individuals from purchasing similar coverage from private insurance companies (also see Viscusi and Zeckhauser, Diamond).

Edgar Browning (1975c) has shown that political forces in a democracy will produce a social-insurance budget that is too large as judged by economic efficiency criteria. In an earlier paper, Browning (1973), using a three-generation model, examines the nature of intergenerational transfers that indicate the windfall gains of the initial generation are paid for in the form of a national debt that is passed forward to the terminal generation. Browning then argues for modifying the social-insurance system into a bond-purchase program along the lines proposed by Buchanan.

Buchanan's proposal advocates the repeal of the payroll tax; however, all income earners would be required to purchase social-insurance bonds with the amount being proportionate to earnings. Workers could purchase more than the required amount of bonds, and the proceeds from bond sales would be utilized to finance current pension payments. Each individual would have the option of purchasing bonds from private firms. Bonds should be nontransferable and converted into an annuity at age 65; their return would be equated to the higher of the rate of interest on long-term U.S. Treasury bonds or the rate of growth in gross national product. Friedman (1972) proposes to terminate the accumulation of further benefits while paying accrued liabilities from general funds, thereby eliminating the social-insurance program in future years.

Benefits

Benefit payments are derived by calculating the average monthly wage subject to the payroll tax over a specified number of years[3] and then applying a progressive computational formula to determine each individual's primary insurance amount. The actual benefits that a worker receives are governed by age at retirement, marital status, and spouse's age; see Table 4.4 (Munnell, 1977a, pp. 25–30). Albert Rettig examines changes in the formulas used to calculate primary insurance amounts from 1954 to 1975.

The 1972 amendments to the Social Security Act provided for automatic adjustments in the benefit formula in response to changes in the cost of living. Although the adjustment mechanism works well in maintaining the real benefits of retirees, high rates of inflation would produce rising replacement rates for those still working. This overindexing of benefits is a function of the manner in which the benefits were determined. Colin Campbell (1976) presents an analysis of the decoupling problem and reviews the two primary proposals for reform. One alternative advocated by the 1975 Social Security Advisory Council would index earnings and the benefit formula so that replacement rates would remain constant over time for workers at the same relative position in the earnings distribution. Another option proposed by the 1976 Consultant Panel on Social Security – usually called the Hsiao proposal – would produce gradually declining replacement rates for the average worker. (Also see Munnell, 1977b.)

In 1977, Congress enacted legislation that indexes future benefits in a manner that stabilizes future replacement ratios. A worker with an average earnings record who retires after 1983 will receive benefits equivalent to approximately 43 percent of his preretirement earnings (Robertson). For an international comparison of this inflation-adjustment mechanism, the interested reader should see Elizabeth Kirkpatrick's analysis. Kirkpatrick examines the more mature European social-insurance system which incorporated inflation-adjustment factors into their plans shortly after World War II. Her study shows that France and Germany base their revaluation on a wage index, whereas Canada, Sweden, and Belgium use a price index, and Norway employs a mixed earnings–price index.

Financing

Social security benefits have been financed through a payroll tax levied in equal portions on the employer and the employee. From the initial tax of 1 percent of the first $3,000 of wage income paid by both parties, the tax rate had risen to 5.08 percent each on the first $22,900 of earnings in 1979 with an additional 1.05 percent for hospital insurance. Thus, the combined tax rate for OASDI was 10.16 percent of taxable payroll with health insurance accounting for an additional 2.1 percent. Table 8.1 illustrates increases in the social security payroll tax over 40 years. As a result of the 600 percent increase in the OASDHI tax and a 550 percent increase in the tax ceiling, the maximum tax that each employer and employee could pay rose from the $30 that was in effect during 1937–49 to $965.25 in 1977. The 1977 social security amendments mandate further increases in the payroll tax rate to 7.65 percent by 1990, a rise of 1.2 percent compared to the previous law. In addition, the taxable wage base is dramatically increased from $17,700 in 1978 to an expected $42,600 in 1987.

This continuing rise in the payroll tax has also increased its relative importance in the federal tax structure. In 1977, payroll tax payment exceeded the federal income tax liabilities for single persons with incomes of $13,000, married couples with earnings

Table 8.1. *Tax rates and earnings ceilings of OASDHI program, 1937–77 (selected year)*

Year	Maximum taxable earnings ($)	Employer and employee each pay the following tax rate (%):					Maximum possible tax paid per year by each employer and each employee ($)
		OASDHI	OASI	DI	HI		
1937–49	3,000	1.000	1.000	—	—		30.00
1950	3,000	1.500	1.500	—	—		45.00
1955	4,200	2.000	2.000	—	—		84.00
1957	4,200	2.250	2.000	0.250	—		94.50
1960	4,800	3.000	2.750	0.250	—		144.00
1965	4,800	3.625	3.375	0.250	—		174.00
1966	6,600	4.200	3.500	0.350	0.350		277.20
1970	7,800	4.800	3.650	0.550	0.600		374.40
1971	7,800	5.200	4.050	0.550	0.600		405.60
1972	9,000	5.200	4.050	0.550	0.600		468.00
1973	10,800	5.850	4.300	0.550	1.000		631.80
1974	13,200	5.850	4.375	0.575	0.900		772.20
1975	14,100	5.850	4.375	0.575	0.900		824.85
1976	15,300	5.850	4.375	0.575	0.900		895.05
1977	16,500	5.850	4.375	0.575	0.900		965.25

up to $15,000, and husband–wife families with two children and incomes of $17,000. OASDHI tax payments were the largest tax liability for about two-thirds of the nation's income recipients, with approximately $2.5 billion being paid by persons below the official poverty level (Pechman, 1977, p. 33). Benjamin Okner further illustrates the increasing relative burden of this tax by noting that in 1960 the payroll tax accounted for only 12 percent of total federal revenue, whereas in 1975 these tax revenues represented 25 percent of total federal receipts.

The increasing burden of the payroll tax combined with its regressive structure has led some researchers to argue for a shift to general revenue financing. John Brittain (1972b) states that the taxing and benefits structure of the system can and should be appraised separately. His conclusion is that a shift to general revenue financing would be desirable (also see Pechman, 1977). Friedman (1977) favors such a modification because he feels that it would limit the growth of the social security system; however, there is some debate on whether general revenue financing would increase or decrease the pressure on Congress to exercise restraint in liberalizing future benefits. A primary argument against any modification of the dependency on a payroll tax by proponents of social security is the fear that this alteration would undermine public support for the program.[4] Munnell (1977a, pp. 93–111 and 149–51) examines the arguments related to social security financing, whereas Okner examines the income-distributional aspects of *general* revenue financing and the use of exemptions for the payroll tax.

The financing of the system is essentially a pay-as-you-go scheme with a small trust fund being created to smooth out annual payments. Questions concerning the solvency of the social security program have three sources. First, short-run cyclical problems have arisen because of the prolonged recession that reduces tax revenues and increases the number of beneficiaries. Second, a significant long-run problem was created by the rising structure of replacement rates due to overindexing. Finally, the demographic pressures of the changing age structure of the population will increase the beneficiary–worker ratio, necessitating a restructuring of the tax and benefit schedule. See Munnell (1977a,b), Clark, and the *1977 Annual Report of the Board of Trustees of the Federal Old-Age and Survivors Insurance and Disability Trust Funds* for a discussion of these issues.

Incidence of the payroll tax

Is the final incidence of the payroll tax shared equally between employer and the employee? Brittain (1971, 1972a,b) has examined the theoretical aspects of the shifting of the tax and estimated the degree of the shift. The tax will be fully shifted to employees in a competitive labor market if the aggregate labor-supply curve has a zero wage elasticity. If labor regards the tax as part of its compensation, there will be no market effect, and labor will bear the entire cost of the system (see also, Pechman, 1966, pp. 169–71 and Smelken). The probable shifting of the employer portion of the tax to the employee was noted much earlier by Spencer Baldwin, Russell Bauden, and James Hall. Using international data, Brittain finds evidence to support the hypothesis that the employer portion of the tax is entirely shifted to labor.[5]

Wayne Vroman illustrates how the degree of progressivity of the tax depends on the final incidence of the employer tax. Forward shifting to higher prices will have the same distributional influence as a general sales tax unless transfers also rise; whereas if the tax is borne by profits, it is clearly progressive. Backward shifting to labor results in taxes that are progressive from the bottom- to middle-income ranges (because of transfer payments not covered by the tax) and regressive from the middle- to top-income levels (capital is not taxed, and neither is income above the ceiling). His empirical tests indicate a backward shifting to labor of between 25 and 50 percent with a lag of six to nine months. Shiv Pratap Singh argues that the employer tax should be proportional to profits rather than wages to prevent backward shifting.

The argument is sometimes presented that even though, in the aggregate, labor as a group bears the final incidence of the tax, no single individual can be assumed to pay the employer portion in the form of lower wages. Myers, who is a leading advocate of this position, concludes: "Even though the employer taxes might, in the aggregate, be considered as part of the remuneration of employees and thus fully assignable to them, it does not follow that the assignment should be on an individual-by-individual basis according to wages" (1975, p. 208). This seems to be an unreasonable distinction; thus it is likely that the employee bears much of the employer's portion of the payroll in the form of reduced compensation.

Duncan MacRae and Elizabeth Chase MacRae illustrate the impact of a payroll tax that has a ceiling on taxable earnings. They show that if leisure is a normal good, workers whose earnings exceed the ceiling will supply additional hours of work because of the income effect. Thus, if individual labor supply is perfectly wage-inelastic, the effect of the payroll tax will be to increase aggregate supply as those workers with earnings above the ceiling seek to increase their work effort. Only if individual labor supply is responsive to wage changes is it possible for decreased work effort by those below the ceiling to cancel out the increased supply of the high earners to leave aggregate supply unaffected. Robert Moffitt notes the possibility of "nonmarginal" shifts in labor supply with the imposition of a kinked budget constraint that is the result of an earnings tax with a ceiling. Moffitt argues that these nonmarginal shifts make the labor-supply response to the payroll tax much more ambiguous.

Browning (1975a) examines the welfare implications of the social security system. His analysis shows that the labor-supply response and welfare changes depend not only on the tax but also on the manner in which benefits are paid to workers. "It is clearly inappropriate in general to evaluate the welfare cost (or incidence) of a tax without some attention to the expenditure programs of the government" (p. 245). Browning finds that the welfare loss is reduced the more benefits are related to taxes paid. The existence of a tax ceiling also serves to reduce the welfare loss. The implication of Browning's analysis is that the effect of the social security program on labor supply can only be assessed in a life-cycle context in which the individual evaluates the payroll tax along with the availability of future benefits.

Rate of return on taxes

Retired workers who have participated in the social security system are generally acknowledged to have received benefits that far exceed the accumulated value of their tax payments. Pechman et al. (1968, p. 237) estimated that workers who were first covered in 1937 and were retiring in 1967 might have a present value of benefits of between two and ten times the accumulated value of their tax payments and accrued interest. Future generations will obviously not fare as well, but will they receive a reasonable "return" on their contributions? The concept of attempting to estimate a rate of return to a tax may seem strange; however, because the system has been promoted as an earnings-related form of deferred compensation or forced savings, such research is of interest. The use of general funds to finance future benefits may further cloud this avenue of investigation.

Estimates of benefit–tax ratios or rates of return have been made by Myers (1967), Pechman et al., Campbell (1969), and Brittain (1972b). Their results show that the benefit–tax values are highly sensitive to assumptions of the growth rate of earnings, interest rate, future changes in the benefit or tax schedules, and the incidence of the employer portion of the tax. The return for any specific workers will also depend on marital status, sex, income level, and age at which taxes were first paid.

Campbell (1969), assuming that the then-existent tax and benefit schedule of future changes remained static, found that with a 4 percent interest rate, costs to the worker would outweigh future benefits. Excluding the employer portion of the tax, Myers (1967) found that benefits would continue to exceed taxes for workers now entering the system. More recently, Myers suggested that "a young entrant at the present time on the average 'pays' with the employee tax for about 70–75 percent of his benefit protection, while for the ultimate new entrant, this proportion will be about 90–95 percent" (1975, p. 211).

Brittain (1972b, pp. 151–183) and Pechman et al. (pp. 231–50) provide a detailed analysis of the rate-of-return question, combined with estimates of future returns using alternative assumptions. Brittain makes the assumption that future benefits increase at the same rate as real earnings. His estimates of the internal rate of return vary from 2.15 to 7.17 percent. The rate of return is positively correlated with the growth rate of real earnings and inversely related to interest rate and the age of entry into the labor force. In his pay-as-you-go model, Brittain suggests that trends in the fertility rate and the ensuing beneficiary–worker ratio also influence the rate of return. Brittain concludes: "If past experience is a plausible guide, social security participants . . . will fare much better than they would if offered the option of a private savings program. On the other hand, these relatively attractive rates of return fall considerably short of the long-run yield on equity capital in recent decades" (1972b, p. 168).

Significant future rises in the payroll tax rate necessitated by continuing low fertility rates and increasing benefit levels will adversely affect the rate of return on contributions. In conjunction with this shift, Yung-Ping Chen and Kwang-Wen Chu estimate that rates of return for 1974 retirees were from 6.7 to 17 percent, whereas the rates for 1974 entrants into the labor force will be between 1 and 8.5 percent. Several more recent unpublished studies project even lower rates of return – perhaps even negative returns – for future beneficiaries.

Aaron (1977) argues that the interaction between educational attainment, differential mortality rates, and age of entry into the labor force implies that the overall tax–benefit structure is regressive. His simulations indicate that variations in mortality rates fully offset the progressivity of the benefit structure, and the correlation between length of formal schooling and entry into the labor force reinforce these effects. He concludes: "Together these factors make the social security benefit–cost ratio rise with educational attainment. . . . In short, retirement benefits are regressive, not progressive . . ." (p. 57). A. B. Atkinson examined the British Labor Party's proposal for the National Superannuation plan introduced to Parliament in 1969. Using Brittain's methodology, he found that the intergenerational transfers in the bill would have created rates of return that declined with increases in income and were greater for women than single men. Atkinson estimated that real returns would be approximately 4.5 percent, which compared favorably to other assets. A. R. Prest noted that the introduction of intragenerational transfers would have been a break from the past. Subsequent national elections precluded passage of the bill.

Impact on savings

Considerable attention has recently been focused on the relationship between pension coverage and individual savings. Friedman (1957) argued that "the availability of assistance from the state would clearly tend to reduce the need for private reserves and so to reduce planned savings" (p. 123).[6] However, a decade later, Pechman et al. concluded that, "The available evidence suggests that, over the long run, individuals covered by government and industrial pension plans tend to save more than those who are not covered" (p. 186) (also see Garvey). This assessment was based in part on the work of Phillip Cagan, who, in examining the saving behavior of members of *Consumers Union,* found that individuals covered by private pension plans saved more than those not covered. Cagan attributed this behavior to a "recognition effect" of retirement needs. In addition, George Katona, using a representative sample of all American families, estimated that pension coverage stimulated individual savings. Katona hypothesized a goal-feasibility effect that suggests people intensify their efforts the closer they come to their savings objective.[7] After reviewing contradictory hypotheses on the influence of social security on savings, Aaron concluded: "The issue cannot be resolved with cross-section data; time series analysis of the impact of Social Security on savings within a number of countries is necessary to discriminate between these hypotheses" (1967, p. 28).

Munnell (1974), using a subset of his data, reexamines Cagan's findings. Her results indicate that contrary to Cagan's conclusions, pension coverage slightly discourages private savings. In a subsequent article employing the National Longitudinal Survey of men in their preretirement years, Munnell reports that pension coverage clearly ". . . reduces savings efforts in other areas – at least for those older men for whom retirement is the primary savings motive" (1976, p. 1014). However, aggregate savings appear to be increased owing to the funding of private pension plans.

Using a life-cycle model of economic decision making, Feldstein (1974) and Munnell (1974) examined the response of individuals to a social security system. They illustrate how individuals incorporate the promise of future benefits into their decision-making process. This social security wealth reduces individual savings. At the same time, these benefits may induce workers to retire at an earlier age, thus increasing savings per year in the labor force. Therefore, the net effect of social security is theoretically indeterminant. In their studies, Feldstein (1974) and Munnell (1974), using aggregate consumption functions, conclude that the social security program has reduced aggregate savings. Their estimates of the magnitude of this effect are quite disparate, with Feldstein arguing that personal saving was reduced by $51 billion in 1969 compared to Munnell's estimate of $3.6 billion (Munnell, 1977a, p. 117).

Munnell (1977a, pp. 119–21) argues that Feldstein's results overstate the impact because of the correlations between unemployment and social security and his omission of the unemployment rate and his exclusion of any variable that would capture the induced-retirement effect. Munnell (1974) and Feldstein (1977b) incorporate reduced labor-force participation of the elderly as a proxy for induced retirement. The inclusion of a retirement variable moderates but does not fully offset the negative impact of social security on savings behavior.

Robert Barro and Merton Miller and Charles Upton present

models that analyze the impact of social security on capital accumulation. In their framework, a type of government debt is created concurrently with the promise of future benefits. If individuals desire to make intergenerational transfers in the form of bequests, reductions in savings for their own retirement will be exactly offset by increases in savings for bequests. Therefore, capital accumulation would be unaffected.

Richard Hemming (1978) tests the Feldstein hypothesis on data from the U.K. Using a gross pension-wealth variable, he finds that the existence of state pensions reduced personal savings by £148 million in 1971 when aggregate contributions to the National Insurance Fund were £1,515 million. Employing a net social security variable adjusted for future taxes, he finds personal savings to be increased. He estimates that a 10 percent increase in benefits and contributions has no effect on savings with the gross social security variable and increases savings by 2.7 percent with net wealth as the pension variable.

In his review of the impact of retirement benefits on private savings, Rosen finds that the results of Feldstein and Munnell are not robust to alternative empirical specification because of the higher correlation between social security wealth and other variables. He concludes with the assessment that "the empirical findings provide weak evidence that Social Security has had a harmful effect on private savings" (p. 99). In his review of recent studies, Esposito is even more skeptical of the empirical finding of a strong negative effect on savings. He states: "The conclusion that seems incontestable is that the empirical results do not support the hypothesis that the social security program decreases private saving" (p. 17).

In an innovative paper, Burkhauser and Turner find that the earnings test changes the relative prices of an individual's time during his life. Workers increase hours during the unconstrained early years, whereas they reduce supply during late life. Additional earnings will raise savings and tend to offset the income effect of social security benefits, which reduces savings.

Several sutdies have indicated how the institution of a social security system might improve social welfare. First, Paul

Samuelson (1958) considered a consumption–loan economy in which real capital accumulation was impossible. Individual savings required the location of a borrower who desired to consume more than his present income and would repay the saver at a later date. In such a model, Samuelson showed that a pay-as-you-go social security system could lead to an unambiguous improvement in social welfare. Illustrating that this result is due to the lack of a store of value, he proves that the introduction of money can also achieve the improvement attributed to the social security system.

Aaron is able to show that with population growing at a steady rate, ". . . if no reserve is accumulated in the financing of old age pensions, each person will receive a larger pension than he has paid for" (1966, p. 372). A universal social insurance system improves the welfare of each person if the sum of the rates of growth of population and real wages exceeds the interest rate. In addition, the existence of the social-insurance program must not lower savings investment and therefore the rate of growth of income. This latter conclusion has, of course, been seriously questioned. Samuelson further extends the analysis of social security and growth. He finds that individual myopia may produce suboptimal savings rates and that ". . . Social Security systems . . . may be deemed most valuable precisely because the myopia ignored by the present models does in fact prevail" (1975, p. 543). A final issue on the funding of social security is raised by Jean Bourgeois-Pichat, who notes the possibility that a fully funded national pension system would require much of the available stock of capital in an economy. The magnitude of the liabilities in mature social-insurance programs may preclude the full funding of the accrued liabilities.

Thomas Pogue and L. G. Sgontz formulate a model in which an income-transfer system from workers to the elderly may permit increased investment in human capital of the young and thereby improve welfare if the return to investment in human capital exceeds the return on physical capital. They estimate that real educational expenditures rise by $0.76 for each dollar of real social security contribution. They conclude that intergenerational transfers and publicly financed education make it ". . . possible for one generation to save for its retirement by investing in the human capital of the next generation" (p. 165).

The authors are aware of a large number of presently unpublished studies by academic and governmental economists examining the nation's retirement programs, which, owing to space limitations, have not been included in this review. Increasing emphasis is being given to placing the savings and labor-supply responses to public and private pensions within a life-cycle context. A shift to general-fund financing will require some modifications and extensions in the analysis of the social security system. Considerable attention is also being given to exploring the long-run implications of retirement programs within a framework of an aging of the population. As the nation's retirement policy increases in importance during the remainder of this century, the economic impact of social security and private pensions should continue to be fertile ground for economic research.

Private pensions
Growth and development
     During the past four decades, private pensions have expanded rapidly throughout the American economy. The number of workers covered by these plans has risen from slightly over 4 million in 1940 to over 30 million in 1975; annual employer contributions have increased from $180 million in 1940 to $1.75 billion in 1950 to $23 billion in 1974; and the book value of the assets of retirement plans had grown to $192 billion by the end of 1974 (Skolnik). Table 8.2 shows that this expansion has increased the number of covered workers as a percent of all workers from 22.5 percent in 1950 to 46.2 percent in 1975. Over the same period, contributions have risen as a proportion of national payroll from 1.67 to 4.73 percent (Yohalem).

     Joseph Melone and Everett Allen attribute this rapid growth in private pensions to preferential tax treatment accorded to this form of compensation and the earnings from its assets. In addition, a pension system ". . . permits employers to terminate superannuated employees in a humanitarian and nondiscrimina-

Table 8.2. *Pension plan and deferred profit-sharing plans of wage and salary workers in private industry*

Year	Coverage (millions)	Coverage as a percent of workers	Employer and employee contributions (millions)	Contributions as a percent of national payroll
1950	9.8	22.5	2,080	1.67
1955	14.2	29.6	3,840	2.19
1960	18.7	37.2	5,490	2.46
1965	21.8	39.5	8,360	2.86
1970	26.1	42.1	14,000	3.25
1971	26.4	42.6	16,640	3.66
1972	27.5	43.1	18,540	3.74
1973	29.2	43.7	21,100	3.82
1974	29.8	44.0	25,020	4.14
1975	30.3	46.2	29,850	4.73

Source: Martha Remy Yohalem, "Employee-Benefit Plans, 1975," *Social Security Bulletin*, Nov. 1977, Tables 1–4.

tory manner" (p. 9). Furthermore, actions by the War Labor Board freezing direct wages but allowing the establishment of fringe-benefits programs and the 1948 ruling by the National Labor Relations Board that employers were legally obligated to bargain over the terms of pension plans stimulated a surge of pension activity.[8]

Interesting overviews of the institutional and operational characteristics of private pension plans are presented by Merton Bernstein, Melone and Allen, and Dan McGill (1975). Robert Tilove provides a recent analysis of public employee pensions, and William Greenough and Francis King present a detailed review of many of the public-policy issues that still remain unsolved as they relate to the nation's pension system. Howard Winklevoss provides a mathematical model to evaluate the effect of alternative assumptions on the funding requirements of pension plans. The papers of McGill (1977) examine the relationship between private pensions and social security and assess the future development of each system.

Factors influencing coverage and vesting
Studies by the government (U.S. DHEW) have shown that the incidence of coverage has a high degree of variability among industries, ranging from 80 percent in communications and public utilities to less than 35 percent for workers in construction and retail trade. Length of job tenure was positively correlated with pension coverage, as was the level of compensation. Males were more likely to be in pension plans than female workers. Donald Bell reported similar relationships for tenure and compensation. In addition, he found that union status and size of the firm were important determinants of pension coverage.

An employee who has attained vesting status may sever his relationship with his employer without forfeiting the accrued pension benefits based on his employer's contributions as specified by the guidelines of his pension plan.[9] Prior to the enactment of the Employee Retirement Income Security Act (ERISA) of 1974, there were no legal standards for vesting of employee benefits; however, vesting provisions were being rapidly incorporated into pension contracts (McGill, 1975, p. 135; Skolnik, p. 14). With the passage of ERISA, employers who offered pension plans were required to meet one of three permissible minimum standards of vesting;[10] however, most plans that were required to amend their vesting standards have chosen full vesting after ten years (Meier). Greenough and King (Chapter 7) review the vesting debate, the cost of liberalized vesting, and recommended changes in vesting standards.

Impact on personal savings and capital accumulation
The preceding discussion outlining the relationship between social security and savings provides a framework to assess the effect of private pensions on capital accumulation. Especially pertinent are the studies by Katona, Cagan, and Munnel, (1974, 1976). A unique perspective of the impact of pension funds on the equity market is provided by Peter Drucker, who argues that at least 25 percent of the equity capital in the United States is owned by workers through their pension funds with at least another 10

percent being held by the pension funds of the self-employed, public employees, and school and college teachers. He believes that within the next ten years, pension funds will increase their holdings of the total business equity from the present one-third to at least 50 or 60 percent. Thus, Drucker labels the American economy one of pension-fund socialism.

Of course, the extent to which the liabilities of a pension are funded is a primary factor determining the net effect of pension on capital accumulation. ERISA has created new guidelines on the funding and operation of pension systems (Treynor et al.). The papers presented at a conference sponsored by the Federal Reserve Bank of Boston entitled *Funding Pensions: Issues and Implications for Financial Markets* shed additional light on the funding questions. For a pre-ERISA view, see Roger Murray.

Labor supply effects

Pensions affect the labor supply of older workers through the income effect of benefits (Barfield and Morgan; Parnes et al.; Quinn; Hemming, 1977). Mandatory retirement from a worker's career has the effect of lowering the wage offers and removes the protection of seniority. (See Chapter 6.) Coverage by a pension also influences the labor-market activity of younger workers. Mobility decisions must include the effect of job changes on accumulated pension benefits, whereas the initial choice of job will depend on the incidence of pension contributions and their link to future benefits (Taggart). Compensating wage differentials are expected in firms that do not offer pension coverage.

Problems

Among the problems confronting the formulation of pension policy, these stand out: adverse changes in age structure that reduce the capacity of the working population to support retirees, migration, and inflation. In this summary, we concentrate on the last two factors because the first is discussed in Chapters 9 and 10.

Internal migration may shrink the basis of support for a localized community or state pension system that is dependent upon tax revenue under a pay-as-you-go arrangement and hence not funded. This can happen when such a community undergoes persisting economic adversity, with the result that significant numbers of its working population emigrate. Pay-as-you-go systems need to be based upon stable closed communities unless the size of the system is very small in comparison with the size of the communal earnings. Flight from some cities, as in the United States, illustrates the risks attendant upon community pay-as-you-go nonfunded systems.

Inflation is the greatest threat to public and private funded pension systems because it is likely to return to the retired pensioners money with less purchasing power than that which they paid into the system. Inflation may introduce "delayed deficits" in social security funds as reported by the Deutsche Bundesbank in its 1976 Report (pp. 41–5). Illustrative difficulties attendant upon annuities designed to afford protection against inflation are discussed by James Stephenson. In the United States expansion of social security is checking growth of private pensions (Munnell, 1978), perhaps in part because of inflation. Unless safeguards against inflation are developed, pay-as-you-go systems or systems dependent upon general revenue are likely to predominate. Thompson illustrates the effect of inflation on the real benefits from private pensions which are not adjusted for inflation compared to the stream of income from social security payments which rise to reflect changes in consumer prices. Munnell (forthcoming) further indicates the problems that would face private firms if they attempted to index their pension benefits.

Demographic fluctuations introduce variation in government outlays on the components of social security, such as retirement pay, medical expenses, and so on (Chesnais). These may affect redistribution policies and thus be of significance for the welfare of the aged (Browning, 1975b,c). Private pensions may also entail intergenerational and other forms of income redistribution (Asimakopulos and Weldon), especially in the presence of inflation (Pesando, Deutsch).

Of greater importance is the prospective long-run change in the age structure and decline in the ratio of workers to retirees should retirement not generally be deferred until the late sixties. Ture attaches less importance to the impact of demographic trends upon private pensions than to "potential developments in the social security system and prospective changes in the laws and regulations governing private pensions" (p. 59), along with the course of inflation.

9

Macroeconomic response to age-structural change

Our concern here is how the economic behavior and productivity of an economy respond to population aging; that is, to increases in the relative number of older persons – those 65 and over. As a population ages owing to the decline of fertility and its approach to the replacement level, both the relative number of persons aged 18–64 and that of those over 64 increase, the latter more rapidly (in the absence of echo effects), until the age composition becomes stable and the ratio of those 65 and over to those aged 18–64 becomes stationary. With the population stationary and stable, the ratio of those aged 18–64 to the total population will fall roughly within a range of 0.58 to 0.6,[1] and, given entry into the labor force at age 18 and withdrawal at age 65, per capita *potential* productivity will be in the neighborhood of a maximum. Of course, given considerable deferment of retirement beyond 64, potential productivity will be higher.

Even given fertility slightly below the replacement level, the fraction of a population aged 18–64 may remain little affected.[2] Under these circumstances, however, two adverse effects may be experienced. First, dependency cost per capita increases insofar as cost per dependent over 65 exceeds that per dependent under 18. Second, output per person aged 18–64 will be somewhat lower if productivity per worker is lower among those over 55 or 60 than among those younger. This decline occurs because a larger fraction of those 18–64 will be over 55 or 60 in a population based on fertility below the replacement level than in a stationary or growing population.

The macroeconomic response of an economy to age-structural change will depend upon (a) aging at the individual level, (b) increase in the relative number of individuals describable as aged, and (c) forms of synergism that make the total effect greater than the sum of the effects initially experienced at the individual level. The total response therefore is twofold in origin; it consists of the sum of the individual responses of autonomous individuals to the incidence of aging and of the collective or synergistic impact of increase in the fraction of a population's members describable as old, along with the impact of changes in the economic, social, and political environment associated with increase in the relative number of older persons.

The age composition of a nation's population, together with the reaction of its economy, is conditioned by the manner in which the age composition has evolved. If fertility has approached, for example, the replacement level gradually and settled there, the age structure will assume the correspondingly smooth pyramidal form. If, on the contrary, the life histories of sets of neighboring cohorts have differed markedly, as has been true in some Western countries since about 1910–20, owing to considerable variation in fertility, the resulting age-structure profile becomes irregular in form and prone to give rise to echo effects in the future until it is evenly smoothed by the advent and continuation of a stable fertility pattern (for illustrations, see United Nations, Chapter 1; U.S. Commission, Part V).

As has been noted, the effects of population aging need to be distinguished from effects of the slowing down of population growth, with which population aging (i.e., increase in the relative number of older persons) is closely associated. The two sets of effects are somewhat similar, of course, in that each reenforces the other, and both may tend to be relatively unfavorable to investment and economic flexibility.

Underlying the economic concomitants of aging both at the

aggregate population level and at the autonomous individual level are mainly the physical and psychological effects of the aging process incident upon individuals, as well as the diminution both of an individual's anticipated remaining life expectancy and of his future prospects as he grows older. The macroeconomic significance of population aging depends on the size of the fraction of the population describable as old (e.g., over 60–65, or over 70) and on the degree to which aging affects a population's productive power, investment behavior, incidences of taxes (Cowell), consumption patterns (e.g., see Crockett, on food, pp. 470–3), and political along with politically affected behavior (Eisele, Pratt, Carlie, Donahue and Tibbitts). William Serow and Thomas Espenshade detail the aggregate response of these factors to decreased rates of population growth.

The economic response of an economy to population aging is dominated by the influence of aging upon a growing number of autonomous individuals. But the impact of increase in the relative number of older persons may be accentuated by the slowness with which a population is growing if it is growing at all, for, as indicated earlier, increase in the *relative* number of older persons is attributable mainly to lowness of fertility and the resulting lowness of the rate of population growth. Slowness of population growth, in turn, may produce changes in the economic environment that affect some forms of economic behavior (e.g., Modigliani, pp. 163–7). Somewhat indicative of the near future is Sweden's population, the percentage of which 65 and over approximates 15 and apparently is destined to increase to 19.

Underlying the behavioral response of an individual to aging are three somewhat interrelated effects of aging. (1) The individual undergoes physical and psychological changes as he ages (e.g., see Bakerman, Eisdorfer and Lawton, Atchley, Botwinick),[3] and these changes influence economic behavior. The incidence of these changes may vary from individual to individual, however, with the result that economic behavior of individuals over their life cycles (e.g., see Ghez and Becker, Lydall, Shorrocks) tends to vary somewhat. (2) As an individual ages, and his preretirement years decrease in number, his options and prospective economic opportunities decline in number and magnitude (e.g., see Modigliani and Brumberg). (3) Response of an individual to the aging process is influenced both by changes in his social and economic status (e.g., stage in family life cycle; e.g., see Glick, 1947, 1955, 1977, Glick and Parke) that can affect his economic behavior (Manney, Cowgill) and by "social expectations about age and aging" that bear upon "the capacities and perception of capacities of older people" (Haber, pp. 14, 162, 165–7; also Lieberman).

Inasmuch as population aging is essentially a twentieth-century phenomenon, its economic significance did not command attention until the present century. The economic significance of individual aging did, however, attract notice in the nineteenth century, as noted earlier in Chapter 5, where we refer to the work of Rae, Cassel, and von Böhm-Bawerk and to Irving Fisher's relating of saving and dissaving to the personal life cycle (see Fisher, Chapter 5; Tobin).

Age and productivity

Among the sources of the macroeconomic impact of aging may be its influence upon individual productivity (e.g., Meier and Kerr, Shatto, Donahue, Welford), earnings (Suzuki), health, and economic behavior (e.g., Modigliani and Brumberg) affected by earnings. Aging may not, of course, affect productivity as much in the future as it did in the past if conditions associated with decline in productivity are reduced or averted (e.g., see Sheppard, 1970; Donahue; Barkin). There are limits, however, to the degree to which work loads can be reduced relative to a body's energy reserve (Karvonen, p. 7).

Note may be taken here of the relation between age and productivity, although it has been touched upon in several earlier chapters. For example, in the United States in 1959–60, earnings peaked before age 65 though wage rates did not decline because hours worked per year per man declined after the late thirties (Ghez and Becker, pp. 84–5, 103, also p. xv where they point out that people "retire at old age when their productivity is low").

Colberg and Wiridham (pp. 34, 35) found that whereas income was lower in 1939, 1949, and 1959 for southern males aged 55–64 than for those currently 45–54, average income of the members of the cohort 35–44 years old in 1939 continued to rise, reaching a peak when its members were 20 years older (also see Colberg). Thurow points out that the distribution of income by age does not correspond to the distribution of needs by age, with family needs tending to exceed income before age 35 and in the late sixties. Kreps (1977, pp. 1425–6) reports that "the age–earning profile for the male is usually steeper during his thirties than in his subsequent years" (see also Kreps, 1971, Part III; H. Miller; Reder). Suzuki finds similarities in the age–earnings profiles across countries and emphasizes the importance of seniority and job tenure. Decline in investment in human capital may affect the relation between age and productivity (Zucker, Dalton and Thompson). Health limitations reportedly affect nearly two-fifths of male workers in their sixties (Andrisani; see also Klarman, Davis).

Although it is often held (e.g., see Lehman; Brennan et al., Chapters 4, 13; also Pelz and Andrews) that peak ability is reached "shortly after biological maturity," some students consider such a negative view of the relation between age and productivity to be invalid (Clemente and Hendricks; Knapp; Kreps, 1977; McLeish; Riley and Foner, pp. 426–33; Sheppard and Rix, Chapter 5). Although there is some correlation between disability and age (Haber, pp. 148–64; Davis), Mincer found little evidence of an intrinsic age difference in learning capacity over the years prior to age 60, together with evidence of the importance of experience (e.g., pp. 22–122; see also Shatto). Friend and Zubek (pp. 412–13) found that although "critical thinking ability" declined after age 35, the performance of older persons generally remained as high as or higher than that of young-adult subjects. Green and Reimanis (pp. 99–116) report that in most respects IQ-test performance did not decline before age 65. Of course, genetic and family environmental differences may give rise to individual differences in learning, performance, and retentiveness (Taubman). The importance of experience has been stressed also by Lazear, Klevmarken and Quigley, and Schwab and Heneman, among others.

The correlation between productivity and age varies not only with individuals but also with the nature of the employment under consideration. Moreover, it may be subject to modification such as when the nature and requirements of particular employments are better adapted to the capacity and skills of an individual worker than according to age (Barkin, Koyl). Population aging is likely to have its most important effect on aggregate productivity in those economies where knowledge is changing rapidly, and highly competitive markets necessitate a high degree of adaptability of the labor force (Chesnais). Presumably, with an increase in the relative number of persons in and beyond their late fifties, greater attention will be given to means intended to preserve the skills and productive capacity of workers as they age into and beyond the fifties (e.g., see Sheppard, Sheppard and Rix).

Age and mobility

Mobility is essential to the optimum employment of human and other resources in dynamic modern economies subject to continuous change in composition of output and occupations. In the United States, for example, the rate of mobility has been high. Employment and location of employment have been subject to frequent change, and many older persons have been inclined to seek new homes upon retirement (e.g., see Prasad and Johnson, Yee and van Arsdol). Sommers and Eck report that 32 percent of all persons working in 1965 had moved to different occupations by 1970 (see also Gallaway, 1969, 1971, Chapter 5; Jaffe and Carlton). Both vertical and horizontal mobility are somewhat inversely related to age, the former as a result of population aging and the latter on physical grounds and because the opportunity to recoup the costs of movement and benefit through movement is inversely related to the age of adults. Under modern conditions, of course, the tendency to migrate may be influenced by such conditions as education and labor-force status (A. R. Miller, pp. 1–18), though, as Barsby and Cox find, older persons may respond differently from younger persons to factors that influence migration decisions. Serow (1978) finds that a higher proportion of elder migrants are characterized by return migration to state of birth, whereas, for young migrants, other characteristics are more important. Vertical mobility is affected by aging (Tissue, 1970); however, it is restrained mainly by absence of population growth (Browning, Keyfitz).

Among the personal characteristics that affect the propensity to migrate, Greenwood (pp. 406–8) found age, education, and race to be important; he points out that older persons have shorter expected working lives over which to realize the advantages of migrating and satisfactory rates of return on the costs of moving (Koltis; Gallaway, 1969, p. 180; Sjaastad). In contrast, young persons with little investment in skill do not have much to lose through changes associated with migration and have many years in which to profit from moving (Sjaastad, pp. 87–91, 93). Schwartz (p. 1159, also 1161, 1167) found that the rate of migration increased with education and decreased with age up to retirement, and then increased slightly. Yee and van Arsdol put forward a life-cycle explanation of residential mobility, showing that not only is age inversely related to mobility, but also mobility is affected through the impact of age upon the family life cycle. Although the potential benefits from moving tend to decline with age, a small household may be attracted to a pleasant climate upon retirement of its head (e.g., from New York to Florida).

The constraint imposed by aging upon vertical mobility may prove important in a comparatively stationary population in which a relatively large and stable fraction of the population of conventional working age (18–64 or 18–69) is over 50. Even so, the flexibility of an economy need not be greatly reduced with approximately 2 percent of the labor force being replaced each year. Moreover, given sufficient education and suitable facilitation of horizontal and vertical movement of members of the labor force, a near-optimum occupational composition of the labor force may be sustained.

More important than constraint upon vertical mobility arising from aging as such is the limitation attributable to the advent of a near-zero population growth and the ensuing replacement of the typical triangular population pyramid by a comparatively cylindrical structure. This structure has been nicely described by Browning on the basis of Coale's estimates:

> In discussing a stationary population, of paramount importance, demographically, is the age composition. As Coale (1972a:592) notes, '. . . the number of persons at any given age (say age 30) does not change from year to year, because 30-year-olds are the survivors (with the same proportion surviving) of the same number of births. Hence, the stationary population is not only constant in size, but also in age composition.' The shape of the distribution is changed from the steeply sloped pyramidal form of today to the cylindrical form of a stationary population . . . (p. 592). [Browning, p. 58]

Keyfitz has constructed a model designed to show how the opportunity of a representative individual to move upward through a hierarchical social structure is associated with life expectancy, the rate of population growth, and the corresponding age structure. He finds that the members of a growing population or organization will be promoted more rapidly on an average than members of a stationary population or organization. For example, a college instructor will require more years to move to a professorship. This slowing down of the progress of the representative individual from lower to higher positions is the result mainly of slowness of population growth, not of increase in life expectancy. Although "the mortality of one's contemporaries is favorable to one's own promotion," this "mortality effect is small in comparison with the population growth effect" (Keyfitz, p. 339; also Henry, 1971, 1976).

As Sauvy (p. 194) and Ryder (pp. 54–5) indicate, the occupational structure may prove less flexible. Solutions may, however, develop, as Browning (pp. 65–70) suggests. Moreover, as Spengler (1971, pp. 45–7; 1975, pp. 8–10, 14) points out, slowing down in status promotion may be compensated partly by reduction in interstatus reward differentials; for the number of younger members of the labor force will be smaller relative to low-status posts in a slowly growing or stationary population, whereas the relative number of older persons will be greater relative to the number of higher-status posts, with the result that the earnings profile will tend to be less steep. Furthermore, potential small entrepreneurs, preferring a relatively high post in a small enterprise, may seek to exploit the many small niches deemed too small for exploitation by large enterprises.

Age and consumption

Spending, consumption, and investment vary with the stage of an individual's life cycle, in part because of the impact of the family cycle. Consumption itself varies with age in response to a variety of physiological, economic, and social reasons (Billing; Clark; Campbell; J. Fisher; Eilenstine and Cunningham, pp. 228–30; Heien). Of primary importance for study of the impact of aging, despite the occasional stress upon the "over-65" market (Unsigned, *Nation's Business,* p. 59ff.), is the comparative lowness of the income of older persons (Goldstein, 1968; Alexis; Hurff) and its dominance of consumption (Nagatani), as well as limited variability in the potential purchase (Alexis; Reinecke) and expenditure patterns of the elderly (Crockett). Changes in the family support system have affected consumption by the aged (Treas). Age change also affects health-care expenditures (Gibson et al.).

Average consumption declines with age as individuals enter their later years, for income usually declines in these years (Brady; Kreps, 1971; Taussig, p. 13, Chapter 13; Nagatani; Thurow; also Binder, 1974, 1976; Creedy; Heckman), as do wealth holdings (J. Fisher; Gallaway, 1966; Goldstein, 1960, Chapter 16, and 1965; Shorrocks; Straw; also Ando and Modigliani) and their availability for conversion into dissavings. The physical demands of some forms of consumption (e.g., some forms of recreation) may limit their use (Cicchetti, pp. 163–4, 172). On the other hand, expenditures on drugs, and health and medical expenditures per capita, are much higher for persons aged 65 and over than for younger persons (Cooper and Piro; Cooper and Worthington; Gibson et al.; Reinecke; Grossman, 1972a,b). In general, Ferber writes (1962, p. 46), "family size and age, next to income appear to exert the main influence on family consumption," in part because of the influence "of age on durable goods purchases," shifts in the response of consumption to the life cycle, the development of consumer buying habits (Ferber, 1973), and other age-connected phenomena (e.g., Gorman; Houthakker and Taylor; Ferber, 1973, pp. 1310–12; Parks and Barten, p. 849). Of importance also is the lifetime of the goods under consideration (Spengler, 1971). For inasmuch as the ratio of expected life of an aged consumer to the average life of the durables and semidurables he has on hand is lower than that of younger consumers, the consumption of older persons is likely to be affected by inventories on hand as well as by consumption habits.[4]

The increase in the absolute and relative number of aged persons may not only increase the demand for products favored by older persons, especially in areas with a considerable fraction of older persons in their populations (e.g., Florida), but also will encourage private and public enterprise to cater more effectively to the needs of older persons than at present (Unsigned, *Business Week*). The impact of the increase in the population 65 and over should be most pronounced in the United States between 2010 and 2030, when, as a result of the post–World War II baby boom, the number of those over age 64 will increase about 20 million, or 58 percent, only to remain virtually stationary over the two following decades (cf. Easterlin). Between 1977 and 2010 those over 64 will increase 11.4 million or nearly 49 percent. Kerr has estimated that there will be only a slight change in the American consumption pattern of the aged between 1965 and 1980; the Science Council of Canada has indicated a number of ways in which aging may affect the structure of demand. Goldstein (1960, Chapters 17–18) has identified categories of goods and services comparatively favored by "the aged segment of the market," a segment

Hurff found relatively free of debt in 1954. According to Parks and Barten (p. 847), "an increase in the relative proportion of old to working age tends to increase threshold levels of some goods (food, clothing and services) but has the reverse effect on housing durables" (p. 847). The Science Council of Canada (Chapters 4–8) points to means whereby health care, transport, communication, housing, and services can be better adapted to the needs of an aging society. Denton and Spencer (1975) employ a simulation model of Canada to illustrate that rapid population growth would decrease health costs per capita. The needs referred to in this discussion are characteristic of a modern household rather than of a developing-country household (Kuznets; Treas). Thus, age-structure changes in conjunction with age-specific product demand may necessitate a restructuring of investment so as to enable a change in the nation's output mix.

Therefore, it can be inferred that the growth of a market heavily supported by the expenditure of older persons (e.g., aged 60) will depend largely upon an increase in the incomes of older persons, upon catering to this market by imaginative entrepreneurs, and upon subsidizing of emerging needs, especially those collective in character, by the state.

Aging and saving

Although the aging of individuals is unfavorable to individual saving on the part of those 65 and over (Hurff, Brady, Nagatani, Modigliani), population aging in the sense of an increase in the fraction of the population of working age may be favorable. In addition the proportion of the population aged 45–64, the principal saving years, also rises. The relationship between aging and saving on the part of an individual is conditioned mainly by the course of his annual-income curve and the pattern of his family expenditures (e.g., Kreps, 1971, Chapters 8–11, and 1977; Denton and Spencer, p. 94), together with whether institutionalized saving (e.g., social security, pension arrangements) discourages private individual saving (e.g., Feldstein; Munnell, 1977, Chapter 6, pp. 152–5) or whether other motives (e.g., the desire to form an estate) encourage saving (Mayer, pp. 28–32, 250–1; Brady) in addition to what is required to meet projected life-cycle requirements. Retirement greatly reduces an individual's income, and its buying power may be reduced further by inflation (Spengler, 1978). Early retirement, of course, reduces income and capacity to save even more (Munnell, 1974, 1977).

Population aging is concomitant with decline in fertility and, within limits, results in a relative increase in the population of working age (Enke; Coale, 1972b). Given a population that is stationary and stable, about three-fifths of its members will be 18–64 and hence of working age and capable of earning and saving. Of course, should fertility decline appreciably below the replacement level, the relative number of persons of working age will decline. Moreover, the composition of the dependent population will change, with those under 18 declining in relative number and those over 64 increasing. As a result, the cost per dependent rises, and capacity to form capital tends to decline.

When a population is stable and stationary, its potential capacity to form capital per head is roughly at its long-run maximum, for the fraction of its population of working age is at or near a maximum, and this population no longer needs to provide capital for the equipment of *net* additions to the population and the labor force. Hence savings can be formed easily and made available to increase capital per head in a stationary population. Whether advantage will be taken of the capacity of a stationary population to raise the aggregate capital–labor ratio at a relatively high rate depends on the degree to which motives to work, save, and invest remain as strong as in a growing population. For, within limits, the population growth process itself can be favorable to saving (Kelley). Carrying population aging to the point where it is stationary and stable entails a risk. Fertility can be reduced to below replacement, with the result that the burden of supporting the aged becomes oppressive and relatively unfavorable to capital formation.

In this connection, it is worth noting that Samuelson (1958, 1975a) has pointed to an advantage associated with some population growth despite the need to "widen" capital in proportion to population growth. "Increased population growth has the advantage of giving retired persons more working individuals to support them." There might, therefore, "be an intermediate rate of population growth – positive, zero or negative – depending upon the parameters of the problem – at which the disadvantages of further growth were just cancelled by the advantages. At such a point we would have the optimal rate of population growth, the one which maximized per capita lifetime utility of consumptions." At this rate "voluntary life-cycle personal savings would just suffice to support the equilibrium without recourse to Social Security alterations of life-cycle consumption patterns" (Samuelson, 1976, p. 516; also 1975a,b). In a comment on Deardorff's critique, Samuelson points out that "it never pays to let population grow at a faster rate than that in which the system is able to keep its capital formation up, even with zero consumption" (1976, p. 523).

Aging and investment

Both individual and population aging tend to be relatively unfavorable to investment characterized by appreciable risk and uncertainty. Such investment is distinguishable from that characterized by much less risk and uncertainty and hence describable as defensive in a world ridden by risk and uncertainty. Perhaps representative of the former is recourse to equities as a hedge against current inflation (cf. Friedman). Too little time remains to the old investor or entrepreneur to recover or compensate for loss.[5] Sauvy argues that, "In countries suffering from ageing, the spirit of enterprise, and hence the willingness to accept risks without which capitalism cannot function, gradually atrophies and is replaced by a new feeling: the desire for security" (p. 118).

Concern has been implied that age so intensifies the propensity to avert risk that underinvestment in new ventures or extension of old ventures often occurs. Hence it is inferred that bodies responsible for policy-shaping decisions (e.g., business, corporate, administrative) need to include enough relatively young members to avoid the supposedly excessive risk aversion associated with old decision makers.

Such concern is accentuated when aging of decision makers is a concomitant of the population aging that accompanies the advent of a stationary or slowly declining population. For, in a stagnant world such as J. M. Keynes and A. H. Hansen at times envisaged, offsets to investment would be in short supply even in the absence of advanced population aging. Of course, given the heavy current taxation and public expenditure, such imbalance as Keynes envisaged is unlikely. Indeed, a dearth of savings is often likely. However, given Samuelson's optimum social security model, the problem disappears (Samuelson, 1975b).

Population aging and support of retirees

The capacity of a population to support its retired population depends upon its age structure and the ratio of persons eligible for benefits (approximated by those aged 65 and over) to those of working age (say 18–64) and in the labor force. When, for example, the American population was growing rapidly, this ratio was quite low; it still approximated 18.2 percent in 1977. With the advent of a stationary or slightly declining population, this ratio will increase, slightly during this century but to between 30 and 40 percent by 2030, when, by current estimates, there will be only about 2.5 to 3.0 persons aged 18–64 per each supposed retiree aged 65 and over. The transfer burden of supporting these retirees along with other public and private expenses will increase significantly and could be reduced by greatly diminishing pensions, and so on, or by deferring retirement until a later age and prolonging worklife in keeping with the prolongation of life expectancy at ages 65 and 70. Deferment of retirement may then be viewed as a substitute for the maintenance of fertility at a relatively high level, together with earlier withdrawal from the labor force.

10

Conclusion

In Chapters 2–9 we have reviewed the literature bearing upon economic and related consequences of population aging and its causes – a phenomenon that, according to Sauvy, tended to escape notice despite its obviousness. The tendency toward population aging will be accentuated should fertility descend below the replacement level or should a "gerontic revolution" get under way. Whether a decline in a nation's fertility and eventually in its population in conjunction with further population aging constitutes a serious economic problem turns on "the capacity of our societal institutions to cope with the changes that can be anticipated" and realize the potential advantages of a longer life (see Myers).

Fertility is currently below the replacement level in a number of highly developed countries, according to the United Nations *Demographic Yearbook*. Among these countries in 1973–4, besides Canada, Japan, and the United States,[1] were Austria, Belgium, Denmark, England and Wales, Finland, both Germanies, Netherlands, Scotland, Sweden, and Switzerland. Should fertility persist at these levels, the age composition will include more persons over 65 than would a corresponding stationary population.

Should life expectancy at higher ages increase, the fraction of the population 65 and over would increase somewhat. For example, in the ultimately stationary population projected for the

United States made in 1975, the median age would be 37.8 years, with 17.05 percent 65 and over and 58.93 percent aged 18–64 years. As a result mainly of the upward adjustment of anticipated life expectancy in the stationary population, projections constructed in 1977 illustrate further population aging in the future stationary state (U.S. Bureau of the Census, July 1977, pp. 1–11). These estimates forecast that the median age will be 38.9 years, with 18.98 percent of the population 65 and over and 57.66 percent aged 18–64 years. Prolongation of life thus slightly reduces the fraction of the working-age population.[2] Therefore, reductions in mortality can increase the dependency burden unless worklife is increased in essentially corresponding measure.

Population aging produces significant changes in a variety of economic, social, and institutional factors, and further analysis of these impending shifts is necessary if society is to be able to adjust satisfactorily. Many of the economic responses to aging have been examined in detail in earlier chapters. A recurring assessment is that our knowledge of the transition mechanism from demographic to economic variables is limited,[3] and many relationships remain to be explained. Although the immediate impact of each of these problems is on the individual older persons affected, a solution frequently must be sought through collective arrangements under public or private auspices. Illustrative is support in old age – to be derived through public social security, through private security in the form of a pension or annuity, or (now more rarely) under a family support system.

Of these problems, the most important is provision of adequate economic security for the aged (Spengler, 1978); that is, for the diverse needs of older persons no longer in the labor force but entitled to support under one of the intergenerational arrangements or sets of "contracts" (e.g., pension, annuity, government social security) in force in a society. Let r denote the average benefits available at any given time for transfer per aged retiree or dependent. Then r approximates $(Lty)/R$, where L denotes the employed members of the labor force; R, the number of aged dependents; y, average produced income per member of L; and t, the fraction of *y* appropriated, in the form of a tax or othrwise, for the support of *R*. Of especial importance is the ratio *L/R* because this ratio conditions the magnitude of *t* and hence the ease with which a given level of *r* can be supplied. The level of *t* that is tolerable for a given average income is conditioned, of course, by the fraction of *y* that is appropriated by the state for other purposes as well as by the extent of private and public outlays upon younger dependents.

Two important determinants of the ratio *L/R* and the related worker/young dependent ratio are the age composition of a population and the age at which individuals withdraw from the labor force and become members of *R*, that is, recipients of *r* instead of contributors of *ty*. Maintenance of replacement-level fertility will lower *L/R* from the 5.5 that prevailed in 1976 to a potential ratio of slightly above 3. A fertility rate of 1.7 would lower *L/R* below 3. Low levels of fertility, however, generate a corresponding rise in the worker/youth ratio, and, as noted in earlier chapters, the total cost of dependency support programs depends on the relative cost of young versus old dependents (Clark and Spengler). The nature and size of payments to both groups needs further study.

Of increasing importance with population aging is the age of retirement. Should half of the 11.25 percent of the population aged 55–64 in the ultimate stationary population transfer from *L* to *R*, this ratio declines to 2.16, and the value of *t* will have to be adjusted upward about 40 percent if *r* is to remain unchanged. A decrease in *L/R* thus entails a decline in *r* or an increase in *t*. However, because there is a limit to the degree to which *t* can be adjusted upward, maintenance of benefits and taxes at satisfactory levels requires older persons to remain in the labor force compatibly with the level of postretirement income they prefer. So doing also offers some protection against the erosion of the purchasing power of current income by inflation.

The availability of publicly financed retirement benefits and other age-related income-supplement programs induces lower labor-force participation by the elderly (see Chapter 6). As has just been noted, further population aging necessitates relatively high rates of labor-market activity by older persons to prevent dramatic increases in the tax rate to finance transfers to the elderly. Thus, the age of eligibility for these programs must be examined closely with gradually rising ages being more compatible with population aging. Additional scrutiny of retirement policy must be forthcoming as policy makers must be aware of the labor-market implications of retirement programs and their long-run cost implications, given further population aging.

The worker–retiree ratio also depends on when the labor force is entered. If primary, secondary, and college education could be completed in 12 instead of the 16 years that is common, most could enter the labor force at 18 instead of at 22, the age of entry when 16 years of education is required. Given 12 instead of 16 years of required time for education, the fraction of those 18–64 free to enter the labor force would be roughly one-tenth higher.

The quality of security of the aged is conditioned by their relative economic condition as well as by their absolute economic status. Their condition can be improved by reducing the forces that subject the aged to greater inequality. Population aging contributes to inequality in post-tax income distribution in that older cohorts experience diminution in relative income owing to withdrawal from the labor force, limited protection against inflation, less opportunity to accumualte assets, and possibly intercohort differences in experience.[4] Given later rather than earlier retirement, together with reduction in intercohort differences in the accumulation of human and other capital assets, the impact of population aging on income inequality will be reduced.

Inflation also may affect the income of the aged adversely and thus contribute to inequality. This effect is reinforced by income-increasing technical progress and investment which tends to augment output and income per member of the labor force but not that of retired persons unless provision is made for the latter. The adverse impact of inflation on the aged can be reduced insofar as income of the aged can be indexed, mainly through national social security systems that draw on public revenue, though not as a rule when the source of a retiree's income is a private pension or an annuity. Retirees can share in the fruits of income-increasing technical progress and investment under a social security system because with $r = (Lty)/R$, and t and L/R constant, r keeps pace with y. This ability to index benefits increases the desirability of social security benefits in contrast to private savings.

The economic security of the aged depends not only upon the amount of income received but also upon the degree to which the economy is adapted to meeting the needs of older persons and delivering the goods and services required, especially on the part of those of more advanced years and with greatly reduced mobility. Inquiry into various aspects of this problem and the means of financing delivery is needed. These factors will increase in importance as the proportion of the elderly over 75 or 85 years of age continues to rise.

The importance of delivery methods for goods and services required by the aged depends upon their health status.[5] As long as older persons are fully mobile, these delivery problems are not essentially distinct from those of the population at large. These problems become distinct, however, when the mobility of one or both spouses is reduced, and the problems are intensified when the living accommodations available are not adapted to the peculiar needs and requirements of older persons.

Further research should be devoted to the ability of private enterprise to meet adequately these needs and requirements. Presumably, a constraint is the high cost of labor along with the failure of potential private suppliers to exploit modern means of economizing on labor inputs. Inquiry is indicated also into whether collective approaches to the solution of this problem can be put on a sufficiently economical basis under private enterprise. One might expect further government regulation of enterprises that affect the well-being of the aged (ERISA, Medicare, etc.).

Companion inquiry is indicated into the problem of providing housing suitable to the real needs of the less mobile aged, needs that are not well met by so-called high-rise housing. Some aspects of the housing problem have been considered by the Science

Council of Canada (pp. 29–30, 53–62), along with the transport problem (ibid., pp. 65–9) and the degree of substitutability of computers and means of communication for transport (ibid., pp. 73–81).

Of general concern is the degree to which private enterprise can well identify the diverse needs of the older population and meet them. As a rule, of course, private enterprise is effective in ferreting out wants and satisfying them. The diverse needs of the aged may be less perceptible, however, particularly to larger-scale enterprise.

Of related concern is the degree to which the medical and related needs of older persons are being met economically, whether under private-, public-, or mixed-enterprise conditions. For if costs per unit are augmented owing to absence of competition, the amount of service purchasable by older persons may be unduly limited inasmuch as the funds available to meet these costs are limited. On the other hand, public subsidies may encourage overuse of the available health resources.

Among other problems in need of further study are the changing nature of the family support system and the vulnerability of alternative support systems to inflation. The nature of the family support system is influenced by the rise in female labor-force participation and by replacement of families in which a single spouse, usually the male, is the sole breadwinner, by the family in which both spouses are fully employed.

When both spouses are employed, the attained level of living is higher, as is the rate at which assets tend to be accumulated. As a result, earlier retirement is likely to be compatible with adequacy of retirement income unless what is considered to be adequate has been greatly increased by the enjoyment of two incomes and the career orientation of both spouses. Additional research is needed to enhance our understanding of the retirement process in dual-career families (see Anderson et al.).

Further examinations, assessing the advantages and disadvantages of alternative means of supporting the aged, should be conducted into their vulnerability to inflation, and into financial and other limits on funding retirement programs (e.g., the availability of satisfactory securities and other assets in which to invest pension and similar accumulations), as well as into the rates of return on contributions to social security, pension, and similar funds. Of possible concern also is the impact of increasing dissaving should fertility remain below the replacement level, and should the fraction of the population 65 and older rise correspondingly. Mechanisms that would guarantee the real value of pension benefits and return to assets upon retirement must be explored.

Economists should consider future modifications of the incentive and reward patterns in the presence of population aging, in part because of the impact of the absence of much, if any, population growth (see Keyfitz; Ryder; Spengler, 1975). First, because vertical mobility will be delayed by both limitations upon expansion and prolongation of participation in the labor force, compensation for such delay will become necessary, together with changes in the life-style pattern of earnings. There may also be increases in the relative number of independent private-enterprise units because their creation often frees the creator of some barriers to upward mobility. Second, because there will be relatively fewer young persons to provide the interoccupational and interindustrial migration essential to maintenance of optimal interoccupational and interindustrial balance in an economy subject to changes in technology and consumption patterns, older persons may be required to supply some of this required mobility. Thus, barriers to the mobility of middle-aged and older workers should be examined critically. Changes in investing standards, accumulation of pension credits, and portability of these credits should be reassessed.

Having noted ways in which population aging may prove less favorable to economic mobility and flexibility than a population experiencing some growth, we ought to inquire into the degree to which population aging may be conducive to unemployment by discouraging longer-term investment and by reducing mobility and hence making for higher wages and inflation (Spengler, 1972). Also the linkage between aging and labor-force productivity needs further study. Inquiry is indicated into the vulnerability of bases of public or private pension arrangements (especially those that are not funded) when these bases are regional or local in character and hence subject to shrinkage in the size of the supportive population and its capacity for supporting retirees directly or indirectly.

Much more attention needs to be given to the aged (Henry), their economy (Fehm), and their politics (Pratt). With increase in the relative number of aged persons there is increasing evidence of lack of geriatric and long-term care for the aged – a lack due both to inadequacy of means available and to the inappropriateness of these means. McKeown recommends that unproductively used medical resources be transferred to "geriatric care," now a "neglected" area of medical care. Robert L. Kane and Rosalie A. Kane outline new approaches to resolve current dilemmas with long-term care-approaches that embody the experience of several European countries.[6] In a symposium on "planning for the elderly," edited by Marvin Wolfgang, the ability to cope with the many problems peculiar to the aged is examined along with those growing out of aging populations. Illustrative of the approach and performance of private enterprise in meeting an important need of the aged – the nursing industry – is the work of Fraundorf, together with Grimaldi's critique.

Our review of the literature concerning aging has posed many important questions and raised relevant issues that define the economics of individual and population aging. The review of the literature indicates that research into the causes and consequences of population aging is a relatively recent phenomenon. Although several facets of aging recently have received considerable attention, much important work remains to be done. Our primary goal has been to outline avenues of future research while noting the prior research that has established the foundations of the economics of aging.

NOTES

Chapter 1. Recognition of the economics of aging

1 However, "old age" was dealt with in an article by Rubinow (1933).
2 Illustrative is Samuel H. Preston's 1976 study of mortality patterns and declines (a sequel to an earlier study of the causes of death), in which he shows that since the 1920s, improvement in income in advanced countries no longer plays the important role it formerly played in facilitating reduction of mortality.

Chapter 2. Population aging: sources

1 Although life tables and survivorship rates date to the second half of the seventeenth century and Euler's stable population theory to 1760, mathematical demography is essentially a twentieth-century product (Keyfitz, 1976). A "comprehensive index of aging" is a recent development (H. Tanaka; also Keyfitz, 1976, p. 16).
2 See also Lopez, Chapter 3, 5; Keyfitz (1968).
3 Coale (1972, Chapters 2–4) explains the mathematics underlying the convergence of a population to a stable form and the adjustment of the age structure to the ruling fertility pattern, the mortality pattern being given.
4 For the underlying mathematical theory, see Coale (1972, Chapter 5).
5 The subject of aging was treated frequently in the French journal *Population*, edited by Alfred Sauvy upon its establishment in 1945. See also Chapter 3.
6 See also Siegel and Passel, pp. 559–66; Dublin et al., Chapter 1; also Rosenfeld and U.S. Bureau of the Census (May 1975, pp. 37–44, 67–8).
7 Account is not taken of illegal immigration into the United States, which probably runs several hundred thousand a year.
8 If all women aged 18–24 regardless of marital status are considered, expected births are only 2.0 per woman.
9 Lifetime births expected have decline along with the drop in the total fertility rate; however, the decline has been less steep. As a result, the 1976 fertility rate lay below the expected number of births per woman, whereas the reverse

was true in 1960 (U.S. Bureau of Census, Series P-20, No. 308, June 1977, p. 2).

10 On demographic aspects of aging see U.S. Bureau of the Census (Feb. 1973, May 1975).

Chapter 3. Population aging and dependency

1 See also Samuelson (1958).
2 Given a stable population, whether stationary, increasing, or declining, the age structure and age-group ratios are stable. Then the ratio of contributors to social security funds no longer is likely to grow much, if at all. Cf. Aaron.
3 In the third edition of *Population Problems*, Warren Thompson explicitly noted the cost of supporting dependent children and how this was dependent on age structure. He estimated that 1 percent of national income was required to support children in 1948 and that this represented a decline compared to 1928.
4 On career prospects, promotion, and total numbers, see also Louis Henry.
5 This fear has recently been reaffirmed in the getting of a special exemption for many highly paid executives from the legislation raising the age of permissible mandatory retirement.

Chapter 4. Economic status of the elderly

1 Parts of the following three sections are based on material contained in R. Clark (1977).
2 This review will concentrate primarily on the economic status of the elderly in the United States during the 1970s. Readers interested in a more detailed historical perspective should examine works by Peter Steiner and Robert Dorfman, and Harold Orbach and Clark Tibbitts, that assess the economic position of the elderly during the 1950s and 1960s. In addition, the results of surveys of the aged conducted by the Social Security Administration in 1963 and 1968 are reported by Lenore Epstein and Janet Murray, and Lenore Bixby et al.
3 For a discussion of this index and other measures of poverty, see U.S. Department of Health, Education and Welfare (1976).
4 Stanley Herren provides a detailed review of the relationship between age and income distribution. He concludes that population aging should not significantly affect aggregate measures of the distribution of income. See also James Morgan on the impact of the use of time and group of affiliation.
5 Using data from the United Kingdom, John Creedy concludes that if all individuals stayed in the same position in the income distribution and received equal percentage changes in earnings, then the inequality of lifetime earnings would be the same as annual inequality. The existence of changes in relative earnings means that relative inequality within each cohort increases with age. A. B. Atkinson, and A. B. Atkinson and A. J. Harrison, find, however, that the shares of the top 1, 5, and 10 percent of income holders within each age group are not greatly different from the total population. Older male cohorts are characterized by increased inequality relative to younger men.

6 Schulz (1978a) examines the distribution of the increase in benefits that would follow an elimination of the earnings test. Using ten alternative tests, he finds that greater liberalization provides a greater proportion of the additional benefits to the high-income elderly.

7 For a discussion of the consumption patterns of the elderly, see Fred Waddell.

Chapter 5. Age and economic activities: life-cycle patterns

1 "A subjective future is supposed in all our activities. Without a tacit belief in a tomorrow nearly everything we do today would be pointless. Expectation, intention, anticipation, premonition and presentiment – all these have forward reference in time. . . . Implicit in all our actions are plans, however vague and inarticulate, for the future, and sometimes, as in saving and investment, this planning is deliberate. As we ascend the evolutionary scale the temporal horizon becomes more and more extended" (Cohen, p. 262, also 264).

2 As Ghez and Becker (pp. 24, 37) suggest in another connection, the formation of human capital is less influenced by the "estate motive" than is that of more transferable capital. Time spent in the production of human capital falls with age to the extent that it cannot be transferred to one's children. On factors affecting the propensity to save, see also Ishikawa.

3 William Serow and Thomas Espenshade discuss the aggregate response of these behavioral patterns to decrease in the rate of population growth.

4 In this paragraph and a number that follow we draw upon the Presidential address of Juanita Kreps to the Southern Economic Association, 1976 (see Kreps, 1977; also 1976a,b).

5 They further note that the shape of the earnings profiles is determined by differential rates of earnings growth at various points over the life cycle. "The effect of economic conditions appears in a substantially reduced rate of earnings increase for all birth cohorts in periods of recession and unemployment, but substantial increases in output and employment do not appear to have as much influence" (p. 129). The use of constant dollars substantially reduces the growth in earnings and leads to actual declines for the oldest age group.

6 Most important is continued improvement in man's health and the potential length of his worklife, together with its impact on the prolongation of postretirement life (Gori and Richter).

Chapter 6. Labor supply of the elderly

1 Replies to such questions may be biased because of desires of the respondent to give a socially acceptable answer. See discussion below as it relates to the health variables.

2 A survey of more than 100 countries indicated that over 80 percent of the social security systems have retirement-tests provisions (Kirkpatrick, p. 3). Tracy described the flexible-retirement features in Japan and many European countries.

Chapter 7. Personal and market characteristics affecting retirement

1 This "elasticity" is calculated by finding the percentage change in labor-force participation rate, given a one-percentage-point change in the overall unemployment rate.

2 Estimates were insignificant for nonmarried men, nonmarried women, and nonwhite married men.

3 See the discussion of their results of other income in our review of social security benefits.

Chapter 8. Pensions and the economy

1 Of course, the opposite case can also be defended. See Friedman (1972).

2 Buchanan argues that requiring individuals to save for retirement does not necessitate a single public-insurance system. Instead, he believes that "competing private and public schemes could exist side by side and considerations of personal preferences along with the comparative efficiency would determine the individual's choice between these" (p. 387).

3 Yves Balcer and Peter Diamond examine the effect of length of the averaging period on the progressivity of benefits. They argue that despite conflicting forces "one would suspect that, considered alone, the larger averaging period will result in a less progressive distribution of benefits" (p. 265).

4 Recent publicity questioning the viability of the social security system and the sharp increase in taxes may be undermining the popular support that this program has received (Eldred).

5 See Feldstein (1972) and Brittain (1972a) for an exchange on the methodology employed in Brittain's research.

6 Although individual savings is expected to fall, Friedman notes that the impact on aggregate savings depends on the extent that social security and pension plans are funded and the rate of decline of private savings relative to the size of accumulated benefits.

7 Baldwin notes similar arguments in a debate over the impact of pension schemes at the turn of the century.

8 For a review of the pre–World War II development of private pensions, see National Industrial Conference Board and Charles Dearing.

9 For an account of horror stories of workers receiving no benefits after long years of service, see Ralph Nader and Kate Blackwell.

10 The legal standards of vesting are that a worker must be fully vested after ten years of service; an employee receives 25 percent vesting of accrued benefits after five years on the job and must be fully vested after 15 years of participation; or an employee with five years of service must be granted 50 percent vesting when his age and years of participation total 45 with an additional 10 percent of benefits being vested annually.

Chapter 9. Macroeconomic response to age-structural change

1 According to the U.S. population projection issued in 1975 and based on anticipated mortality conditions, the ultimate stationary population would consist of 17.05 percent of persons aged 65 years and over and 58.93 percent of persons aged 18–64 years. According to the 1977 projection, the corresponding fractions would be 18.98 and 57.66 percent, owing to decline in age-specific mortality in middle and older adult ages. See *Current Population Reports,* P-25, No. 601, p. 142; ibid., P-25, No. 704, pp. 2–4, 86. Sheppard and Rix, Chapter 5, examine the biodmedical dimension and age of death.

2 For illustrations we may turn to the stable populations development by Coale and Demeny.

3 Although the incidence of temporary disability due to acute conditions is lower among those over 64 than among those younger, limitation of activity due to chronic conditions is higher among those 65 and over than among those under 65. For example, see U.S. Department of Health, Education and Welfare, 1973; also cf. idem, 1977.

4 Sexauer points out that some effects on consumer demand attributed to habit may be due to the size of the stock on hand. See also Ferber (1973, pp. 1309–12).

5 It may be true as Samuelson has pointed out that "our present sins do gradually wash out, and so do our good deeds!" (1975a, pp. 5–6). But if we are old, is there enough time?

Chapter 10. Conclusion

1 According to the U.S. Bureau of the Census (June 1977) lifetime births expected per 1,000 wives 18–24 numbered 2,137 in 1977 compared with 2,375 in 1971; thus expected fertility sufficed for population replacement in 1977.

2 The above data are from U.S. Bureau of the Census (July 1977, pp. 1–2; Oct. 1975, p. 142).

3 The demographic–economic relationships are simultaneous in nature with interactive effects prominent among these variables.

4 Sahota (pp. 26–7), in his review of theories of personal-income distribution, touches upon "the proportion of point-in-time estimates of inequalities accounted for by age" as well as life-cycle theory. M. Paglin (1975) proposes a method of correcting for age and life-cycle effects upon income distribution. This paper prompted a number of comments by E. R. Nelson and others, to which Paglin replied (1977). See also Bronfenbrenner and Herren on the impact of changes in age structure upon income distribution. Account needs to be taken, of course, of the effect of distribution of income in kind by age, if significant.

5 This point has been stressed by Professor Allen Kelley in private discussion. It has been treated also by the Science Council of Canada in its 1976 study and by Vera R. Kivett.

6 The Kanes summarize their proposals as follows:

Long-term care for the aged in the United States is overly dependent upon the nursing home. This hospital-like model for long-term care is particularly inappropriate since it imposes a medical solution on a variety of social problems. An adequate long-term care program requires a range of resources in the community as well as in institutions; sheltered housing options seem a desirable alternative to the nursing home. To ensure the quality of nursing home care, the present focus on setting standards for care activities should be abandoned in favor of a focus on care outcomes (physical, mental, and social). In an effort to change our present perverse incentives in the nursing home industry, the proposal is made that nursing homes be reimbursed according to the degree to which patient outcomes meet predicted outcomes. (p. 913).

BIBLIOGRAPHY

Chapter 1. Recognition of the economics of aging

Achenbaum, W. Andrew. *Old Age in the New Land*. Baltimore, Md.: Johns Hopkins Press, 1978.

Arrow, Kenneth J. "The Future and the Present in Economic Life." *Economic Inquiry*. April 1978, pp. 157–70.

Beveridge, Sir William. *Full Employment in a Free Society*. New York: W. W. Norton and Company, 1945.

Browning, Edward K. *Redistribution and the Welfare System*. Washington, D.C.: American Enterprise Institute, 1975.

Cannan, Edwin. *Economic Scares*. London: P. S. King, 1933.

Charles, Don C. "Literary Old Age: A Browse Through History." *Educational Gerontology* 2: 237–63 (July–Sept. 1977).

Charles, Enid. "The Effect of Present Trends in Fertility and Mortality Upon the Future Population of Great Britain and Upon its Age Composition." In Lancelot Hogben, ed., *Political Arithmetic*. New York: Macmillan, 1938.

De Beauvoir, Simone. *The Coming of Age*. New York: Putnam, 1972.

Dublin, Louis I., and Lotka, Alfred J. *The Money Value of a Man*. New York: Ronald Press, 1930, 1946.

Haanes-Olsen, Leif. "Earnings-Replacement Rate of Old Age Benefits, 1965–75, Selected Countries." *Social Security Bulletin* 41:3–14 (Jan. 1978).

Hareven, Tamara K. "Historical Adulthood and Old Age. *Daedalus* 105:13–28 (Fall 1976).

Hareven, Tamara K., and Vinovskis, Maris, eds. *Demographic Processes and Family Organization in Nineteenth-Century American Society: Quantitative Studies in History*. Princeton: Princeton University Press, 1978.

Hutchinson, E. P. *The Population Debate*. Boston: Houghton-Mifflin Co., 1967.

Mangoldt, Hans von. *Volkswirthschaftslehre,* 1868.

Notestein, Frank W., Taeubner, Irene B., Kirk, Dudley, Coale, Ansley J., and Kiser, Louise K. *The Future Population of Europe and the Soviet Union, Population Projections 1940–1970*. Geneva: League of Nations, 1944.

Parnes, Herbert S., and King, Randy. "Middle-Aged Job Losers," *Industrial Gerontology* 4:77–95 (Spring 1977).

Preston, Samuel H. *Mortality Patterns in National Populations.* New York: Academic Press, 1976.

Royal Commission on Population. *Report.* London: His Majesty's Stationary Office, 1949.

Rubinow, I. M. "Old Age." *Encyclopaedia of the Social Sciences,* 11. New York: Macmillan, 1933. Pp. 452–62.

Quest for Security. New York: H. Holt Co., 1934.

"Social Insurance." *Encyclopaedia of the Social Sciences,* 14. New York: Macmillan, 1934. Pp. 134–8.

Spengler, Joseph J. *Facing Zero Population Growth; Reactions and Interpretations, Past and Present.* Durham, N.C.: Duke University Press, 1978.

Svoboda, Cyril B. "Senescence in Western Philosophy." *Educational Gerontology* 2:219–35 (July–Sept. 1977).

Thompson, W. S., and Whelpton, P. K. *Population Trends in the United States.* New York: McGraw-Hill Book Co., 1933.

Treas, Judith. "Family Support Systems for the Aged: Some Demographic Considerations," *The Gerontologist* 17:481–91 (Dec. 1977).

United Nations. *The Aging of Populations and Its Economic and Social Implications,* Population Studies, No. 26. New York: United Nations, 1956.

The Concept of a Stable Population: Application to the Study of Populations of Countries with Incomplete Demographic Statistics, Population Studies, No. 39. New York: United Nations, 1968.

The Determinants and Consequences of Population Trends, Population Studies, No. 50. New York: United Nations, 1973a.

World Population As Assessed in 1968, Population Studies No. 53. New York: United Nations, 1973b.

Whelpton, P. K. "Increase and Distribution of Elders in Our Population," *Journal of American Statistical Association,* Supplement, 27:92–101 (March 1932).

Chapter 2. Populating aging: sources

Blackner, J. C. G. "The Estimation of Adult Mortality in Africa from Data on Orphanhood." *Population Studies* 31:107–28 (March 1977).

Brass, William, Coale, Ansley J., Demeny, Paul, Heisel, Don F., Lorimer, Frank, Romaniuk, Anatole, and Van DeWalle, Etienne. *The Demography of Tropical Africa.* Princeton: Princeton University Press, 1968.

Brotman, Herman B. "Life Expectancy: Comparison of National Levels in 1900 and 1974 and Variations in State Levels, 1969–1971." *The Gerontologist* 17(1):12–22 (Feb. 1977).

Bumpass, Larry. "Is Low Fertility Here to Stay?" *Family Planning Perspectives* 5:67–9 (1973).

Busse, Ewald W., and Pfeiffer, Eric, eds. *Behavior and Adaptation in Late Life.* 2d ed. Boston: Little Brown and Co., 1977.

Carré, J. J., Dubois, P., and Malinvaud, E. *French Economic Growth*. Stanford: Stanford University Press, 1975.

Coale, Ansley J. "Increases in Expectation of Life and Population Growth." *International Population Conference*. Vienna, 1958. Vienna: Im Selbstverlag, 1959. Pp. 36–41. [Presented by Louis Henry and Wilhelm Winkler.]
The Growth and Structure of Human Populations: A Mathematical Investigation. Princeton: Princeton University Press, 1972.

Coale, Ansley J., and Demeny, Paul. *Regional Model Life Tables and Stable Populations*. Princeton: Princeton University Press, 1966.

Curtis, Howard J. "Underlying the Aging Process," *Science*. Aug. 23, 1963, pp. 686–94.

Cutler, Richard G., ed. *Cellular Aging. Concepts and Mechanisms*. Basel: Karger, 1976.

DeJong, G. F., and Sell, R. R. "Changes in Childlessness in the United States: A Demographic Path Analysis." *Population Studies* 31:129–42 (March 1957).

Depoid, Francoise. "La mortalité des grands viellards," *Population*. 28:755–92 (July–Oct. 1973).

Dublin, L. I., Lotka, A. J., and Spiegelman, Mortimer. *Length of Life*. Rev. ed. New York: Ronald Press, 1949. Pp. 241–56.

Easterlin, Richard A. "On the Relation of Economic Factors to Recent and Projected Fertility Changes." *Demography* 3:131–53 (1966).
"Population." In Neil W. Chamberlin, ed., *Contemporary Economic Issues*. Rev. ed. Homewood, Ill.: Richard D. Irwin, Inc., 1973. Pp. 301–52.

Easterlin, Richard, Wachter, Michael, and Wachter, Susan. "The Changing Impact of Population Swings on the American Economy." *Proceedings of the American Philosophical Society*. June 9, 1978, pp. 119–31.

Feinstein, C. H. *Statistical Tables of National Income, Expenditure and Output of the U.K. 1855–1965*. Cambridge, England: Cambridge University Press, 1972.

Fowles, Jib. "The Impending Society of Immortals." *The Futurist*. June 1978, pp. 175–84.

Fulop, Marcel. "A Survey of the Literature on the Economic Theory of Fertility Behavior." *The American Economist* 21:5–13 (Spring 1977).

Glass, D. V. *Population Policies and Movements in Europe*. Oxford: Clarendon Press, 1940.

Gori, Gio B., and Richter, Brian J. "Macroeconomics of Disease Prevention in the United States." *Science*. June 9, 1978, pp. 1124–30.

Hall, H. R. "Of Baby Booms and Marriage Slumps." *Economic Record*. March 1976, pp. 36–52.

Henschen, Folke. *The History of Diseases*. London: Longmans, Green and Co., 1962.

Keyfitz, Nathan. *Introduction to the Mathematics of Population*. Reading, Mass.: Addison-Wesley Publishing Co., 1968.
"Mathematical Demography: A Bibliographical Essay," *Population Index* 42:9–38 (1976).
"What Difference Would It Make if Cancer Were Eradicated? An Examination of the Tauber Paradox." *Demography* 14:411–18 (Nov. 1977).

Keyfitz, Nathan, and Wilhelm Flieger. *World Population: An Analysis of Vital Data.* Chicago: University of Chicago Press, 1968.

Kitigawa, Evelyn. "On Mortality." *Demography* 14(4):381–90 (Nov. 1977).

Kuczynski, Robert R. *The Balance of Births and Deaths,* I. New York: Macmillan Company, 1928.

The Balance of Births and Deaths, II. Washington, D.C.: Brookings Institution, 1931.

Kurtzman, Joel, and Prillit, Gordon, *No More Dying: The Concept of Aging and the Extension of Life.* New York: Hawthorn Books, 1976.

Le Bras, Hervé. "Lois de mortalité et âge limite." *Population* 31:655–91 (May–June 1976).

Lopez, Alvaro. *Problems in Stable Population Theory.* Princeton: Office of Population Research, 1961.

Lotka, A. J. "Relation Between Birth Rates and Death Rates." *Science,* 26(653):21–2 (1907).

Elements of Physical Biology. Baltimore, Md.: Williams and Wilkins, 1925.

Metropolitan Life Insurance Co. "Centenarians." *Statistical Bulletin* 52:2–4 (Nov. 1971).

"Frequency and Days of Disability." *Statistical Bulletin* 55:9–11 (July 1974).

"Potential Gains in Longevity After Midlife." *Statistical Bulletin* 56:8–9 (Sept. 1975), also 59(3):7–9 (July–Sept. 1978),

"Socioeconomic Mortality Differentials by Leading Causes of Death." *Statistical Bulletin* 58:5–9 (Jan. 1977).

Paillat, Paul. "La vieillissement de la France rurale." *Population* 31:1147–88 (Nov.–Dec. 1976).

Preston, Samuel H., Keyfitz, Nathan, and Schoen, Robert. *Causes of Death, Life Tables for National Population.* New York: Seminar Press, 1972.

Rosenfeld, Albert. *Prolongevity.* New York: Alfred A. Knopf, Inc., 1976.

Sharpe, F. R., and Lotka, A. J. "A Problem in Age-Distribution," *Philosophical Magazine.* April 11, 1911, pp. 435–8.

Sheppard, Harold L., and Rix, Sara E. *The Graying of Working America.* New York: The Free Press, 1977.

Shock, Nathan W., ed. *Aging: Some Social and Biological Aspects.* Washington, D.C.: American Academy for the Advancement of Science, 1960.

Shryock, Henry S., Siegel, Jacob S., and Associates. *The Method and Materials of Demography.* Washington, D.C.: U.S. Bureau of the Census, 1971.

Siegel, J. S., and Passel, J. S. "New Estimates of the Number of Centenarians in the United States." *Journal of American Statistical Association* 71:559–66 (Sept. 1976).

Spengler, Joseph J. *France Faces Depopulation.* Durham, N.C.: Duke University Press, 1938.

"Demographic Factors and Early Economic Development." *Daedalus* 72(2):433–46 (Spring 1968).

"Population Aging and Security of the Aged." *Atlantic Economic Journal* 6(1):1–7 (March 1978).

Strehler, Bernard L. *Time, Cells, and Aging.* 2d ed. New York, Academic Press, 1977.

Strehler, Bernard L., and Mildvan, Albert S. "General Theory of Mortality and Aging." *Science*. July 1, 1960, pp. 14–21.

Tanaka, H., et al. ["Symptoms of Senility and Life Expectancy"]. *Japanese Journal of Hygiene* (Kyoto) 30:199 (1975) [in Japanese].

Thomas, Lewis. "Biostatistics in Medicine." *Science*. Nov. 18, 1977, p. 675.

Thompson, W. S., and Whelpton, P. K. *Population Trends in the United States*. New York: McGraw-Hill, 1933.

United Nations. "Some Quantitative Aspects of the Aging of Western Populations." *Population Bulletin* 1:42–57 (Dec. 1951).

"The Cause of the Aging Populations: Declining Mortality or Declining Fertility." *Population Bulletin* 4:30–8 (Dec. 1954).

The Aging of Populations and Its Economic and Social Implications, Population Studies, No. 26. New York: United Nations, 1956.

Population Bulletin of the United Nations, No. 6, 1962.

The Concept of a Stable Population, Population Studies, No. 39. New York: United Nations, 1968.

The World Population Situation in 1970, Population Studies, No. 49. New York: United Nations, 1971, chap. 2.

The Determinants and Consequences of Population Trends, Population Studies, No. 50. New York: United Nations, 1973.

Statistical Yearbook, 1974. New York: United Nations, 1975.

Demographic Yearbook, 1975 and 1976. New York: United Nations, 1976, 1977.

U.S. Bureau of the Census. *Current Population Reports:* Special Studies, Series P-23, No. 43. "Some Demographic Aspects of Aging in the United States." Washington, D.C.: U.S. Government Printing Office, Feb. 1973.

Current Population Reports: Special Studies, Series P-23, No. 57. "Social and Economic Characteristics of the Older Population 1974." Washington, D.C.: U.S. Government Printing Office, No. 1975.

Current Population Reports: Special Studies, Series P-23, No. 59. "Demographic Aspects of Aging and the Older Population in the United States." Washington, D.C.: U.S. Government Printing Office, May 1975.

Current Population Reports, Series P-25, No. 601. "Projections of the Population of the United States: 1975 to 2050." Washington, D.C.: U.S. Government Printing Office, Oct. 1975.

Current Population Reports, Series P-20, No. 308. "Fertility of American Women: June 1976." Washington, D.C.: U.S. Government Printing Office, June 1977.

Current Population Reports, Series P-25, No. 704. "Projections of the Population of the United States: 1977 to 2050." Washington, D.C.: U.S. Government Printing Office, July 1977.

U.S. Department of Health, Education and Welfare. *United States Life Tables by Causes of Death: 1969–71*, Vol. I, No. 5. DHEW Publication No. (HRA) 75-1500, May 1975.

Unsigned. "Old Age Pensions: Level, Adjustment and Coverage." *The OECD Observer*. Sept. 1975, pp. 19–24.

"La population stable et la population stationnaire selon Laplace et Quetelet." *Population*. March/April 1976, pp. 485–87.

Population Projections 1975–2015, by the Government Actuary. London: H.S.O., 1977.

Wachter, Michael L. "A Time-Series Fertility Equation: The Potential for a Baby Boom in the 1980s." *International Economic Review* 16:609–23 (Oct. 1975).

Chapter 3. Population aging and dependency

Aaron, Henry. "The Social Insurance Paradox." *Canadian Journal of Economics* 32:371–4 (Aug. 1966).

Advisory Council on Social Security. *Reports* of the 1974 Council. Washington, D.C., March 6, 1975.

The Annals of the American Academy of Political and Social Science, Vol. 415, Sept. 1974. [This number is devoted to "Political Consequences of Aging," edited by F. R. Eisele.]

Best, Fred, and Stern, Barry. "Education, Work, Leisure: Must They Come in That Order?" *Monthly Labor Review* 100:3–10 (July 1977).

Bixby, Lenore E. "Retirement Patterns in the United States: Research and Policy Interaction." *Social Security Bulletin* 39:3–19 (Aug. 1976).

Bourgeois-Pichat, J. "La structure de la population et la sécurité sociale." *Population* 5(3):435–92 (July–Sept. 1950).

Browning, Edgar K. "Social Insurance and Intergenerational Transfers," *Journal of Law and Economics* 16:215–37 (Oct. 1973).

Browning, Harvey L. "Speculation on Labor Mobility in a Stationary Population." In Spengler, ed., 1975.

Cannan, Edwin. *Economic Scares*. London: P. S. King, 1933.

Chaddock, Robert E. "Age and Sex in Population Analysis." *The Annals of the American Academy of Political and Social Science* 188:185–93 (Nov. 1936).

Chen, Yung-Ping, and Chu, Kwang-Wen. "Total Dependency Burden and Social Security Solvency." *Proceedings* of the 29th Annual Meeting of the Industrial Relations Research Association, Sept. 1976, pp. 43–51.

Clark, Robert. "The Influence of Low Fertility Rates and Retirement Policy on Dependency Costs," prepared for the American Institutes for Research in the Behavioral Sciences, Washington, D.C., 1976. Summarized in Harold Sheppard and Sara Rix, *The Graying of Working America*. New York: The Free Press, 1977a.

"Increasing Income Transfers to the Elderly Implied by Zero Population Growth." *Review of Social Economy*, 35(1):37–54 (April 1977b).

Clark, Robert, and Spengler, Joseph J. "Changing Demography and Dependency Costs: The Implications of New Dependency Ratios and Their Composition." In Barbara Herzog, ed., *Income and Aging: Essays on Policy Prospects*. New York: Human Science Press, 1978.

Coale, Ansley J., and Demeny, Paul. *Regional Model Life Tables and Stable Populations*. Princeton: Princeton University Press, 1956.

Corson, J. J., and McConnell, J. W. *Economic Needs of Older People*. New York: The Twentieth Century Fund, 1956.

Cowgill, Donald O. "The Aging of Population and Societies." *Annals of the American Academy of Political and Social Science* 415:1–18 (Sept. 1974).

Daric, Jean. *Vieillissement de la population et prolongation de la vie active* (Institut National d'Études Démographiques). Paris: Presses Universitaires de France, 1948.

Deardorff, A. V. "The Growth Rate for Population: Comment." *International Economic Review* 17:510–15 (June 1976).

Durand, John. "Age Distribution of the Population." In New York State Joint Legislative Committee on Aging [see below], *Birthdays Don't Count,* pp. 60–5.

Ehrbar, A. F. "Those Pension Funds are Even Weaker Than You Think." *Fortune* 96(5):104–16 (Nov. 1977).

Eldred, G. W. "Does the Public Support the Social Security Program?" *Journal of Risk and Insurance* 44(2):179–91 (June 1977).

Faltermayer, Edmund. "A Steeper Climb Up Pension Mountain." *Fortune* 95(1):78–81, 157–65 (Jan. 1975).

Foltman, Felician F., and McClelland, Peter D. *New York State's Economic Crisis: Jobs, Incomes and Economic Growth.* Part I. Ithaca, N.Y.: New York State School of Industrial and Labor Relations, Cornell University, 1977.

Fullerton, Howard N., Jr. "A Table of Expected Working Life for Men, 1968." *Monthly Labor Review* 94:49–55 (June 1971).

Gujarati, Damodar. *Pensions and New York City's Fiscal Crisis.* Washington, D.C.: American Enterprise Institute, 1978.

Hareven, Tamara K. "The Last Stage: Historical Adulthood and Old Age." In *American Civilization: New Perspectives,* issued as *Daedalus,* vol. 105, No. 4, of the Proceedings of the American Academy of Arts and Sciences, 1976.

Harrod, R. F. *The Trade Cycle.* Oxford: The Clarendon Press, 1936.

Henry, Louis. "Pyramids, statuts et carrieres," in 3 parts. *Population* 26:463–86 (1971); 27:599–636 (1972); 31:839–56 (1976).

Hicks, J. R. "Economic Foundations of Wage Policy." *Economic Journal* 65:389–404 (Sept. 1955).

Hogan, Timothy. "The Implications of Stationarity for Social Security." *Social Science Quarterly* 55:151–8 (1974).

Hopkin, W. A. B. "The Economics of an Ageing Population." *Lloyd's Bank Review,* New Series, No. 27:25–36 (Jan. 1953).

Hurff, George B., ed. *Economic Problems of Retirement.* Gainesville, Fla.: University of Florida Press, 1954.

Kelley, Allen C. "Population Growth, the Dependency Rate, and the Pace of Economic Development." *Population Studies* 27(3):405–14 (Nov. 1973).

Keyfitz, Nathan." Individual Mobility in a Stationary Population." *Population Studies* 27:335–52 (July 1973).

Kreps, Juanita M. "Social Security in the Coming Decade: Questions for a Mature System." *Social Security Bulletin* 29(3):21–9 (March 1976).

"Age, Work, and Income." *Southern Economic Journal* 4(4):1438–52 (April 1977).

Lampman, Robert J. "The Future of Social Security, 1977–2050." *Proceedings* of the 29th Annual Meeting of the Industrial Relations Research Association. Sept. 1976, pp. 25–42.

Lehman, Harvey C. *Age and Achievement.* Princeton: Princeton University Press, 1953.

Leibenstein, Harvey. "The Impact of Population Growth, on Economic Welfare – Nontraditional Elements." In Roger Revelle et al., ed., *Rapid Population Growth.* Baltimore, Md.: Johns Hopkins Press (for National Academy of Sciences), 1971. Pp. 175–98.

Munnell, Alicia H. *The Future of Social Security.* Washington, D.C.: The Brookings Institution, 1977.

Muny, Gene E. "The Economics of Local Government Pensions and Pension Funding." *Journal of Political Economy,* 505–16 (June 1978).

National Resources Committee. *The Problems of a Changing Population.* Washington, D.C.: U.S. Government Printing Office, 1938.

Nuefeld, Maurice F. "Lifetime Jobs and Wage Security: Vintage Wine in New Containers." *Monthly Labor Review* 100:27–8 (Sept. 1977).

New York State Joint Legislative Committee on Problems of Aging. *Birthdays Don't Count.* Albany, N.Y.: Legislative Document 1948. No. 61, pp. 102–22.

Owens, Aaron J. "Will Zero-Population Growth Hamper Scientific Creativity?" *Physics Today* 26:9–13 (Oct. 1973).

Page, Irvine H. "Age and Creativity." *Science.* Nov. 30, 1962, p. 947.

PEP (Political and Economic Planning). *Population Policy in Great Britain.* London: 16 Queen Anne's Gate, 1948.

Reddaway, W. B. "The Economic Consequences of Zero Population Growth." *Lloyd's Bank Review* 124:14–30 (April 1977).

Reder, M. W. "The General Level of Money Wages." *Proceedings* of the Third Annual Meeting of the Industrial Relations Research Association, 1951, pp. 186–202.

Reimers, Cordelia. "Is the Average Age at Retirement Changing?" *Journal of the American Statistical Association* 71:552–8 (Sept. 1976).

Rejda, George, and Shepler, Richard. "The Impact of Zero Population Growth on the OASHDI Program." *Journal of Risk and Insurance* 40:313–25 (Sept. 1973).

Roe, Anne. "Changes in Scientific Activities With Age." *Science.* Oct. 15, 1965, pp. 313–18.

"Patterns in Productivity of Scientists." *Science.* May 26, 1972, pp. 940–1.

Royal Commission on Population. *Papers.* London: His Majesty's Stationery Office, 1950.

Ryder, N. B. "Notes on Stationary Populations." *Population Index* 41:3–28 (1975).

Samuelson, Paul A. "An Exact Consumption-Loan Model of Interest with or without the Social Contrivance of Money." *Journal of Political Economy* 66:467–82 (Dec. 1958).

"The Optimum Growth Rate for Population." *International Economic Review* 16:531–8 (Oct. 1975a).

"Optimum Social Security in a Life-Cycle Growth Model." *International Economic Review* 16:539–44 (Oct. 1975b).

"The Optimum Growth Rate for Population: Agreement and Evaluations." *International Economic Review* 17:516–25 (June 1976).

Sauvy, Alfréd. "Social and Economic Consequences of the Ageing of Western European Populations." *Population Studies* 2(1):115–24 (June 1948).

General Theory of Population (translated by Christophe Campos). New York: Basic Books, 1969.

Science Council of Canada. *Implications of the Changing Age Structure of the Canadian Population.* Ottawa, Canada: Minister of Supply and Services, 1976.

Skolnik, Alfred M. "Private Pension Plans, 1950–74." *Social Security Bulletin* 39(6):3–20 (June 1976).

Spengler, Joseph J. *France Faces Depopulation.* Durham, N.C.: Duke University Press, 1938.

"The Economic Effects of Changes in Age Composition." In New York State Joint Legislative Committee on Problems of Aging, *Birthdays Don't Count,* 1948. Pp. 102–22. Reprinted in Spengler and Duncan, eds., *Demographic Analysis.*

"Prospective Population and Income Growth and Fiscal Policy." *National Tax Journal* 3:36–63 (March 1950).

"Wage-Price Movements and Old-Age Security." In Webber, ed., *Aging, A Current Appraisal.* Pp. 105–19.

"Prospective Population and Price Level Tendencies." *Southern Economic Journal* 38:459–67 (April 1972).

Zero Population Growth: Implications. Chapel Hill, N.C.: Carolina Population Center, 1975.

"Population Aging and Security of the Aged." *Atlantic Economic Journal* 6:1–7 (March 1978a).

Facing Zero Population Growth: Reactions and Interpretations, Past and Present. Durham, N.C.: Duke University Press, 1978b.

Spengler, Joseph J., and Duncan, Otis Dudley, eds. *Demographic Analysis: Selected Readings.* Glencoe, Ill.: The Free Press, 1956.

Stassart, Joseph. *Les avantages et les inconvénients économiques d'une population stationnaire.* The Hague: Martinus Nijhoff, 1965.

Stein, Rona B. "New York City's Economy – A Perspective on its Problems." *Quarterly Review* of the Federal Reserve Bank of New York 2:49–59 (Summer 1977).

Sweezy, Alan, and Owens, Aaron. "The Impact of Population Growth on Employment." *American Economic Review* 64(2):44–50 (May 1974).

Thompson, Warren S. *Population Problems.* 3d ed. New York: McGraw-Hill Book Co., 1942.

Thompson, W. S., and Whelpton, P. K. *Population Trends in the United States.* New York: McGraw-Hill Book Co., 1933.

Turchi, Boone A. "Stationary Populations: Pensions and the Social Security System." In Spengler, ed., 1975.

United Nations. *The Aging of Populations and Its Economic and Social Implications* (St/SOA/Series A/26). New York: United Nations, 1956.

The Determinants and Consequences of Population Trends, Population Studies No. 50. New York: United Nations, 1973.

U.S. Bureau of the Census. *Current Population Reports,* Series P-60, No. 101. Washington, D.C.: U.S. Government Printing Office, Jan. 1976.

Current Population Reports, Series P-25, No. 704. "Projections of the Population of the United States: 1977-2050." Washington, D.C.: U.S. Government Printing Office, July 1977.

Webber, Irving L. *Aging and Retirement.* Gainesville, Fla.: University of Florida Press, 1955

ed. *Aging: A Current Appraisal.* Gainesville, Fla.: University of Florida Press, 1956.

Weldon, J. C. "Presidential Address: On the Theory of Intergenerational Transfers." *Canadian Journal of Economics* 9:559-79 (Nov. 1976).

Chapter 4. Economic status of the elderly

Atkinson, A. B. "The Distribution of Wealth and the Individual Life-Cycle." *Oxford Economic Papers* 23(2):239-54 (July 1971).

Atkinson, A. B., and Harrison, A. J. *Distribution of Personal Wealth in Britain.* Cambridge: Cambridge University Press, 1978.

Bach, G. L., and Stephenson, James. "Inflation and the Redistribution of Wealth." *Review of Economics and Statistics* 56(1):1-13 (Feb. 1974).

Bixby, Lenore, Finegar, W. W., Grad, S., Kolodrubetz, W. W., Lauriat, P., and Murray, Janet. *Demographic and Economic Characteristics of the Aged,* Office of Research and Statistics, SSA, Research Report No. 45. Washington, D.C.: U.S. Government Printing Office, 1975.

Borzilleri, Thomas. "The Need for a Separate Consumer Price Index for Older Persons." *The Gerontologist* 18(3):230-6 (June 1978).

Brimmer, Andrew. "Inflation and Income Distribution." *Review of Economics and Statistics* 53(1):37-48 (Feb. 1971).

Brotman, Herman. "Income and Poverty in the Older Population in 1975." *The Gerontologist* 17(1)23-6 (Feb. 1977).

Clark, Robert. *The Role of Private Pensions in Maintaining the Level of Income in Retirement.* Washington, D.C.: National Planning Association, 1977.

Creedy, John. "The Distribution of Lifetime Earnings." *Oxford Economic Papers* 29(3):412-29 (Nov. 1977).

Diamond, Peter. "A Framework for Social Security Analysis." *Journal of Public Economics* 8(3):275-98 (Dec. 1977).

Epstein, Lenore, and Murray, Janet. *The Aged Population of the United States,* Office of Research and Statistics, SSA, Research Report No. 19. Washington, D.C.: U.S. Government Printing Office, 1967.

Freeman, Richard. *The Overeducated American.* New York: Academic Press, 1976.

Fullerton, Howard, and Flaim, Paul. "New Labor Force Projections to 1990." *Monthly Labor Review* 99(12):3-13 (Dec. 1976).

Grad, Susan. *Income of the Population Aged 60 and Older, 1971.* Office of Research and Statistics, HEW Publication No. (SSA) 77-11851, Staff Paper No. 26, 1977.

Haanes-Olsen, Leif. "Earnings-Replacement Rate of Old-Age Benefits, 1965-75, Selected Countries." *Social Security Bulletin* 41(1):3-14 (Jan. 1978).

Henle, Peter. "Trends in Retirement Benefits Related to Earnings." *Monthly Labor Review* 95(6):12–20 (June 1972).

Henson, Mary F. *Trends in the Income of Families and Persons in the United States: 1947–1964*. U.S. Bureau of Census, Technical Paper No. 17. Washington, D.C.: U.S. Government Printing Office, 1967.

Herren, Stanley. "The Relationship Between Age Structure and Income Distribution." In *Economics of a Stationary Population: Implications for Older Americans*. Washington, D.C.: U.S. Government Printing Office (No. NSF/RA-770024), 1977.

Hodgens, Evan. "Key Changes in Major Pension Plans." *Monthly Labor Review* 98(7):22–7 (July 1975).

Hollister, Robinson, and Palmer, John L. "The Impact of Inflation on the Poor." In Kenneth Boulding and M. Pfaff, eds., *Redistribution to the Rich and Poor: The Grants Economics of Income Distribution*. Belmont, Calif.: Wadsworth Publishing Co., 1972. Pp. 240–70.

Horlick, Max. "The Earnings Replacement Rate of Old Age Benefits: An International Comparison." *Social Security Bulletin* 33(3):3–15 (March 1970).

Kolodrubetz, Walter. "Private Retirement Benefits and Relationship to Earnings: Survey of New Beneficiaries." *Social Security Bulletin* 36(5):16–36 (May 1973).

Moon, Marilyn. *The Measurement of Economic Welfare: Its Application to the Aged Poor*. New York: Academic Press, 1977.

Morgan, James. "The Anatomy of Income Distribution." *Review of Economics and Statistics* 44(3):270–81 (Aug. 1962).

Munnell, Alicia. *The Future of Social Security*. Washington, D.C.: The Brookings Institution, 1977a.

"Social Security." In *Setting National Priorities, the 1978 Budget*. Washington, D.C.: The Brookings Institution, July 1977b.

Okun, Arthur. "Inflation: The Problems and Prospects Before Us." In Arthur Okun, Henry Fowler, and Milton Gilbert, eds., *Inflation: The Problems It Creates and the Policies It Requires*. New York: New York University Press, 1970.

Orbach, Harold L., and Tibbitts, Clark, eds. *Aging and the Economy*. Ann Arbor, Mich.: University of Michigan Press, 1963.

Palmore, Erdman. "Retirement Patterns Among Aged Men: Findings of the 1963 Survey of the Aged." *Social Security Bulletin* 27(8):3–10 (Aug. 1964).

Schulz, James. "The Economics of Mandatory Retirement." *Industrial Gerontology* 1(1):1–10 (Winter 1974).

The Economics of Aging. Belmont. Calif.: Wadsworth Publishing Co., 1976.

"Pension Adequacy and Pension Costs." *Aging* Nos. 279–80:14–21 (Jan.–Feb. 1978a).

"Liberalizing the Social Security Retirement Test: Who Would Receive the Increased Pension Benefits." *Journal of Gerontology* 33(2):262–8 (March 1978b.)

Schulz, James, Currin, Guy, Krupp, Hans, Paschke, Manfred, Sclar, Elliot, and Van Steenberge, J. *Providing Adequate Retirement Income*. Hanover, N.H.: University Press of New England, 1974.

Sherman, Sally. "Assets on the Threshold of Retirement." *Social Security Bulletin* 36(8):3–17 (Aug. 1973).

Steiner, Peter O., and Dorfman, Robert. *The Economics Status of the Aged.* Berkeley, Calif.: University of California Press, 1957.

Tilove, Robert. *Public Employee Pension Funds.* New York: Columbia University Press, 1976.

Torda, Theodore. "The Impact of Inflation on the Elderly." *Federal Reserve Bank of Cleveland Monthly Review.* Oct./Nov. 1972, pp. 3–19.

U.S. Bureau of the Census. *Census of Population: 1970,* Subject Reports, Final Report PC(2)-5B. "Educational Attainment." Washington, D.C.: U.S. Government Printing Office, 1973.

Current Population Reports: Special Studies, Series P-23, No. 57. "Social and Economic Characteristics of the Older Population 1974." Washington, D.C.: U.S. Government Printing Office, Nov. 1975.

Current Population Reports: Special Studies, Series P-23, No. 59. "Demographic Aspects of Aging and the Older Population in the United States." Washington, D.C.: U.S. Government Printing Office, 1976.

Current Population Reports, Series P-60, No. 102. "Characteristics of the Population Below the Poverty Level: 1974." Washington, D.C.: U.S. Government Printing Office, 1976.

Current Population Reports, Series P-25, No. 704. "Projections of the Population of the United States: 1977–2050." Washington, D.C.: U.S. Government Printing Office, 1977.

Current Population Reports, Series P-60, No. 106. "Characteristics of the Population Below the Poverty Level: 1975." Washington, D.C.: U.S. Government Printing Office, 1977.

Current Population Reports, Series P-60, No. 107. "Money, Income and Poverty Status of Families and Persons in the United States: 1976" (Advanced Report). Washington, D.C.: U.S. Government Printing Office, 1977.

U.S. Department of Health, Education and Welfare. *The Measure of Poverty,* A Report to the U.S. Congress. Washington, D.C.: U.S. Government Printing Office, 1976.

U.S. House Select Committee on Aging. *Funding of Federal Programs Benefiting Older Persons.* Hearings, Washington, D.C., June 1976.

U.S. Social Security Administration. "Income of Newly Entitled Beneficiaries, 1970." Report No. 10 in *Preliminary Findings from the Survey of New Beneficiaries.* Washington, D.C.: U.S. Government Printing Office, June 1973.

Waddell, Fred E. *The Elderly Consumer.* Columbia, Md.: The Human Ecology Center, Antioch College, 1976.

Chapter 5: Age and economic activity: life-cycle patterns

Ando, Albert, and Modigliani, Franco. "The 'Life Cycle' Hypothesis of Saving: Aggregate Implications and Tests." *American Economic Review* 53:55–84 (1963).

Bancroft, Gertrude, and Garfinkle, Stuart. "Job Mobility in 1961." *Monthly Labor Review* 86:897–906 (Aug. 1963).

Becker, Gary S. *Human Capital.* New York: National Bureau of Economic Research, 1964.

"A Theory of the Allocation of Time." *Economic Journal* 75:493–517 (Sept. 1965).

Becker, Gary S., and Chiswick, B. R. "Education and the Distribution of Earnings." *American Economic Review* 66:358–69 (May 1966).

Belbin, R. M. *Training Methods,* Series on Employment of Older Workers, No. 2. Paris: Organization for Economic Cooperation and Development, 1965.

Ben-Porath, Yoram. "Lifetime Income and Economic Growth – Comment." *American Economic Review* 56:869–72 (Sept. 1966).

"The Production of Human Capital and the Life Cycle of Earnings." *Journal of Political Economy* 75:352–65 (Aug. 1967).

Bernstein, Marvin H. *Regulating Business by Independent Commission.* Princeton: Princeton University Press, 1966.

Best, Fred, and Stein, Barry. "Education, Work, and Leisure: Must they Come In That Order?" *Monthly Labor Review* 100:3–10 (July 1977).

Birren, James E. "Age Changes in Skill and Learning." In Wilma Donahue, ed., *Earning Opportunities for Older Workers.* Ann Arbor, Mich.: University of Michigan Press, 1955.

Blaug, Mark. "Human Capital Theory: A Slightly Jaundiced Survey." *Journal of Economic Literature* 14:827–55 (Sept. 1976).

Blinder, Alan S. *Toward an Economic Theory of Income Distribution.* Cambridge, Mass.: MIT Press, 1974.

"Intergenerational Transfers and Life Cycle Consumption." *American Economic Review* 66:87–93 (May 1976).

Blinder, Alan S., and Weiss, Y. "Human Capital and Labor Supply: A Synthesis." *Journal of Political Economy* 84:449–72 (June 1976).

Boskin, Michael. "Social Security and Retirement Decision." *Economic Inquiry* 15:1–25 (Jan. 1977).

Bosworth, D. L. "The Rate of Obsolescence of Technological Knowledge – A Note." *Journal of Industrial Economics* 26(3):273–79 (March 1978).

Botwinick, J. *Age and Behavior.* New York: Springer Publishing Company, 1973.

Brennan, M. J., Taft, P., and Schupack, M. B. *The Economics of Age.* New York: W. W. Norton, 1967.

Burkhauser, Richard, and Turner, John. "A Time Series Analysis on Social Security and Its Effects on the Market Work of Men at Younger Ages." *Journal of Political Economy* 86(4):701–15 (Aug. 1978).

Carp, Frances M. "Impact of Improved Living Environment on Health and Life Expectancy." *The Gerontologist* 17(3):242–9 (June 1977).

Cassel, Gustav. *The Theory of Social Economy.* New York: Harcourt, Brace and Co., 1932.

Clark, L. H., ed. *The Life Cycle and Consumer Behavior.* New York: New York University Press, 1955.

Clay, H. M. "A Study of Performance in Relation to Age at Two Printing Works." *Journal of Gerontology* 11:417–24 (Oct. 1956).

Cohen, John. "Subjective Time." In Fraser, pp. 257–75.

Colberg, M. R., and Windham, D. M. "Age-Income Profiles and Invidious Comparison." *Mississippi Valley Journal of Economics and Business* 5:28–40 (Winter 1970).

Collver, Andrew. "The Family Cycle in India and the United States." *American Sociological Review* 28(1):86–96 (Feb. 1963).

Creedy, J. "Income Changes Over the Life Cycle." *Oxford Economic Papers* 26:405–23 (Nov. 1974).

Davis, M. J. "Impact of Health on Earnings and Labor Market Activity." *Monthly Labor Review* 95:46–9 (Oct. 1972).

De La Mare, G. C., and Shepherd, R. D. "Ageing: Changes in the Speed and Quality of Work Among Leather Cutters." *Occupational Psychology* 31:204–9 (July 1958).

Donahue, W., ed. *Earnings Opportunities for Older Workers.* Ann Arbor, Mich.: University of Michigan Press, 1955.

Eisele, F. R., ed. "Political Consequences of Aging." *The Annals of the American Academy of Political and Social Science,* Vol. 415, Sept. 1974.

Espenshade, T. J. "How A Trend Towards A Stationary Population Affects Consumer Demand." *Population Studies* 32(1):147–58 (March 1978).

Esposito, Louis. "The Effect of Social Security on Savings: Review of Studies Using U.S. Time Series Data." *Social Security Bulletin* 41(5):9–17 (May 1978).

Feldstein, Martin. "Social Security, Induced Retirement, and Aggregate Capital Accumulation." *Journal of Political Economy* 82:905–26 (Sept./Oct. 1974).

"Social Security and Saving: The Extended Life Cycle Theory." *American Economic Review* 66:77–86 (May 1976).

Fisher, Irving. *The Theory of Interest.* New York: Macmillan, 1930.

Fraser, J. T., ed. *The Voices of Time.* New York: George Braziller, 1966.

Friedman, M. *A Theory of the Consumption Function.* Princeton: Princeton University Press for the National Bureau of Economic Research, 1957.

Ghez, Gilbert, and Becker, G. S. *The Allocation of Time and Goods Over the Life-Cycle.* New York: National Bureau of Economic Research, 1975.

Glick, P. C. "The Family Cycle." *American Sociological Review* 12:164–74 (April 1947).

"The Life Cycle of the Family." *Marriage and Family Living* 17:3–9 (Feb. 1955).

"Updating the Life Cycle of the Family." *Journal of Marriage and Family* 39:1–13 (Feb. 1977).

Glick, P. C., and Norton, Arthur, J. "Marrying, Divorcing, and Living Together in the U.S. Today." *Population Bulletin* 32(5):1–39 (Oct. 1977).

Glick, P. C., and Parke, R., Jr. "New Approaches in Studying the Life Cycle of the Family." *Demography* 2:187–202 (1965).

Gori, Gio B., and Richter, Brian. "Macroeconomics of Disease Prevention in the United States." *Science.* June 9, 1978, pp. 1126–38.

Hanoch, G. "An Economic Analysis of Earnings and Schooling." *Journal of Human Resources* 2:310–29 (Summer 1967).

Hareven, Tamara K. "The Last Stage: Historical Adulthood and Old Age." *Daedalus* 195(4):13–28 (Fall 1976).

Heckman, J. J. "A Life-Cycle Model of Earnings, Learning and Consumption." *Journal of Political Economy* 84:511–49 (Aug. 1976).

Houthakker, H. S. "Education and Income." *Review of Economics and Statistics* 41:24–8 (Feb. 1959).

Irvine, Ian. "Pitfalls in the Estimation of Optimal Lifetime Consumption Patterns." *Oxford Economic Papers* 30(2):301–9 (July 1978).

Ishikawa, T. "Family Structure and Family Values in the Theory of Income Distribution." *Journal of Political Economy* 83:987–1008 (Oct. 1975).

Johnson, T. "Returns from Investment in Human Capital." *American Economic Review* 60:546–60 (Sept. 1970).

Jordan, Winthrop D. "Searching for Adulthood in America." *Daedalus* 105(4):1–12 (Fall 1976).

Keyfitz, Nathan. "Individual Mobility in a Stationary Population." *Population Studies* 27:335–52 (1973).

Kossoris, Max. "Absenteeism and Injury Experience of Older Workers." *Monthly Labor Review* 71:16–19 (July 1948).

Kreps, Juanita. *Lifetime Allocation of Work and Income.* Durham, N.C.: Duke University Press, 1971.

"The Economy and the Aged." In Robert Binstock and Ethel Shanas, eds., *Handbook of Aging and The Social Sciences.* New York: Van Nostrand Reinhold Company, 1976a.

"Social Security in the Coming Decade: Questions for a Mature System." *Social Security Bulletin* 39(3):21–9 (March 1976b).

"Age, Work and Income." *Southern Economic Journal* 44:1423–37 (April 1977).

Kreps, Juanita, and Pursell, Donald. *Lifetime Earnings and Income in Old Age.* In Hearings on Old Age Income Assistance, Joint Economic Committee, 90th Congress, First Session, Vol. II, pp. 260–279, 1967.

Landesberger, Michael. "The Life Cycle Hypothesis: A Reinterpretation and Empirical Test." *American Economic Review* 60:175–83 (March 1976).

Lazear, E. "Age, Experience, and Wage Growth," *American Economic Review* 66:548–58 (Sept. 1976).

Le Bras, Hervé, and Chesnais, Jean-Claude. "Cycle de l'Habitat et âge des habitants." *Population* 31:269–98 (March–April 1976).

Leibenstein, Harvey. "The Impact of Population Growth on Economic Welfare – Nontraditional Elements." In Roger Revelle, ed., *Rapid Population Growth: Consequences and Policy Implications.* Baltimore, Md.: Johns Hopkins Press, 1971.

Leigh, D. E. "The Effect of Job Experience on Earnings Among Middle Aged Men." *Industrial Relations* 15:130–46 (May 1976).

Levhari, D., and Mirman, L. J. "Savings and Consumption with an Uncertain Horizon." *Journal of Political Economy* 85:65–81 (April 1977).

Long, Clarence D. *The Labor Force Under Changing Income and Employment.* Princeton: Princeton University Press, 1958.

Lydall, H. "The Life Cycle in Income, Saving and Ownership." *Econometrica* 23:131–50 (April 1955).

McFarland, Ross. "The Need for Functional Age Measurements in Industrial Gerontology." *Industrial Gerontology* 1:1–19 (Fall 1973).

McFarland, Ross, and O'Doherty, Brian. "Work and Occupational Skills." In James Birren, ed., *Handbook on Aging and the Individual.* Chicago: University of Chicago Press, 1959. Pp. 452–500.

Mack, Jerome. "Comparative Job Performance by Age." *Monthly Labor Review* 80:1467–71 (Dec. 1957).

Mayer, Thomas. *Permanent Income, Wealth and Consumption.* Berkeley, Calif.: University of California Press, 1972.

Miller, Herman. "Lifetime Income and Economic Growth." *American Economic Review* 64:869–72 (Sept. 1966).

Mincer, J. "The Distribution of Labor Incomes: A Survey with Special Reference to the Human Capital Approach." *Journal of Economic Literature* 8:1–26 (March 1970).

Modigliani, Franco. "The Life Cycle Hypothesis of Saving, the Demand for Wealth and the Supply of Capital." *Social Research* 33:160–217 (1966).

"The Life Cycle Hypothesis of Saving and Intercountry Differences in the Saving Ratio." In W. A. Eltis, M. F. G. Scott, and J. M. Wolfe, eds., *Induction, Growth and Trade. Essays in Honour of Sir Roy Harrod.* New York: Oxford University Press, 1970.

Modigliani, Franco, and Ando, A. K. "Tests of the Life Cycle Hypothesis of Savings: Comments and Suggestions." *Bulletin of Oxford Institute of Statistics* 19:99–124 (May 1957).

Modigliani, Franco, and Brumberg, R. "Utility Analysis and the Consumption Function: An Interpretation of Cross-Section Data." In K. Kurihara, ed., *Post Keynesian Economics.* New Brunswick, N.J.: Rutgers University Press, 1954. Pp. 388–436.

Munnell, Alicia. *The Effect of Social Security on Personal Savings.* Cambridge, Mass.: Ballinger Publishing Co., 1974.

"The Impact of Private Pensions on Savings." *Journal of Political Economy* 84:1013–32 (Oct. 1976).

Nagatani, K. "Life Cycle Saving: Theory and Fact." *American Economic Review* 62:344–53 (June 1972).

Oppenheimer, V. K. "The Life Cycle Squeeze: The Interaction of Men's Occupational and Family Life Cycles." *Demography* 11:227–45 (May 1974).

Patton, Carl V. "Early Retirement in Academia: Making the Decision." *The Gerontologist* 17(4):347–54 (Aug. 1977).

Peterson, James L. "Research on the Socioeconomic Life Cycle." *Items* (Social Science Research Council, 605 Third Ave., New York). June 1978, pp. 27–31.

Poitrenaud, M., and Moreaux, C. "Rapports entre performances intellectuelles et maintien d'une activité professionale à un âge avance." *Population* 31(2):607–16 (May–June 1976).

Rae, John. *The Sociological Theory of Capital* [1834]. New York: Macmillan, 1905.

Reimers, Cordelia. "Is the Average Age at Retirement Changing?" *Journal of the American Statistical Association* 71:552–8 (Sept. 1976).

Riley, Matilda, and Foner, Anne. *Aging and Society,* Vol. 1. New York: Russell Sage Foundation, 1968.

Rosen, Benson, and Irde, T. H. "Too Old or Not Too Old." *Harvard Business Review.* Nov.–Dec. 1977, pp. 97–106.

Rosen, Sherwin. "Human Capital: A Survey of Empirical Research." In Ronald Ehrenberg, ed., *Research in Labor Economics,* Vol. 1. Greenwich, Conn.: JAI Press, Inc., 1977.

Ruggles, Nancy, and Ruggles, Richard. "The Anatomy of Earnings Behavior. In F. Thomas Juster, ed., *The Distribution of Economic Well-Being.* Cambridge, Mass.: Ballinger Publishing Co., 1977. Pp. 115–58.

Ryder, Harl E., Stafford, Frank P., and Stephan, Paula E. "Labor, Leisure and Training Over the Life Cycle." *International Economic Review* 17:651–74 (Oct. 1976).

Rylands, George, ed. *A Shakespeare Anthology: The Ages of Man.* New York: Harper & Row, 1963.

Sadik, Ali T., and Johnson, T. "Consuming, Learning and Earnings: A Life-Cycle Model." Unpublished memograph, Raleigh, North Carolina: North Carolina State University, 1976.

Schwab, Donald P., and Heneman, Herbert G., III. "Effects of Age and Experience on Productivity." *Industrial Gerontology* 4:113–17 (Spring 1977).

Science Council of Canada. *Implications of the Changing Age Standard of the Canadian Population.* Ottawa: 1976.

Serow, William J. "Slow Population Growth and the Relative Size and Productivity of the Male Labor Force." *Atlantic Economic Journal* 4:62–8 (Spring 1976).

Serow, William J., and Espenshade, Thomas. "The Economics of Declining Population Growth: An Assessment of the Current Literature." In William Serow and Thomas Espenshade, eds., *The Economic Consequences of Slowing Population Growth.* New York: Academic Press, 1978.

Shock, Nathan W. "The Contribution of Psychology." In *The Aged and Society.* Champaign, Illinois: Industrial Relations Research Association, 1950. Pp. 168–80.

Shorrocks. A. F. "The Age-Wealth Relationship: A Cross-Section and Cohort Analysis." *Review of Economics and Statistics* 57:155–63 (May 1975).

Spengler, Joseph J. "The Economic Effects of Changes in Age Composition." In New York Joint Legislative Committee on Problems of the Aging, *Birthdays Don't Count.* Albany, N.Y.: Legislative Document, 1948. No. 61, pp. 102–22.

Stafford, F., and Stephan, P., "Labor, Leisure and Training Over the Life-Cycle." Unpublished paper presented at Econometric Society Meeting, Dec. 1972.

Stassart, Joseph. *Les avantages et les inconvences économiques d'une population stationaire.* The Hague: Nijhoff, 1967.

Thorndike, E. L. *Human Nature and the Social Order.* New York: Macmillan, 1940.

Thurow, L. C. "The Optimum Lifetime Distribution of Consumption Expenditures." *American Economic Review* 59:324–30 (June 1969).

Tobin, James. "Life Cycle Saving and Balanced Growth." In *Ten Economic Studies in the Tradition of Irving Fisher*. New York: John Wiley and Sons, 1967.

Treas, Judith. "Family Support Systems for the Aged: Some Social and Demographic Conditions." *The Gerontologist* 17(6):486–91 (Dec. 1977).

U.S. Bureau of Labor Statistics. "Job Performance and Age: A Study in Measurement," Bulletin No. 1203. Washington, D.C.: U.S. Government Printing Office, Sept. 1956.

"Comparative Job Performance by Age," Bulletin No. 1223. Washington, D.C.: U.S. Government Printing Office, Nov. 1957.

"Comparative Job Performance by Age: Office Workers," Bulletin No. 1273. Washington, D.C.: U.S. Government Printing Office, Feb. 1960.

"A Study of the Performances of Older Workers," Bulletin No. 1368. Washington, D.C.: U.S. Government Printing Office, June 1963.

U.S. Department of Labor. *The Older American Worker: Age Discrimination in Employment*. Washington, D.C.: U.S. Government Printing Office, June 1965.

von Böhm-Bawerk, Eugene. *The Positive Theory of Capital* [1888]. New York: G. E. Stechert and Company, 1923.

Wachter, Michael. "The Demographic Impact on Unemployment." In *Demographic Trends and Full Employment*. National Commission for Manpower Policy, Special Report No. 12. Washington, D.C.: U.S. Government Printing Office, 1976. Pp. 27–99.

Walker, James. "The Job Performance of Federal Mail Sorters by Age." *Monthly Labor Review* 87:296–301 (March 1964).

Weaver, Paul. H. "Regulation, Social Policy, and Class Conflict." *The Public Interest* No. 50:45–63 (Winter 1978).

Welford, A. T. *Ageing and Human Skill*. London: Oxford University Press, 1958.

Woytinski, W. S. *Earnings and Social Security in the United States*. Washington, D.C.: Committee on Social Security, Social Science Research Council, 1943.

Yaari, M. E. "On the Consumer's Lifetime Allocation Process." *International Economic Review* 5:304–17 (Oct. 1964).

Yee, William, and Van Arsdol, Maurice D. "Residential Mobility, Age, and the Life Cycle." *Journal of Gerontology* 32:211–26 (March 1977).

Young, C. M. "A Note on Demographic Influences on the Economic Contributions of Wives and Children During the Family Life Cycle." *Economic Record*, 51:84–92 (March 1975).

Zeller, A. F., and Moseley, H. G. "Accidents as Related to Pilot Age and Experience." *Journal of Aviation Medicine*. 28:171–9 (1957).

Chapter 6. Labor supply of the elderly

Anonymous. *A Panel Study of Income Dynamics*, Vols. 1, 2. Ann Arbor, Mich.: Institute for Social Research, University of Michigan, 1972.

Barfield, Richard. *The Automobile Worker and Retirement: A Second Look*. Ann Arbor, Mich.: Institute of Social Research, University of Michigan, 1970.

Barfield, Richard, and Morgan, James. *Early Retirement: The Decision and the Experience*. Ann Arbor, Mich.: Institute of Social Research, University of Michigan, 1969.

Becker, Gary S. "A Theory of the Allocation of Time." *Economic Journal* 75:299 493-517 (Sept. 1975).

Best, Fred. "Recycling People: Work-Sharing Through Flexible Life Scheduling." *The Futurist* 12(1):5-17 (Feb. 1978).

Bixby, Lenore. "Retirement Patterns in the United States: Research and Policy Interactions." *Social Security Bulletin* 39(8):3-19 (Aug. 1976).

Boskin, Michael. "Social Security and Retirement Decision." *Economic Inquiry*. 15(1):1-25 (Jan. 1977).

Bowen, William, and Finegan, T. Aldrich. *The Economics of Labor Force Participation*. Princeton: Princeton University Press, 1969.

Burkhauser, Richard. *The Early Pension Decision and Its Effect on Exit From the Labor Market*. Unpublished Ph.D. dissertation, University of Chicago, 1976.

Burkhauser, Richard, and Turner, John. "The Effects of Pension Policy Across Life." In Robert Clark, ed., *Retirement Policy and Further Population Aging*. Durham, N.C.: Duke University Press, forthcoming.

Cain, Glen G., and Watts, Harold. "Toward a Summary and Synthesis of the Evidence." In Cain, G. G. and Watts, H., eds., *Income Maintenance and Labor Supply*. New York: Academic Press, 1973.

Campbell, Colin, and Campbell, Rosemary. "Conflicting Views on the Effect of Old-Age and Survivors Insurance on Retirement." *Economic Inquiry*. 14(3):369-88 (Sept. 1976).

Carré, J. J., Dubois, P., and Malinvaud, E. *French Economic Growth*. Stanford, Calif.: Stanford University Press, 1975.

Clark, Robert, and Spengler, Joseph. "Economic Responses to Population Aging With Special Emphasis on Retirement Policy." In Robert Clark, ed., *Retirement Policy and Further Population Aging*. Durham, N.C.: Duke University Press, forthcoming.

Colberg, Marshall. *The Social Security Retirement Test Right or Wrong?* Washington, D.C.: American Enterprise Institute, 1978.

Dernberg, Thomas, and Strand, Kenneth. "Hidden Unemployment, 1953-62: A Quantifiable Analysis by Age and Sex." *American Economic Review* 56(1):71-95 (March 1966).

Epstein, Lenore, and Murray, Janet. *The Aged Population of the United States,* Office of Research and Statistics, SSA, Research Report No. 19, Washington, D.C.: U.S. Government Printing Office, 1967.

Feldstein, Martin. "Social Security, Induced Retirement, and Aggregate Capital Accumulation." *Journal of Political Economy* 82(5):905-26 (Sept./Oct. 1974).

Fleisher, Belton. *Labor Economics*. Englewood Cliffs, N.J.: Prentice-Hall, 1970.

Gallaway, L. E. *The Retirement Decision, an Exploratory Essay*. Division of Research and Statistics, SSA, Research Report No. 9. Washington, D.C., 1965.

Manpower Economics. Homewood, Ill.: Richard R. Irwin, Inc., 1971.

Gordon, Margaret. *The Economics of Welfare Policies.* New York: Columbia University Press, 1963a.

"Income Security Programs and the Propensity to Retire." In Richard Williams, Clark Tibbets, and Wilma Donahue, eds., *Processes of Aging,* Vol. II. New York: Atherton Press, 1963b. Pp. 436–58.

Halpern, Janice. "Raising the Mandatory Retirement Age: Its Effect on the Employment of Older Workers." *New England Economic Review.* May–June 1978, pp. 23–35.

Harris, Louis, and Associates. *The Myth and Reality of Aging in America: A Study Conducted for the National Council on the Aging, Inc.* Washington, D.C.: National Council on the Aging, 1975.

Heckman, J. J. "A Life-Cycle Model of Earnings, Learning and Consumption." *Journal of Political Economy* 84(1):511–44 (Part II) (Aug. 1976).

Hemming, R. C. L. "The Effect of State and Private Pensions on Retirement Behavior and Personal Capital Accumulation." *Review of Economic Studies* 44(1):169–72 (Feb. 1977).

Henderson, J. M., and Quandt, R. E. *Microeconomic Theory.* New York: McGraw-Hill Book Co., 1971.

Hicks, J. R. *Value and Capital.* Oxford: Clarendon Press, 1939.

Irelan, Lola. "Retirement History Story: Introduction." *Social Security Bulletin* 35 (11):3–8 (Nov. 1972).

Kane, R. L., and Kane, R. A. "Care of the Aged: Old Problems in Need of New Solutions." *Science.* May 20, 1978, pp. 913–18.

Kirkpatrick, Elizabeth K. "The Retirement Test: An International Study." *Social Security Bulletin* 37(7):3–16 (July 1974).

Kittner, Dorothy. "Forced Retirement: How Common Is It?" *Monthly Labor Review* 100(1):60–1 (Dec. 1977).

Kosters, Marvin. "Income and Substitution Effects in a Family Labor Supply Model." Santa Monica, Calif.: The Rand Corporation, Dec. 1966.

Kreps, Juanita. *Lifetime Allocation of Work and Leisure,* Office of Research and Statistics, Research Report No. 22. Washington, D.C., 1967.

Leon, Carol, and Bednarzik, Robert. "A Profile of Women on Part-Time Schedules." *Monthly Labor Review* 101(10):3–12 (Oct. 1978).

Long, Clarence. *The Labor Force Under Changing Income and Employment.* Princeton: Princeton University Press, 1958.

Macdonald, Robert. *Mandatory Retirement and the Law.* Washington, D.C.: American Enterprise Institute, 1978.

Marshall, G. P. "The U.K. Retirement Pension and Negative Taxation." *Bulletin of Economic Research* 30(1):33–8 (May 1978).

Morgan, James, ed., *Five Thousand Families – Patterns of Economic Progress,* Vols. 1 and 2. Ann Arbor, Mich.: Institute for Social Research, University of Michigan, 1974.

Motley, D. K. "Availability of Retired Persons for Work: Findings from the Retirement History Study." *Social Security Bulletin* 41(4):18–29 (April 1978).

Munnell, Alicia. *The Effect of Social Security on Personal Savings.* Cambridge, Mass.: Ballinger Publishing Co., 1974.

Palmore, Erdman. "Retirement Patterns Among Aged Men: Findings of the 1963 Survey of the Aged." *Social Security Bulletin* 27(8):3–10 (Aug. 1964).

Parnes, Herbert, Adams, Arvil V., Andrisani, Paul J., Kohen, Andrew I., and Nestel, Gilbert. *The Pre-Retirement Years,* Vol. 4, Manpower Research and Development Monograph No. 15, U.S. Department of Labor. Washington, D.C.: U.S. Government Printing Office, 1975.

Pechman, Joseph, Aaron, Henry, and Taussig, Michael. *Social Security: Perspectives for Reform.* Washington, D.C.: The Brookings Institution, 1968.

Quinn, Joseph F. *The Microeconomics of Early Retirement: A Cross-Sectional View.* Unpublished report prepared for the Social Security Administration, Washington, D.C., 1975.

"Retirement Patterns of Self-Employed Workers." In Robert Clark, ed., *Retirement Policy and Further Population Aging.* Durham, N.C.: Duke University Press, forthcoming.

Rees, Albert. *The Economics of Work and Pay.* New York; Harper & Row, 1973.

Reimers, Cordelia. "Is the Average Age at Retirement Changing?" *Journal of the American Statistical Association* 71(355):552–8 (Sept. 1976).

Reno, Virginia. "Incidence of Compulsory Retirement Policies." *Reaching Retirement Age.* Social Security Administration, Research Report No. 47, 1976a. Pp. 53–64.

"Why Men Stop Working Before Age 65." *Reaching Retirement Age.* Social Security Administration, Research Report No. 47, 1976b. Pp. 41–51.

Robbins, Lionel. "On the Elasticity of Demand for Income in Terms of Effect." *Economica* 10(29):123–9 (June 1930).

Sadik, Ali T., and Johnson, T. "Consuming, Learning and Earnings: A Life-Cycle Model." Unpublished memograph, Raleigh, North Carolina: North Carolina State University, 1976.

Sander, K. G. "The Retirement Test: Its Effect on Older Workers' Earnings." *Social Security Bulletin* 31(6):3–6 (June 1968).

Schulz, James. "The Economics of Mandatory Retirement." *Industrial Gerontology* 1(1):1–10 (Winter 1974).

Slavick, Fred. *Compulsory and Flexible Retirement in the American Economy.* Ithaca, N.Y.: Cornell University, School of Industrial and Labor Relations, 1966.

Spengler, Joseph. "Adam Smith on Human Capital." *American Economic Review.* Feb. 1977, pp. 32–6.

Tella, Alfred. "Labor Force Sensitivity to Employment by Age, Sex." *Industrial Relations.* Feb. 1965, pp. 69–83.

Tolley, G. S., and Burkhauser, R. V., "Integrating Social Security into an Incomes Policy." In G. S. Tolley and R. V. Burkhauser, eds., *Income Support Policies for the Aged.* Cambridge, Mass.: Ballinger Publishing Co., 1977.

Tracy, Martin B. "Flexible Retirement Features Abroad." *Social Security Bulletin* 41(5):18–36 (May 1978).

U.S. Department of Labor. *Pre-Retirement Years,* Manpower Research Monograph No. 15, Vol. 1 (1970), Vol. 2 (1970), Vol. 3 (1973), Vol. 4 (1975). Washington, D.C.: U.S. Government Printing Office.

1977 Employment and Training Report of the President. Washington, D.C.: U.S. Government Printing Office, 1977.

"Work Experience of the Population in 1976." Bureau of Labor Statistics, Special Labor Force Report No. 201, 1977.

U.S. Social Security Administration. "Income of Newly Entitled Beneficiaries, 1970." Report No. 10 in *Preliminary Findings from the Survey of New Beneficiaries.* Washington, D.C., June 1973.

Unsigned. "Old Age Pensions: Level, Adjustments and Coverage." *The OECD Observer* No. 77:19–24 (Sept. 1975).

Vroman, Wayne. *Older Worker Earnings and the 1965 Social Security Act Amendments.* Social Security Administration, Research Report No. 38, 1971.

Wentworth, E. C., "Why Beneficiaries Retire." *Social Security Bulletin* 8(1):16–20 (Jan. 1945).

Chapter 7. Personal and market characteristics affecting retirement

Barfield, Richard. *The Automobile Worker and Retirement: A Second Look.* Ann Arbor, Mich.: Institute of Social Research, University of Michigan, 1970.

Bixby, Lenore. "Retirement Patterns in the United States: Research and Policy Interaction." *Social Security Bulletin* 39(8):3–19 (Aug. 1976).

Boskin, Michael. "Economics of Labor Supply." In G. G. Cain and H. Watts eds., *Income Maintenance and Labor Supply.* New York: Academic Press, 1973.

"Social Security and the Retirement Decision." *Economic Inquiry* 15(1):1–25 (Jan. 1977).

Bowen, William, and Finegan, T. Aldrich. *The Economics of Labor Force Participation.* Princeton: Princeton University Press, 1969.

Brennan, M. J., Taft, P., and Schupack, M. B. *The Economics of Age.* New York: W. W. Norton, 1967.

Burkhauser, Richard. *The Early Pension Decision and Its Effect on Exit from the Labor Market.* Unpublished Ph.D. dissertation, University of Chicago, 1976.

Cain, Glen G. *Married Women in the Labor Force.* Chicago: The University of Chicago Press, 1966.

Cain, Glen G., and Watts, Harold. "Toward a Summary and Synthesis of the Evidence." In G. G. Cain and H. Watts, eds., *Income Maintenance and Labor Supply.* New York: Academic Press, 1973.

Campbell, Colin, and Campbell, Rosemary. "Conflicting Views on the Effect of Old-Age and Survivors Insurance on Retirement." *Economic Inquiry* 14(3):369–88 (Sept. 1976).

Da Vanzo, Julie, De Tray, Denis, and Greenberg, David. "The Sensitivity of Male Labor Supply Estimates to Choice of Assumptions." *Review of Economics and Statistics* 58(3):313–25 (Aug. 1976).

Davidson, Donald, and Eaton, B. C. "Firm-Specific Human Capital: A Shared Investment or Optimal Entrapment." *Canadian Journal of Economics* 9(3):462–72 (Aug. 1976).

Dernberg, Thomas, and Strand, Kenneth. "Hidden Unemployment, 1953–62: A Quantifiable Analysis by Age and Sex." *American Economic Review* 56(1):71–95 (March 1966).

Dorfman, Robert. "The Labor Force Status of Persons Aged Sixty-Five and Over." *American Economic Review* 44(2):634–44 (May 1954).

Dougherty, C. R. S. "Substitution and the Structure of the Labor Force." *Economic Journal* 82(325):170–82 (March 1972).

Gallaway, Lowell E. *Manpower Economics.* Homewood, Ill.: Richard R. Irwin, Inc., 1971.

Hall, Robert E. "Wages, Income and Hours of Work in the U.S. Labor Force." In G. G. Cain and H. Watts, eds., *Income Maintenance and Labor Supply.* New York: Academic Press, 1975. Pp. 102–62.

Humphrey, Don. "Alleged 'Additional Workers' in the Measurement of Unemployment." *Journal of Political Economy* 48(3):412–19 (June 1940).

Humphrey, D. B., and Moroney, J. R. "Substitution Among Capital, Labor, and Natural Resources: Products in American Manufacturing." *Journal of Political Economy* 83(1):57–82 (Feb. 1975).

Jacobson, D. "Fatigue Producing Factors in Industrial Work and Preretirement Attitudes." *Occupational Psychology* No. 4:193–200 (1972).

"Willingness to Retire in Relation to Job Strain and Type of Work." *Industrial Gerontology* No. 13:65–74 (Spring 1972).

Kreps, Juanita. *Lifetime Allocation of Work and Leisure,* Office of Research and Statistics, Social Security Administration, Research Report No. 22. Washington, D.C., 1967.

Long, Clarence D. *The Labor Force Under Changing Income and Employment.* Princeton: Princeton University Press, 1958.

Mincer, Jacob. "Labor Force Participation and Unemployment: A Review of Recent Evidence." In R. A. Gordon and M. S. Gordon, eds., *Prosperity and Unemployment.* New York: John Wiley and Sons, 1966. Pp. 73–112.

Schooling, Experience and Earnings. New York: National Bureau of Economic Research, 1974.

Munnell, Alicia. *The Effect of Social Security on Personal Savings.* Cambridge, Mass.: Ballinger Publishing Co., 1974.

Parnes, Herbert, Adams, Arvil, Andrisani, Paul, Kohen, Andrew, and Nestel, Gilbert. *The Pre-Retirement Years,* Vol. 4, Manpower Research and Development Monograph No. 15, U.S. Department of Labor. Washington, D.C.: U.S. Government Printing Office, 1975.

Pechman, Joseph, Aaron, Henry, and Taussig, Michael. *Social Security: Perspectives for Reform.* Washington, D.C.: The Brookings Institution, 1968.

Perry, George L. "Potential Output and Productivity." *Brookings Papers on Economic Activity,* No. 1. Washington, D.C.: The Brookings Institution, 1977. Pp. 11–60.

Quinn, Joseph F. *The Microeconomics of Early Retirement: A Cross-Sectional View.* Unpublished report prepared for the Social Security Administration, Washington, D.C., 1975.

Reno, Virginia. "Incidence of Compulsory Retirement Policies." *Reaching Re-*

tirement Age. Social Security Administration, Research Report No. 47, 1976. Pp. 53–64.

Rosenblum, Marc. "The Last Push: From Discouraged Worker to Involuntary Retirement. *Industrial Gerontology* 1(1):14–22 (Winter 1975).

Schwab, Karen. "Early Labor-Force Withdrawal of Men: Participants and Non-participants Aged 58–63." *Social Security Bulletin* 37(8):24–38 (Aug. 1974).

Shanas, Ethel, Townsend, P., Wedderburn, D., Friis, H., Milhoj, P., and Stehouwer, J. *Old People in Three Industrial Societies.* New York: Atherton Press, 1968.

Sheldon, Henry D. *The Older Population of the United States.* New York: Social Science Research Council, 1958.

Sherman, Sally. "Labor Force Status of Unmarried Women on the Threshold of Retirement." *Social Security Bulletin* 37(9):3–15 (Sept. 1974).

Steiner, Peter O., and Dorfman, Robert. *The Economic Status of the Aged.* Berkeley, Calif.: University of California Press, 1957.

Tella, Alfred. "Labor Force Sensitivity of Employment by Age, Sex." *Industrial Relations* 4(2):69–83 (Feb. 1965).

Wentworth, Edna. *Employment After Retirement.* U.S. Department of Health, Education and Welfare, Social Security Administration, Research Report No. 21. Washington, D.C., 1968.

Woytinsky, Wladimir. *Additional Workers and the Volume of Unemployment,* Pamphlet Series No. 1. Washington: Committee on Social Security of the Social Science Research Council, 1940.

Chapter 8. Pensions and the economy

Aaron, Henry. "The Social Insurance Paradox." *Canadian Journal of Economics and Political Science* 32(3):371–4 (Aug. 1966).

"Social Security: International Comparisons." In Otto Eckstein, ed., *Studies in the Economics of Income Maintenance.* Washington, D.C.: The Brookings Institution, 1967. Pp. 13–48.

"Demographic Effects on the Equity of Social Security Benefits." In Martin Feldstein and Robert Inman, eds., *The Economics of Public Services.* London: Macmillan, 1977. Pp. 151–73.

Altmeyer, Arthur. *The Formative Years of Social Security.* Madison, Wisc.: University of Wisconsin Press, 1966.

Asimakopulos, A., and Weldon, J. C. "On Private Plans in the Theory of Pensions." *Canadian Journal of Economics* 3(2):223–38 (May 1970).

Atkinson, A. B. "National Superannuation: Redistribution and Value for Money." *Bulletin Oxford University Institute of Economics and Statistics* 32(3):171–86 (Aug. 1970).

Balcer, Yves, and Diamond, Peter. "Social Security Benefits with a Lengthening Averaging Period." *Journal of Risk and Insurance* 44(2):259–65 (June 1977).

Baldwin, F. Spencer. "Old Age Pension Schemes: A Criticism and a Program." *Quarterly Journal of Economics* 24:713–42 (Aug. 1910).

Barfield, Richard, and Morgan, James. *Early Retirement: The Decision and the Experience*. Ann Arbor, Mich.: Institute of Social Research, University of Michigan, 1969.

Barro, Robert. "Are Government Bonds Net Wealth?" *Journal of Political Economy* 86(6):1095–118 (Nov./Dec. 1974).

Bauden, Russell. "The Probable Incidence of Social Security Taxes." *American Economic Review* 26(3):463–5 (Sept. 1936).

Bell, Donald. "Prevalence of Private Retirement Plans." *Monthly Labor Review* 98(10):17–20 (Oct. 1975).

Bernstein, Merten. *The Future of Private Pensions*. London: Collier-Macmillan, 1964.

Bourgeois-Pichat, Jean. "Le financement des retraites par capitalisation." *Population* 33(6):1115–37 (Nov.–Dec. 1978).

Brittain, John. "The Incidence of Social Security Payroll Taxes." *American Economic Review* 61(1):110–25 (May 1971).

"The Incidence of Social Security Payroll Tax: Reply." *American Economic Review* 62(4):739–42 (Sept. 1972a).

The Payroll Tax for Social Security. Washington, D.C.: The Brookings Institution, 1972b.

Browning, Edgar. "Social Insurance and Intergenerational Transfers." *Journal of Law and Economics* 16(2):215–37 (Oct. 1973).

"Labor Supply Distortions of Social Security." *Southern Economic Journal* 42(2):243–52 (Oct. 1975a).

Redistribution and the Welfare System. Washington, D.C.: American Enterprise Institute, 1975b.

"Why the Social Insurance Budget is Too Large in a Democracy." *Economic Inquiry* 13(3):373–88 (Sept. 1975c).

Buchanan, James M. "Social Insurance in a Growing Economy: A Proposal for Radical Reform." *National Tax Journal* 21(4):386–95 (Dec. 1968).

Burkhauser, Richard, and Turner, John. "A Time-Series Analysis on Social Security and Its Effects on the Market Work of Men at Younger Ages." *Journal of Political Economy* 86(4):701–15 (Aug. 1978).

Cagan, Phillip. *The Effect of Pension Plans on Aggregate Savings*. New York: National Bureau of Economic Research, 1965.

Campbell, Colin. "Social Insurance in the United States: A Program in Search of an Explanation." *Journal of Law and Economics* 12(2):249–65 (Oct. 1969).

Over-Indexed Benefits: The Decoupling Proposals for Social Security. Washington, D.C.: American Enterprise Institute, 1976.

Chen, Yung-Ping, and Chu, Kwang-Wen. "Tax-Benefit Ratios and Rates of Return Under OASI: 1974 Retirees and Entrants." *Journal of Risk and Insurance* 41(2):189–206 (June 1974).

Chesnais, Jean-Claude. "Fluctuations démographiques et dépenses de sécurité sociale." *Population* 32(2):373–404 (March–April 1977).

Clark, Robert. "Increasing Income Transfers to the Elderly Implied by Zero Population Growth." *Review of Social Economy* 35(1):37–54 (April 1977).

Dearing, Charles. *Industrial Pensions*. Washington, D.C.: The Brookings Institution, 1954.

Deutsch, Antal. "Inflation and Guaranteed Formula Pension Plans." *Canadian Journal of Economics* 8(3):447–8 (Aug. 1975).

Diamond, P. A. "A Framework for Social Security Analysis." *Journal of Public Economics* 8(3):275–98 (Dec. 1977).

Douglas, Paul H. *Social Security in the United States.* 2d ed. New York: McGraw-Hill Book Co., 1939.

Drucker, Peter. *The Unseen Revolution.* New York: Harper & Row, 1976.

Eldred, G. W. "Does the Public Support the Social Security Program?" *Journal of Risk and Insurance* 44(2):179–92 (June 1977).

Esposito, Louis. "Effect of Social Security on Savings: Review of Studies Using U.S. Time-Series Data." *Social Security Bulletin* 41(5):9–17 (May 1978).

Federal Reserve Bank of Boston. *Funding Pensions: Issues and Implications for Financial Markets.* Boston, 1976.

Feldstein, Martin. "The Incidence of the Social Security Payroll Tax: Comment." *American Economic Review* 62(4):735–8 (Sept. 1972).

――― "Social Security, Induced Retirement, and Aggregate Capital Accumulation." *Journal of Political Economy* 82(5):905–26 (Sept./Oct. 1974).

――― "Toward a Reform of Social Security." *The Public Interest* No. 40:75–95 (Summer 1975).

――― "Social Security." In Michael Boskin, ed., *The Crisis in Social Security.* San Francisco: Institute for Contemporary Studies, 1977a. Pp. 17–24.

――― "Social Security and Private Savings: International Evidence in an Extended Lifecycle Model." In Martin Feldstein and Robert Inman, eds., *The Economics of Public Services.* London: Macmillan, 1977b. Pp. 174–205.

Flowers, Marilyn. *Women and Social Security: An Institutional Dilemma.* Washington, D.C.: American Enterprise Institute, 1977.

Freidman, M. *A Theory of the Consumption Function.* Princeton: Princeton University Press for the National Bureau of Economic Research, 1957.

――― "Second Lecture." In Wilbur Cohen and Milton Friedman, *Social Security: Universal or Selective?* Washington, D.C.: American Enterprise Institute, 1972.

――― "Payroll Taxes, No; General Revenues, Yes." In Michael Boskin, ed., *The Crisis in Social Security.* San Francisco: Institute of Contemporary Studies, 1977. Pp. 25–30.

Garvey, George. "The Effect of Private Pension Plans on Personal Savings." *Review of Economics and Statistics* 32(3):223–6 (Aug. 1950).

Gelber, Sylva. "Social Security and Women: A Partisan View." *International Labor Review* 112(6):431–44 (Dec. 1975).

Greenough, William, and King, Francis. *Pension Plans and Public Policy.* New York: Columbia University Press, 1976.

Hall, James. "Incidence of Federal Social Security Payroll Taxes." *Quarterly Journal of Economics* 53(1):38–63 (Nov. 1938).

Harris, Seymour. *Economics of Social Security.* New York: McGraw-Hill Book Co., 1941.

Hemming, R. C. L. "The Effect of State and Private Pensions on Retirement Behavior and Personal Capital Accumulation." *Review of Economic Studies* 44(1):169–72 (Feb. 1977).

Hemming, Richard. "State Pensions and Personal Savings." *Scottish Journal of Political Economy* 25(2):135–47 (June 1978).

Katona, George. *Private Pensions and Individual Savings*, Monograph No. 40. Ann Arbor, Mich.: Survey Research Center, Institute for Social Research, University of Michigan, 1965.

Kirkpatrick, Elizabeth. *Protecting Social Security Beneficiary Earnings Against Inflation: The Foreign Experience*, SSA, Office of Research and Statistics, Staff Paper No. 25. Washington, D.C., 1976.

Kreps, Juanita. "Social Security in the Coming Decade: Questions for a Mature System." *Social Security Bulletin* 39(3):21–9 (March 1976).

McGill, Dan. *Fundamentals of Private Pensions*. Homewood, Ill.: Richard D. Irwin, 1975.

ed. *Social Security and Private Pensions Plans: Competitive or Complementary?*, Homewood, Ill.: Richard D. Irwin, 1977.

MacRae, C. Duncan, and MacRae, Elizabeth Chase. "Labor Supply and the Payroll Tax." *American Economic Rview* 66(3):408–9 (June 1976).

Meier, Elizabeth. "ERISA and the Growth of Private Pension Income." *Industrial Gerontology* 4(3):147–57 (Summer 1977).

Melone, Joseph, and Allen, Everett. *Pension Planning*. Homewood, Ill.: Richard D. Irwin, 1972.

Miller, Merton, and Upton, Charles. *Macroeconomics: A Neoclassical Introduction*. Homewood, Ill.: Richard D. Irwin, 1974.

Moffitt, Robert. "Labor Supply and the Payroll Tax: Note." *American Economic Review* 69(5):1004–5 (Dec. 1977).

Munnell, Alicia. *The Effect of Social Security on Personal Savings*. Cambridge, Mass.: Ballinger Publishing Co., 1974.

"Private Pensions and Savings: New Evidence." *Journal of Political Economy* 84(5):1013–32 (Oct. 1976).

The Future of Social Security. Washington, D.C.: The Brookings Institution, 1977a.

"Social Security." In *Setting National Priorities, the 1978 Budget*. Washington, D.C.: The Brookings Institution, 1977b.

"Are Private Pensions Doomed?" *New England Economic Review*. March–April 1978, pp. 5–20.

"The Impact of Inflation on Private Pensions." In Robert Clark ed. *Retirement Policy and Further Population Aging*. Durham, N.C.: Duke University Press, forthcoming.

Murray, Roger. *Economic Aspects of Pensions*. New York; National Bureau of Economic Research, 1968.

Musgrave, Richard. "The Role of Social Insurance in an Overall Program for Social Welfare." In William Bowen, Frederick Harbison, Richard Lester, and Herman Somers, eds., *The American System of Social Insurance*. New York: McGraw-Hill Book Co., 1968. Pp. 23–40.

Myers, Robert. "Analysis of Whether the Young Worker Receives His Money's Worth Under Social Security." Memorandum in *Presidential Proposals for Revision in the Social Security System*, Hearings Before the House Committee on Ways and Means on H.R. S-710, 90th Congress, First Session, 1967, Pt. 1, pp. 331–2.

Social Security. Homewood, Ill.: Richard D. Irwin, Inc., 1975.

Nader, Ralph, and Blackwell, Kate. *You and Your Pension.* New York: Grossman Publishers, 1973.

National Industrial Conference Board. *Industrial Pensions in the United States,* 1925.

1977 Annual Report of the Board of Trustees of the Federal Old-Age and Survivors Insurance and Disability Trust Funds. Washington, D.C.: U.S. Government Printing Office, 1977.

Okner, Benjamin. "The Social Security Payroll Tax: Some Alternatives For Reform. *Journal of Finance* 30(2):567–78 (May 1975).

Organization for Economic Cooperation and Development. *Old Age Pension Schemes.* Paris, 1977.

Parnes, Herbert, Adams, Arvil, Andrisani, Paul, Kohen, Andrew, and Nestel, Gilbert. *The Pre-Retirement Years,* Vol. 4, Manpower Research and Development Monograph, No. 15, U.S. Department of Labor. Washington, D.C.: U.S. Government Printing Office, 1975.

Pechman, Joseph. *Federal Tax Policy.* Washington, D.C.: The Brookings Institution, 1966.

"The Social Security System: An Overview." In Michael Boskin ed., *The Crisis in Social Security.* San Francisco: Institute of Contemporary Studies, 1977. Pp. 31–9.

Pechman, Joseph, Aaron, Henry, and Taussig, Michael. *Social Security: Perspectives for Reform.* Washington, D.C.: The Brookings Institution, 1968.

Pesando, James. "Inflation and Guaranteed Formula Pension Plans: An Additional Issue." *Canadian Journal of Economics* 9(3):529–31 (Aug. 1976).

Pogue, Thomas, and Sgontz, L. G. "Social Security and Investment in Human Capital." *National Tax Journal* 30(2):157–70 (June 1977).

Prest, A. R. "Some Redistributional Aspects of the National Superannuation Fund." *The Three Banks Review* No. 86:3–22 (June 1970).

Quinn, Joseph. *The Microeconomics of Early Retirement: A Cross-Sectional View.* Unpublished report prepared for the Social Security Administration, Washington, D.C., 1975.

Rettig, Albert. *A Precise Formula for Primary Insurance Amounts,* SSA, Office of Research and Statistics, Staff Paper No. 22. Washington, D.C., 1975.

Robertson, A. Haeworth. "Financial Status of Social Security Program After the Social Security Amendments of 1977." *Social Security Bulletin* 41(3):21–9 (March 1978).

Rosen, Sherwin. "Social Security and the Economy." In Michael Boskin, ed., *The Crisis in Social Security.* San Francisco: Institute for Contemporary Studies, 1977. Pp. 87–106.

Samuelson, Paul. "An Exact Consumption-Loan Model of Interest With and Without Social Contrivance of Money." *Journal of Political Economy* 66(6):467–82 (Dec. 1958).

"Optimum Social Security in a Life-Cycle Growth Model." *International Economic Review* 16(3):539–44 (Oct. 1975).

Singh, Shiv Pratap. "Social Security Financing and Income Redistribution." *Indian Journal of Economics* 54(212):57–72 (July 1973).

Skolnik, Alfred. "Private Pension Plans, 1950–74." *Social Security Bulletin* 39(6):3–17 (June 1976).

Smelken, Mary. "The Impact of Federal Income and Payroll Taxes on the Distribution of After-Tax Income." *National Tax Journal* 21(4):448–56 (Dec. 1968).

Spengler, Joseph. *Facing Zero Population Growth.* Durham, N.C.: Duke University Press, 1978.

Stephenson, James. "The High Protection Annuity." *Journal of Risk and Insurance* 45(4):593–610 (Dec. 1978).

Taggart, Robert. *The Labor Market Impact of the Private Retirement System.* In Joint Economic Committee, U.S. Congress, Studies in Public Welfare No. 11. Washington, D.C.: U.S. Government Printing Office, 1973.

Thompson, Gayle. "Pension Coverage and Benefits: Findings From the Retirement History Study," *Social Security Bulletin* 41(2):2–17 (Feb. 1978).

Tilove, Robert. *Public Employee Pension Funds.* New York: Columbia University Press, 1976.

Tracy, M. B. "Flexible Retirement Features Abroad." *Social Security Bulletin* 41(5):18–39 (May 1978).

Treynor, Jack, Regan, Patrick, and Priest, William. *The Financial Reality of Pension Funding Under ERISA.* Homewood, Ill.: Dow Jones–Irwin, 1976.

Ture, Norman. *The Future of Private Pensions.* Washington, D.C.: American Enterprise Institute, 1976.

Turnbull, John G., Williams, Arthur, and Cheit, Earl. *Economic and Social Security.* 3d ed. New York: Ronald Press, 1968.

U.S. Department of Health, Education and Welfare. *Coverage and Vesting of Full-Time Employees Under Private Retirement Plans,* Publication No. (SSA)74-11908. Washington, D.C.: U.S. Government Printing Office, Sept. 1973.

U.S. Senate Special Committee on Aging. "Women and Social Security: Adapting to a New Era." 94th Congress, First Session, Washington, D.C., 1975.

U.S. Social Security Administration. *Social Security Programs Throughout the World,* 1975, Office of Research and Statistics, Research Report No. 48. Washington, D.C., 1975.

Unsigned. "The Transition From Work to Retirement." *The OECD Observer* No. 81:28–30 (May 1976).

Viscusi, W. Kip, and Zeckhauser, Richard. "The Role of Social Security in Income Maintenance." In Michael Boskin, ed., *The Crisis in Social Security.* San Francisco: Institute for Contemporary Studies, 1977. Pp. 41–64.

Vroman, Wayne. "Employer Payroll Taxes and Money Wage Behavior." *Applied Economics* 6(3):189–204 (Sept. 1974).

Wilson, Thomas. "The Welfare State and the Elderly in Europe." *The Three Banks Review* No. 101:55–72 (March 1974).

Winklevoss, Howard. *Pension Mathematics.* Homewood, Ill.: Richard D. Irwin, 1977.

Witte, Edwin. *The Development of the Social Security Act.* Madison, Wisc.: University of Wisconsin Press, 1962.

Yohalem, Martha Remy. "Employee-Benefit Plans, 1975." *Social Security Bulletin* 40(1):19–28 (Nov. 1977).

Chapter 9. Macroeconomic response to age-structural change

Alexis, M. "The Changing Consumer Market, 1935–1959." *Journal of Marketing* 26:42–6 (Jan. 1962).

Ando, Albert, and Modigliani, Franco. "The 'Life-Cycle' Hypothesis of Saving." *American Economic Review* 53:55–84 (March 1963).

Andrisani, Paul J. "Effect of Health Problems on the Work Experience of Middle-Aged Men." *Industrial Gerontology* 4:97–112 (Spring 1977).

Atchely, R. C. *Social Forces in Later Life*. Belmont, Calif.: Wadsworth Publishing Co., 1972.

Bakerman, S. *Aging Life Processes*. Springfield, Ill.: Charles C. Thomas, 1969.

Barkin, Solomon. "Retraining and Job Design: Positive Approaches to the Continued Employment of Older Persons." In Sheppard, ed., 1970, pp. 17–30.

Barsby, S. L., and Cox, D. R. *Interstate Migration of the Elderly: An Economic Analysis*. Lexington, Mass.: Heath, Lexington Books, 1975.

Billing, G. C. "Some Economic Effects of a Stationary Population." *Economic Record* 41:167–75 (Dec. 1965).

Blinder, A. S. *Toward an Economic Theory of Income Distribution*. Cambridge, Mass.: MIT Press, 1974.

"Intergenerational Transfers and Life Cycle Consumption." *American Economic Review* 66:87–93 (May 1976).

Botwinick, J. *Age and Behavior*. New York: Springer Publishing Co., 1973.

Brady, D. "Influence of Age on Saving and Spending Patterns." *Monthly Labor Review* 78:1240–4 (Nov. 1955).

Brennan, M. J., Taft, P., and Schupack, M. B. *The Economics of Age*. New York: W. W. Norton, 1967.

Browning, H. L. "Speculation on Labor Mobility in a Stationary Population." In Joseph J. Spengler, ed., *Zero Population Growth: Implications*. Chapel Hill, N.C.: Carolina Population Center, 1975.

Campbell, Z. "Spending Patterns of Older Persons." *Management Record* 21:85–7 (1963).

Carlie, M. K. "The Politics of Age: Interest Group or Social Movement." *The Gerontologist* 12:265–80 (1972).

Chesnais, Jean-Claude. "Age, productivité et salaires." *Population* 33(6):155–89 (Nov.–Dec. 1978).

Cicchetti, C. C. "Outdoor Recreation and Congestion in the United States." In R. G. Ridker, ed., *Population, Resources, and the Environment*. Washington, D.C.: U.S. Commission on Population Growth and the American Future, Commission Research Reports, 1972.

Clark, L. H., ed. *The Life Cycle and Consumer Behavior*. New York: New York University Press, 1955.

Clemente, F., and Hendricks, J. "A Further Look at the Relationship Between Age and Productivity." *The Gerontologist* 13:106–10 (Spring 1973).

Coale, A. J. "Alternate Paths to a Stationary Population." In C. F. Westoff and R. Parke, Jr., eds., *Demographic and Social Aspects of Population Growth*. Washington, D.C.: Commission on Population Growth and the American Future, U.S. Government Printing Office, 1972a.

The Growth and Structure of Human Populations: A Mathematical Investigation. Princeton: Princeton University Press, 1972b.

Coale, A. J., and Demeny, Paul. *Regional Model Life Tables and Stable Populations.* Princeton: Princeton University Press, 1966.

Colberg, M. R. "Age–Human Capital Profiles for Southern Men." *Review of Business and Economic Research* 11(2):63–73 (Winter 1975–76).

Colberg, M. R. and Windham, D. M. "Age-Income Profiles and Invidious Comparison." *Mississippi Valley Journal of Economics and Business* 5:28–40 (1970).

Cooper, B. S., and Piro, P. A. "Age Differences in Medical Care Spending, Fiscal Year 1973." *Social Security Bulletin* 36:3–14 (May 1974).

Cooper, B. S., and Worthington, N. L. "Age Differences in Medical Care Spending Fiscal Year 1972." *Social Security Bulletin* 36(5):3–15 (May 1973).

Cowell, F. A. "Income Tax Incidence in An Aging Population." *European Economic Review.* Oct. 1975, pp. 343–8.

Cowgill, D. O. *Aging and Modernization.* New York: Appleton-Century Crofts, 1972.

Creedy, J. "Income Changes Over the Life Cycle." *Oxford Economic Papers* 26:405–23 (Nov. 1974).

Crockett, J. A. "Population Change and the Demand for Food." In A. J. Coale, ed., *Demographic and Economic Change in Developed Countries.* Princeton: Princeton University Press, 1960.

Dalton, Gene W., and Thompson, Paul H. "Accelerating Obsolescence of Older Engineers." *Harvard Business Review* 49:57–67 (Sept.–Oct. 1971).

Davis, J. M. "Impact of Health on Earnings and Labor Market Activity." *Monthly Labor Review* 95:46–9 (Oct. 1972).

Deardorff, A. V. "The Growth Rate for Population: Comment." *International Economic Review* 17:510–15 (June 1976).

Denton, Frank, and Spencer, Byron. "Health-Care Costs When the Population Changes." *Canadian Journal of Economics* 8(1):34–48 (Feb. 1975).

Donahue, W., ed. *Earnings Opportunities for Older Workers.* Ann Arbor, Mich.: University of Michigan Press, 1955.

Donahue, Wilma, and Tibbitts, Clark, eds. *Politics of Age.* Ann Arbor, Mich.: University of Michigan Press, 1962.

Donahue, Wilma, Roy, J., and Strand, K. *Rehabilitation of the Older Worker.* Ann Arbor, Mich.: University of Michigan Press, 1953.

Easterlin, Richard. "What Will 1984 Be Like?" Socioeconomic Implications of Recent Twists in Age Structure." *Demography* 15(4):397–432 (Nov. 1978).

Eilenstine, D., and Cunningham, J. P. "Projected Consumption Patterns for a Stationary Population." *Population Studies* 26:223–31 (July 1972).

Eisdorfer, C., and Lawton, M. P. *The Psychology of Adult Development and Aging.* Washington, D.C.: American Psychological Association, 1973.

Eisele, F. R., ed. "Political Consequences of Aging." *The Annals of the American Academy of Political and Social Science,* Vol. 415, Sept. 1974.

Enke, S. "Economic Consequences of Rapid Population Growth." *Economic Journal* 81:800–11 (Dec. 1971).

Feldstein, Martin. "Social Security and Saving: The Extended Life Cycle Theory." *American Economic Review* 66:87–93 (May 1976).

Ferber, R. "Research on Household Behavior." *American Economic Review* 52:19–63 (March 1962).

"Consumer Economics, A Survey." *Journal of Economic Literature* 11:1303–42 (Dec. 1973).

Fisher, Irving. *The Theory of Interest.* New York: Macmillan, 1930.

Fisher, J. *Consumption Patterns of the Aged: A Study of Consumer Expenditures, Incomes and Savings in the United States.* Philadelphia: University of Pennsylvania Press, 1960.

Friedman, M. "Nobel Lecture: Inflation and Unemployment." *Journal of Political Economy* 85:451–72 (June 1977).

Friend, C. M., and Zubek, J. P. "The Effects of Age on Critical Thinking Ability." *Journal of Gerontology* 13:406–13 (Oct. 1958).

Gallaway, L. E. "The Aged and the Extent of Poverty in the United States." *Southern Economic Journal* 32:212–22 (Oct. 1966).

"Age and Labor Mobility Patterns." *Southern Economic Journal* 35:171–80 (Oct. 1969).

Manpower Economics. Homewood, Ill.: Richard D. Irwin, Inc., 1971.

Ghez, Gilbert, and Becker, G. S. *The Allocation of Time and Goods Over the Life-Cycle.* New York: National Bureau of Economic Research, 1975.

Gibson, Robert M., Mueller, Marjorie Smith, and Fisher, Charles R. "Age Differences in Health Care Spending, Fiscal Year 1976." *Social Security Bulletin* 40:3–14 (Aug. 1977).

Glick, P. C. "The Family Cycle." *American Sociological Review* 12:167–74 (April 1947).

"The Life Cycle of the Family." *Marriage and Family Living* 17:3–9 (Feb. 1955).

"Updating the Life Cycle of the Family." *Journal of Marriage and Family* 39:1–13 (Feb. 1977).

Glick, P. C., and Parke, R., Jr. "New Approaches in Studying the Life Cycle of the Family." *Demography* 2:187–202 (1965).

Goldstein, S. *Study of Consumer Expenditures, Incomes and Savings in the United States.* Philadelphia: Wharton School of Finance and Commerce, University of Pennsylvania, 1960.

"Changing Income and Consumption Patterns of the Aged, 1950–1960." *Journal of Gerontology* 20(4):453–61 (Oct. 1965).

"The Aged Segment of the Market, 1950 and 1960." *Journal of Marketing* 32:62–8 (April 1968).

Gorman, W. M. "Tastes, Habits and Choices." *International Economic Review* 8:218–22 (June 1967).

Green, R. F., and Reimanis, G. "The Age Intelligence Relationship – Longitudinal Studies Can Mislead." In G. Shatto, ed., *Employment of the Middle-Aged.* Springfield, Ill.: Charles C. Thomas, 1972. Pp. 99–116.

Greenwood, Michael. "Research on Internal Migration in the United States: A Survey." *Journal of Economic Literature* 13:397–433 (June 1975).

Grossman, M. *The Demand for Health: A Theoretical and Empirical Investigation.* New York: National Bureau of Economic Research, 1972a.

"On the Concept of Health Capital and the Demand for Capital." *Journal of Political Economy* 80:223–55 (March/April 1972b).

Haber, L. D. "Age and Capacity Devaluation." In G. Shatto, ed., *Employment of the Middle-Aged.* Springfield, Ill.: Charles C. Thomas, 1972.

Heckman, James J. "A Life-Cycle Model of Earnings, Learning, and Consumption." *Journal of Political Economy* 84(4, Part 2):511–49 (Aug. 1976).

Heien, D. M. "Demographic Effects and the Multiperiod Consumption Function." *Journal of Political Economy* 80:125–38 (Jan./Feb. 1972).

Henry, Louis, "Pyramides, statuts et carrières I. Advancement à l'ancienneté— Sélection." *Population* 26(3):463–6 (May 1971).

Henry, Louis. "Pyramides, statuts et carrières III. Corps de petit effectif." *Population* 31:839–56 (July 1976).

Houthakker, H. S., and Taylor, L. D. *Consumption, Demand in the United States: Analysis and Projections.* Cambridge, Mass.: Harvard University Press, 1971.

Hurff, G. B. "Our Older People: New Markets for Industry." *Journal of Business* 27:131–6 (April 1954).

Jaffe, A. J., and Carlton, R. O. *Occupational Mobility in the U.S. 1930–60.* New York: King's Crown Press, 1934.

Karvonen, M. J. "Women and Men at Work." *World Health.* Jan. 1971, pp. 3–9.

Kelley, A. C. "Demographic Changes and American Economic Development: Past, Present and Future." In Elliott R. Morse and R. H. Reed, eds., *Economic Aspects of Population Change,* U.S. Commission on Population Growth and the American Future, Vol. II, Commission Research Reports. Washington, D.C.: U.S. Government Printing Office, 1972.

Kerr, J. B. "Income and Expenditure: The Over-65 Age Group." *Journal of Gerontology* 23:79–81 (Jan. 1968).

Keyfitz, Nathan. "Individual Mobility in a Stationary Population." *Population Studies* 27:335–52 (July 1973).

Klarman, Herbert, ed. *Empirical Studies in Health Economics.* Baltimore, Md.: Johns Hopkins Press, 1970.

Klevmarken, A., and Quigley, J. M. "Age, Experience, Earnings, and Investments in Human Capital." *Journal of Political Economy* 84:47–72 (Feb. 1976).

Knapp, Martin, R. J. "The Activity Theory of Aging: An Examination in the English Context." *The Gerontologist* 17:553–9 (Dec. 1977).

Koltis, A. "Mobility and Human Capital Theory: The Education, Age, Race and Income Characteristics of Migrants." *Annals of Regional Science* 6(1):41–60 (June 1972).

Koyl, Leon F. *Employing the Older Worker: Matching the Employee to the Job.* Fairfax, Va.: National Publications Center, 1974.

Kreps, Juanita. *Lifetime Allocation of Work and Income.* Durham, N.C.: Duke University Press, 1971.

"Age, Work and Income." *Southern Economic Journal* 43:1243–1437 (April 1977).

Kuznets, Simon. "Size and Age Structure of Family Households: Exploratory Comparisons." *Population and Development Review* 4:187–224 (June 1978).

Lazear, E. P. "Age, Experience, and Wage Growth." *American Economic Review* 66:548–58 (Sept. 1976).

Lehman, H. *Age and Achievement*. Princeton: Princeton University Press, 1953.

Levhari, D., and Mirman, L. J. "Savings and Consumption with an Uncertain Horizon." *Journal of Political Economy* 85:65–81 (April 1977).

Lieberman, M. A. "Institutionalization of the Aged: Effects on Behavior." *Journal of Gerontology* 24:330–40 (July 1969).

Lydall, H. "The Life Cycle in Income, Saving and Ownership." *Econometrica* 23:131–50 (April 1955).

McLeish, John A. B. *The Ulyssean Adult: Creativity in the Middle and Later Years*. New York: McGraw-Hill Book Co., 1976.

Manney, J. D. *Aging in American Society*. Ann Arbor, Mich.: Institute of Gerontology, University of Michigan–Wayne State University, 1975.

March, S. "Human Capital Determination and Net Investment." *Review of Income and Wealth* 19:279–302 (Sept. 1973).

Mayer, Thomas. *Permanent Income, Wealth, and Consumption*. Berkeley, Calif.: University of California Press, 1977.

Meier, E. L., and Kerr, E. "Capabilities of Middle-Aged and Older Workers: A Survey of the Literature." *Industrial Gerontology* 3:147–55 (Summer 1976).

Miller, Ann R. "Interstate Migrants in the United States: Some Social Economic Differences by Type of Move." *Demography* 14:1–18 (Feb. 1977).

Miller, Herman. "Lifetime Income and Economic Growth." *American Economic Review* 55:834–44 (Sept. 1965).

Mincer, Jacob. *Schooling, Experience and Earnings*. New York: National Bureau of Economic Research, 1974.

Modigliani, Franco. "The Life Cycle Hypothesis of Saving, the Demand for Wealth and the Supply of Capital." *Social Research* 33:160–217 (Summer 1966).

Modigliani, Franco, and Brumberg, R. "Utility Analysis and the Consumption Function: An Interpretation of Cross-Section Data." In K. Kurihara, ed., *Post Keynesian Economics*. New Brunswick, N.J.: Rutgers University Press, 1954. Pp. 388–436.

Munnell, Alicia. *The Effect of Social Security on Personal Savings*. Cambridge, Mass.: Ballinger Publishing Co., 1974.

The Future of Social Security. Washington, D.C.: The Brookings Institution, 1977.

Nagatani, Keizo. "Life Cycle Saving: Theory and Fact." *American Economic Review* 62:344–53 (June 1972).

Parks, R. W., and Barten, A. P. "A Cross-Country Comparison of the Effects of Prices, Income and Population Composition on Consumption Patterns." *The Economic Journal* 83:834–52 (Sept. 1973).

Pelz, D., and Andrews, F. *Scientists in Organizations*. New York: John Wiley and Sons, 1966.

Prasad, S. B., and Johnson, A. C. "Residential Mobility and the Retired Worker," *Land Economics* 40:220–3 (May 1964).

Pratt, Henry J. *The Gray Lobby*. Fairfax, Va.: National Publications Center, 1977.

Reder, M. W. "Age and Income." *American Economic Review* 44:661–70 (May 1954).

Reinecke, John. "The 'Older' Market – Fact or Fiction?" *Journal of Marketing* 28:60–4 (Jan. 1964).

Riley, Matilda, and Foner, Anne. *Aging and Society*, Vol. I. New York: Russell Sage Foundation, 1968.

Ryder, Norman. "Two Cheers for ZPG." In M. Olson and H. Landsberg, *The No-Growth Society*. New York: W. W. Norton and Company, 1973. Pp. 45–62.

Samuelson, Paul. "An Exact Consumption-Loan Model of Interest with and without Social Contrivance of Money." *Journal of Political Economy* 66:467–82 (Dec. 1958).

"The Optimum Growth Rate For Population." *International Economic Review* 16:531–8 (Oct. 1975a).

"Optimum Social Security in a Life-Cycle Growth Model." *International Economic Review* 16:539–44 (Oct. 1975b).

"The Optimum Growth Rate for Population: Agreement and Evaluation." *International Economic Review* 17:516–25 (June 1976).

Sauvy, Alfred. "Social and Economic Consequences of the Aging of Western European Populations." *Population Studies* 2(1):115–24 (June 1948).

Schulz, James H. *The Economics of Aging*. Belmont, Calif.: Wadsworth Publishing Co., 1976.

Schwab, Donald P., and Heneman, Herbert G., III. "Effects of Age and Experience on Productivity." *Industrial Gerontology* 4:113–17 (Spring 1977).

Schwartz, Aba. "Interpreting the Effect of Distance on Migration." *Journal of Political Economy* 81:1153–69 (Sept./Oct. 1973).

Science Council of Canada. *Implications of the Changing Age Standard of the Canadian Population*. Ottawa: 1976.

Serow, William J. "Return Migration of the Elderly in the United States: 1955–60 and 1965–70." *Journal of Gerontology* 33(2):288–95 (March 1978).

Serow, William J., and Espenshade, Thomas. "The Economics of Declining Population Growth: An Assessment of the Current Literature." In T. Espenshade and W. Serow, eds., *The Economic Consequences of Slowing Population Growth*. New York: Academic Press, 1978.

Sexauer, Benjamin. "The Role of Habits and Stocks in Consumer Expenditure." *Quarterly Journal of Economics* 41:127–42 (Feb. 1977).

Shatto, Gloria M., ed. *Employment of the Middle Aged: Papers from Industrial Gerontology Seminars*. Springfield, Ill.: Charles C. Thomas, 1972.

Sheppard, Harold L., ed. *Towards an Industrial Gerontology*. Cambridge, Mass.: Schenkman Publishing Co., 1970.

Sheppard, Harold L., and Rix, Sara E. *The Graying of Working America. The Coming Crisis in Retirement Age Policy*. New York: Free Press, Macmillan, 1977.

Shorrocks, A. F. "The Age-Wealth Relationship: A Cross-Section and Cohort Analysis." *Review of Economics and Statistics* 57:155–63 (May 1975).

Sjaastad, Larry A. "The Costs and Returns of Human Migration." *Journal of Political Economy,* Supplement, 70(5):80–93 (Oct. 1962).

Sommers, Dixie, and Eck, Alan. "Occupational Mobility in the American Labor Force." *Monthly Labor Review* 100:3–19 (Jan. 1977).

Spengler, Joseph J. *Declining Population Growth Revisited,* Monograph 14. Chapel Hill, N.C.: Carolina Population Center, 1971.

"Stationary Populations: Economic and Educational Implications." *Canadian Studies in Population* 2:1–14 (1975).

"Population Aging and Security of the Aged." *Atlantic Economic Journal* 6:1–7 (March 1978).

Straw, K. H. "Consumers' Net Worth: The 1953 Savings Survey." *Bulletin of the Oxford Institute of Statistics* 18:1–60 (Feb. 1956).

Suzuki, H. "Age, Seniority, and Wages." *International Labor Review* 113(1):67–84 (Jan./Feb. 1976).

Taubman, P. "The Determinants of Earnings: Genetics, Family and Other Environments: A Study of White Twins." *American Economic Review* 66:858–70 (Dec. 1976).

Taussig, Michael K. *Alternative Measures of the Distribution of Economic Welfare.* Princeton: Princeton Industrial Relations Section, Princeton University, 1973.

Thurow, L. C. "The Optimum Lifetime Distribution of Consumption Expenditures." *American Economic Review* 59:423–30 (June 1969).

Tissue, T. "Downward Mobility in Old Age." *Social Problems* 18:67–77 (Summer 1970).

Tobin, James. "Life Cycle Saving and Balanced Growth." *Ten Economic Studies in the Tradition of Irving Fisher.* New York: John Wiley and Sons, 1967.

Treas, Judith. "Family Support System for the Aged: Some Social and Demographic Conditions." *The Gerontologist* 17:486–91 (Dec. 1977).

United Nations. *The Concept of a Stable Population,* No. 39. New York: United Nations, 1968.

U.S. Bureau of the Census. *Current Population Reports,* Series P-25, No. 601. "Projections of the Population of the United States: 1975 to 2050." Washington, D.C.: U.S. Government Printing Office, 1975.

Current Population Reports, Series P-25, No. 704. "Projections of the Population of the United States, 1977–2050." Washington, D.C.: U.S. Government Printing Office, 1977.

U.S. Commission on Population Growth and the American Future. *Demographic and Social Aspects of Population Growth,* edited by Charles F. Westoff and Robert Parke, Jr., Vol. I of Commission Research Reports. Washington, D.C.: U.S. Government Printing Office, 1972. Part V.

U.S. Department of Health, Education and Welfare. "Limitation of Activity Due to Chronic Conditions, United States – 1960 and 1970," Publication No. (HSM) 73-1506. Washington, D.C.: U.S. Government Printing Office, April 1973.

"Current Estimates from the Health Interview Survey, United States – 1975," Series 10, No. 115, DHEW Publication No. (HRA) 77-1543. Washington, D.C.: U.S. Government Printing Office, March 1977.

Unsigned. "The Power of the Aging in the Market Place." *Business Week* No. 2203:52–8 (Nov. 1971).

"The Over-65 Set: A Bonanza for Business?" *Nation's Business* 59(11)34–6 (Nov. 1971).

Welford, A. T. *Aging and Human Skill.* London: Oxford University Press, 1958.

Yee, William, and Van Arsdol, Maurice, D., Jr. "Residential Mobility, Age, and the Life Cycle." *Journal of Gerontology* 32:211–26 (March 1977).

Zucker, A. "A Note on the Declining Tendency with Age for Investment in Human Capital." *Journal of Human Resources* 2:538–40 (1967).

Chapter 10. Conclusion

Anderson, Kathryn, Clark, Robert, and Johnson, Thomas. "Retirement in Dual Career Families." In Robert Clark, ed., *Retirement Policy and Further Population Aging.* Durham, N.C.: Duke University Press, forthcoming.

Bronfenbrenner, Martin. "Ten Issues in Distribution Theory." In Sidney Weintraub, *Modern Economic Thought.* Philadelphia: University of Pennsylvania Press, 1977.

Clark, Robert, and Spengler, Joseph. "Changing Demography and Dependency Costs: The Implications of New Dependency Ratios and Their Composition." In Barbara Herzog, ed., *Income and Aging: Essays on Policy Prospects.* New York: Human Science Press, 1978.

Fehm, Kurt. *Elemente Einer Systematischen Altersökonomie.* Nürnberg, 1971.

Fraundorf, Kenneth. "Competition and Public Policy in the Nursing Home Industry." *Journal of Economic Issues* 11(3):601–34 (Sept. 1977).

Grimaldi, Paul. "The Nursing Home Industry." *Journal of Economic Issues,* Dec. 1978, pp. 911–21.

Henry, Jules. *Culture Against Man.* New York: Random House, 1963.

Herren, Stanley. "The Relationship Between Age Structure and Income Distribution." In *Economics of a Stationary Population: Implications for Older Americans.* Washington, D.C.: U.S. Government Printing Office (No. NSF/RA 770024), 1977.

Kane, Robert, and Kane, Rosalie. "Care of the Aged: Old Problems in Need of New Solutions." *Science.* May 26, 1978, pp. 913–19.

Keyfitz, Nathan. "Individual Mobility in A Stationary Population." *Population Studies* 27:335–52 (July 1973).

Kivett, Vera. "Characteristics and Needs of an Aging Population in a Southern Metropolitan Area." In Joseph J. Spengler, ed., *Zero Population Growth: Implications.* Chapel Hill, N.C.: Carolina Population Center, 1975.

McKeoun, Thomas. "Determinants of Health." *Human Nature.* April 1978, pp. 60–7.

Myers, George C. "Future Age Projections and Society," forthcoming in the *Proceedings of the World Conference on Aging,* Vichy, France, April 24–30, 1977.

Nelson, Eric, R. "The Measurement and Trend of Inequality: Comment." *American Economic Review* 67:497–519 (June 1977).

Paglin, M. "The Measurement and Trend of Inequality: A Basic Revision." *American Economic Review* 65:598–609 (Sept. 1975).

"The Measurement and Trend of Inequality: Reply." *American Economic Review* 67:520–31 (June 1977).

Pratt, Henry. *The Gray Lobby*. Chicago: University of Chicago Press, 1976.

Ryder, Norman B. "Notes on Stationary Population." *Population Index* 41:3–27 (1975).

Sahota, Gian Singh. "Theories of Personal Income Distribution: A Survey." *Journal of Economic Literature* 16:1–55 (March 1978).

Sauvy, Alfred. "Social and Economic Consequences of the Aging of Western European Populations." *Population Studies* 2:115–24 (1948).

Science Council of Canada. *Study on Population and Technology. Perceptions 2. Implications of the Changing Age Structure of the Canadian Population.* Ottawa: Minister of Supply and Services, 1976.

Spengler, Joseph J. "Prospective Population Changes and Price Level Tendencies." *Southern Economic Journal* 28:459–67 (April 1972).

"Stationary Populations: Economic and Educational Implications." *Canadian Studies in Population* 2:1–14 (1975).

"Population Aging and Security of the Aged." *Atlantic Economic Journal* 6:1–7 (March 1978).

United Nations. *Demographic Yearbook, 1975.* New York: United Nations, 1975.

U.S. Bureau of the Census. *Current Population Reports,* Series P-25, No. 601. Washington, D.C.: U.S. Government Printing Office, Oct. 1975.

Current Population Reports, Series P-25. "Projections of the Population of the United States: 1977-2050." Washington, D.C.: U.S. Government Printing Office, July 1977.

Current Population Reports, Series P-20, No. 308. "Fertility of American Women: June 1976." Washington, D.C.: U.S. Government Printing Office, June 1977.

Wolfgang, Marvin, ed. "Planning for the Elderly." *The Annals of the American Academy of Political and Social Science* 438:vii (July 1978).

INDEX